COLD
CUISINE

Cold Cuisine

**400 recipes for cold buffets,
cocktails, entrées
and desserts**

Exact conversion to metric from imperial (28.35) does not always give convenient working quantities. Therefore metric quantities have been given in units of the nearest 25 grams, except where a different amount is necessary to produce a balanced recipe.

Do be careful to follow 1 type of measure throughout the recipe.

All recipes are for four people unless otherwise stated.

ISBN 1-85129-043-5

Printed in West Germany.

CONTENTS

PREFACE

In this book we intend to show you how fresh, healthy and rich in vitamins the new "Cold Cuisine" is - and above all, how easily you can, with a little imagination, prepare the most delectable salads, cold soups and complete, delicious suppers. All the methods , ideas, serving tips and dressings have been tried and tested in the Dr. Oetker kitchens. The recipes should be read from left to right, starting at the method and including the ingredients as you progress through the recipe.

COCKTAILS

Greenland prawns au naturel
(Recipe on p.14)

Broccoli cocktail

Broccoli cocktail

Discard outer leaves of	**250 g/8 oz broccoli**
Remove florets and peel stalks; and make crossways cuts into them, almost up to the florets	
Add broccoli to a pan of	**boiling salted water**
Bring back to the boil, cook until tender, drain, and allow to cool	
Cut into small pieces, and put some aside for garnishing	
Dip	**3 tomatoes**
first into boiling water, then into cold water	
Skin and dice	
Dice	**125 g/4 oz Camembert**

For the cocktail sauce

Stir together	**125 g/4 fl oz double cream**
	200 ml/6 fl oz Pernod
Season with	**salt**
	pepper
Line 4 cocktail glasses with	**washed lettuce leaves**
Arrange cocktail ingredients in them, and pour the sauce over	
Garnish with the reserved broccoli and	**chopped pistachio nuts**

Cooking time: 10 - 12 minutes

Serve with:	**French bread and butter**

Asparagus cocktail Hawaii

Drain	**500 g/1 lb cooked asparagus**
and cut into pieces 2 cm/l in long	
Thaw	**about 250 g/8 oz frozen prawns**
and mix with the asparagus	
For the cocktail sauce	
Stir together	**5 tbsp mayonnaise**
	2 tbsp cream
	2 tbsp sherry
Add	**lemon juice**
to taste	
Mix the cocktail ingredients with the sauce	
Cut	**2 oranges**
in half, scoop out the fruit and cut into small pieces	
Stir into the cocktail mixture, and spoon into the orange halves	
Serve with:	**toast and butter**

Greek Farmer's cocktail

Discard outer leaves of	**½ head of lettuce**
Leaving the heart whole, tear remaining leaves into small pieces and shake dry	
Peel	**1 onion**
and cut into rings	
Thinly slice, cutting slices in half if necessary	**½ cucumber**

Asparagus cocktail Hawaii

Cut	4 tomatoes
into eighths and remove stalks	
Rinse	8 tinned sardine fillets
under running cold water	
Crumble	125 g/4 oz feta (sheep's cheese)

For the cocktail sauce

Stir	150 ml/5 fl oz double cream
Peel and crush	1 garlic clove
Stir this into the cream with	3 - 4 tbsp finely chopped chives
Season with	salt
	pepper

Arrange the cocktail ingredients in 4 cocktail glasses, and pour the sauce over

| Garnish with | black olives |
| Serve with: | wholemeal bread |

Seafood cocktail

| Wash | 2 sole fillets (150 g/5 oz) |

under running cold water and pat dry

Bring to the boil	125 ml/4 fl oz white wine
	125 ml/4 fl oz water
	1 peppercorn
	1 slice lemon
	salt
	pepper

Add the sole fillets, bring back to the boil, and cook until tender
Remove from liquid and allow to cool

| Wash (optional) and drain | 150 g/5 oz bottled mussels |
| Thaw | 125 g/4 oz frozen |

Seafood cocktail

| Drain | prawns |
| | 125 g/4 oz cooked asparagus stalks |

and cut these into pieces, reserving the tips for garnishing

| Drain and slice | 100 g/4 oz sautéed button mushrooms |

For the cocktail sauce

Stir together	2 tbsp mayonnaise
	2 tbsp double cream
	1 tbsp brandy
	2 tbsp orange juice
	1 tsp grated horse-radish
	1 tbsp tomato ketchup
Season with	salt
	cayenne pepper
Line 4 cocktail glasses with	washed lettuce leaves

Arrange the cocktail ingredients in them, and pour the sauce over
Garnish with asparagus tips
Cooking time: 10 - 15 minutes

| Serve with: | toast and butter |

Crab meat cocktail

| Boil | 500 ml/1 pint salted water |
| Add | 50 g/2 oz long grain rice |

and bring back to the boil
Simmer rice until tender, transfer it to a colander, rinse with cold water and drain

| Pour liquid off | 200 g/6 oz tinned crab meat |

and break into bite-sized pieces

| Wash and halve | 125 g/4 oz black and white grapes |

Remove pips and cut grapes into quarters

| Drain and halve | 1 heaped tbsp tinned mandarin segments |

For the cocktail sauce

Mix together	3 tbsp stiffly whipped cream
	2 heaped tbsp mayonnaise
	1 - 2 tbsp mandarin juice
Add	salt
	pepper
	sugar
	lemon juice
to taste	

Mix cocktail ingredients with the sauce, allow to marinate, then adjust seasoning if necessary

Line 4 cocktail glasses with **washed lettuce leaves** and arrange the cocktail ingredients in them

Garnish with **lemon slices**
mandarin segments
parsley

Cooking time: about 20 minutes
Serve with **toast and butter**

Exotic fruit cocktail

Cut top third of **4 small cantaloupe melons**

into star shapes with a small kitchen knife and remove the seeds
Scoop out the flesh, dice and place in dish
Drain **250 g/8 oz tinned**

Exotic fruit cocktail

lychees
250 g/8 oz tinned
mangos
150 g/5 oz bottled
diced kumquats

Dice mangos, and mix fruit together

For the cocktail sauce
Combine the juice of **1 lemon**
with **2 tbsp cherry brandy**
or cherry liqueur
4 tbsp brandy
1 - 2 tbsp sieved icing
sugar
$\frac{1}{2}$ tsp vanilla essence

Pour over the fruit, cover, and stand in a cold place for at least an hour
Fill a shallow dish with **crushed ice cubes**
and arrange the melon stars on the bed of ice
Carefully stir the fruit mixture and pile it into the melon stars, straining off the juices

Garnish with **lychees**
kumquats
candied cherries
Serve with: **sponge fingers**

Indian prawn cocktail

Peel and dice **2 bananas**
Peel, quarter, core and dice **2 small apples**
Mix fruit with **250 g/8 oz fresh**
peeled prawns
Sprinkle with **lemon juice**
Add **2 tsp chopped hazel-**
nuts
1 level tsp curry
powder
1 level tsp ground
ginger
Stir **300 ml/10 fl oz**
double cream
and mix with the other ingredients
Add **salt**
sugar
to taste
Spoon mixture into cocktail glasses, and decorate with **tomato ketchup**
Serve with: **toast and butter**

Fruit cocktail with prawns

Peel **1 orange**
1 banana
Peel, core and quarter **1 apple**
Finely dice all the fruit
Drain **300 g/10 oz bottled**

Mix all the fruit with	cherries, stoned 150 g/5 oz fresh peeled prawns
For the cocktail sauce Combine	150 ml/5 fl oz yoghurt 1 tbsp lemon juice
Stir in	25 g/1 oz blanched chopped almonds
Add	salt pepper
to taste Carefully stir fruit and prawns into sauce Line 4 cocktail glasses with	washed lettuce leaves
and arrange the cocktail ingredients in them Garnish with	tomato roses
Serve with:	toast and butter

Lobster cocktail

Break	150 g/5 oz cooked lobster
into small pieces Drain and slice	3 tbsp sautéed button mushrooms 2 - 3 slices tinned pineapple
Cut the pineapple into small pieces	
For the cocktail sauce Beat together until thick	1 egg yolk 1 - 2 tsp mustard 1 tbsp vinegar or lemon juice salt 1 tsp sugar

Gradually beat in	125 ml/4 fl oz salad oil
Stir in	4 tbsp cream 1 tbsp sherry
Add salt and sugar to taste Spoon ingredients into 4 cocktail glasses, and pour the sauce over Garnish with	washed lettuce leaves lobster meat parsley
Serve with:	toast and butter

Avocado and crab meat cocktail

Cut	2 ripe avocados
in half lengthways and remove the stones Carefully scoop out flesh without damaging the shells, and dice Sprinkle with juice of	$\frac{1}{2}$ lemon
Drain	125 g/4 oz sautéed button mushrooms
Break up	125 g/4 oz crab meat
and mix with mushrooms and avocados *For the cocktail sauce* Stir together	150 ml/5 fl oz double cream 3 tbsp tomato ketchup 1 tbsp brandy
Stir in	1 tsp grated horse-radish
Season with	salt coarsely ground black pepper
and add	1 - 2 tbsp chopped mixed herbs
Fill the avocado shells with the cocktail	

Lobster cocktail

Avocado and crab meat cocktail

ingredients, and pour the sauce over

Garnish with **dill sprigs**

Lobster Loren cocktail

Break	**500 g/1 lb cooked lobster meat**
into bite-sized pieces	
Dip	**2 tomatoes**
first into boiling water, then into cold water	
Skin them, scoop out centres, and cut flesh into strips	
Drain	**125 g/4 oz sweetcorn ($\frac{1}{2}$ large tin)**
Slice	**12 stuffed Spanish olives**

For the cocktail sauce

Stir together	**150 ml/5 fl oz yoghurt**
	1 tbsp chopped mixed herbs
Season with	**salt**
	pepper

Arrange the ingredients in 4 cocktail glasses, and pour the sauce over

Garnish with	**dill sprigs**
Serve with:	**toast and butter**

Lobster Loren cocktail

Greenland prawns au naturel

(1 serving)(Illustrated on pages 8-9)

Shell	**250 g/8 oz Greenland prawns (cooked)**
and sprinkle with	**juice of 1 lemon**
Sprinkle with	**coarsely ground pepper**
	salt

and leave in a cool place for about 1 hour
(Pour off any liquid that accumulates)

Garnish with	**sprigs of dill**
	halved lemon slices
Serve with:	**toast and butter**

Tuna fish cocktail

Drain and flake	**300 g/10 oz tinned tuna fish**
Peel and finely dice	**3 shallots or 1 small onion**
Drain	**1 tbsp bottled capers**
and cut into small pieces if necessary	

Mix all ingredients together

For the cocktail sauce

Stir together	**150 ml/5 fl oz double cream**
	1 - 2 tbsp milk if necessary
Stir in	**1 tbsp mustard**
	1 tbsp chopped dill
	Worcester sauce
	lemon juice
Season with	**garlic salt**
	sugar
Line 4 cocktail glasses with	**washed lettuce leaves**

Arrange the cocktail ingredients in them, and pour the sauce over

Garnish with	**egg slices**
	parsley
Serve with:	**white bread**
	herb butter
	(page 95)

Lord of the Manor beef cocktail

Dice	**250 g/8 oz cooked beef**
	125 g/4 oz raw smoked ham
Peel and finely chop	**1 onion**
Drain and finely chop	**2 tbsp bottled capers**
	2 pickled gherkins
Shell and finely chop	**4 hard boiled eggs**
Mix all the ingredients in a bowl with	**4 tbsp finely chopped chives**

Season with	**salt**
	sugar
	Worcester sauce

For the cocktail sauce
Stir together	**125 ml/4 fl oz sour cream**
	4 tbsp mayonnaise
	2 tbsp mustard
Reserving a little for garnishing, stir in	**90 g/3 oz bottled caviar**
Line 4 cocktail glasses with	**washed lettuce leaves**
Arrange cocktail ingredients in them, and pour the sauce over	
Garnish with the remaining caviar and	
Serve with:	**egg slices**
	wholemeal or rye bread and butter

Button mushroom cocktail

Drain and thinly slice	**250 g/8 oz sautéed button mushrooms**
Reserving a little for garnishing, cut	**250 g/8 oz cooked chicken**

into small pieces	
Mix chicken with mushrooms and season with	**salt**
	sugar
	lemon juice

For the cocktail sauce
Beat until thick	**1 egg yolk**
	1 tsp mustard
	1 tsp vinegar or lemon juice
	salt
	1 tsp sugar
Gradually beat in	**125 ml/4 fl oz salad oil**
Using a fork, cream	**50 g/2 oz cream cheese**
and stir into the sauce, with	**celery salt**
	3 tbsp sour cream
Line 4 cocktail glasses with	**washed lettuce leaves**
Arrange the cocktail ingredients in them, and pour the sauce over	
Garnish with the reserved chicken	
Serve with:	**French bread and butter**

STARTERS/ENTREES

Fresh figs with pastrami
(Recipe on p.26)

Avocado with roquefort cream

Avocado with roquefort cream

Wash, dry and halve lengthways	**2 ripe avocado pears**
Remove stones, and scoop out flesh, leaving about $\frac{1}{2}$ cm/$\frac{1}{4}$ in lining skin Press flesh through a sieve, or purée with an electric mixer	
Add	**150 ml/5 fl oz double cream**
and beat until creamy	
Peel and grate and stir it in	**1 small onion**
Season to taste with	**salt**
	pepper
Mash	**75 g/3 oz roquefort cheese**
with a fork and stir together with	**2 tbsp cream**
Fold cheese cream into avocado mixture Put mixture into a piping bag, and pipe it into avocado halves	
Garnish with	**black olives washed lettuce leaves**

Stuffed tomato baskets

Halve crossways and remove pulp	**4 large tomatoes**
Halve	**1 green pepper**
Remove the stalk, and pith and cut the pepper into strips	
Add to	**250 ml/8 fl oz boiling salted water**
Bring back to the boil, and cook for 5 minutes Drain, and allow to cool	
Cut	**250 g/8 oz cooked pork**

into strips	**75 g/3 oz ham**
For the salad dressing	
Stir together	**2 tbsp mayonnaise**
	2 tbsp yoghurt
	1 - 2 tbsp vinegar
Season with	**salt**
	pepper
	sweet paprika

Mix all the ingredients together with the dressing and leave to absorb flavours
Put mixture into tomato halves and arrange on a serving dish

Tomatoes with mozzarella cheese
(5 - 6 servings)

Slice	**750 g/1 $\frac{1}{2}$ lb tomatoes**
Remove cores	
Slice	**300 g/10 oz mozza-rella cheese**

Overlap the 2 ingredients alternately on a large platter or lay them out on individual small plates

For the dressing	
Stir together	**4 tbsp olive oil**
	2 tbsp wine vinegar
	salt
Sprinkle dressing over tomato and cheese	
Sprinkle with	**freshly ground black pepper**
Wash and drain	**2 bunches basil**
Pluck off basil leaves and arrange them over tomato and cheese slices	
Serve with:	**French bread**

Tomatoes with mozzarella cheese

Savoury mussel dish

Peel and finely dice	**1 onion**
Melt	**50 g/2 oz butter**
and use to sauté onions	
Add	**125 g/4 oz frozen prawns, defrosted**
and cook for about 3 minutes	
Shell and dice	**1 hard-boiled egg**
Drain	**250 g/8 oz tinned Spanish mussels**
and add to the prawns, together with the egg and	**1 bunch chopped parsley**
Heat them all together, and season with	**salt**
	pepper
	tabasco
Garnish, as desired, with	**egg slices**
	chopped parsley
Serve with:	**French bread**

Leeks with vinaigrette dressing

Cut	**5 medium leeks (about 1 kg/2 lb)**
lengthways	
Wash thoroughly, and add to	**1 1/2 pints boiling water**

Bring to the boil and cook for 12 - 15 minutes
Drain and allow to cool, then arrange on a serving dish

For the vinaigrette dressing	
Stir together	**3 tbsp salad oil**
	2 tbsp white wine vinegar
	1 tsp mustard
Season to taste with	**salt**
	pepper
Stir in	**2 tbsp finely chopped chives**

Pour vinaigrette dressing over leeks and leave for 1 - 2 hours to absorb flavours

Shell and chop	**1 - 2 hard-boiled eggs**

and sprinkle them over the leeks just before serving

Lobster slices

Cream	**50 g/2 oz butter**
Stir in	**10 g/$\frac{1}{2}$ oz concentrated crab soup**
Toast	**4 thick slices white bread**

Leeks with vinaigrette dressing

Spread butter on toast	
Shell and chop	**2 hard-boiled eggs**
Stir eggs together with	**1 heaped tbsp mayonnaise**
	1 generous tbsp double cream
Season to taste with	**salt**
	pepper
Flake	**about 150 g/5 oz tinned lobster meat**

Put egg mayonnaise on to toast slices with lobster meat on top
Arrange lobster slices on **washed lettuce leaves**
and garnish with **parsley**

Prawns on a bed of artichokes

Drain	**14 - 16 tinned artichoke hearts**

and arrange on a glass dish
Sprinkle with **lemon juice**
Worcester sauce
Allow **250 g/8 oz frozen prawns**
to thaw at room temperature and spread them over artichokes
Arrange **washed lettuce leaves**
around artichokes

For the dressing
Stir together **4 - 5 tbsp tomato ketchup**
3 tbsp cream
1 tbsp brandy
Season with **salt**
pepper
sugar

Pour dressing over prawns
Slice **stuffed Spanish olives**
and use to garnish artichokes

Prawn ramekins
(6 servings)

Stir together	**300 g/10 oz fresh peeled prawns**
	peel of 1 lemon
	3 tbsp lemon juice
	2 tbsp finely chopped dill
	3 tbsp medium sweet sherry
Season with	**pepper**

Cover, and leave for about 1 hour to absorb flavours, stirring occasionally
Remove lemon peel, and put mixture into 6 ramekins, flattening it slightly
Gently melt **200 g/6 oz butter**
(do not allow it to foam)

Celery with roquefort

Pour the butter over the prawns, and allow to cool
Garnish with **dill sprigs**
lemon slices
Serve with: **hot toast**

Celery with roquefort

Clean and dry	**4 sticks celery**
Arrange them on a serving dish, and sprinkle with	**salt**
	lemon juice
Mash	**125 g/4 oz roquefort cheese**
with a fork	
Gradually stir in	**2 - 3 tbsp cream**

Stir until creamy, put into a piping bag with a rosette nozzle, and pipe on to celery stalks

Weinberg snails

Wash	**24 tinned snails and shells**

in hot water and allow to drain
Put $\frac{1}{2}$ tsp of the tinned snail liquid into

and stir together with	2 tbsp double cream
	1 tbsp milk
	1 tsp finely chopped
	dill
Add	salt
	pepper
	sugar
	lemon juice
	Worcester sauce
to taste	

For the filling	
Halve	3 medium tomatoes
Remove cores and pips, and dice	
Mix avocado and tomato with	125 g/4 oz fresh
	peeled prawns
and the dressing	
Leave for a while to absorb flavours	
Sprinkle the avocado halves with	onion salt
and fill with prawn mixture	
Arrange on	washed lettuce leaves
and garnish with	lemon slices
	dill sprigs
Serve with:	French bread or toast
Variation:	
Spread dressing over filling	

Caviar slices

Cream	75 g/3 oz butter
Mash about half of	50 g/2 oz bottled
	caviar
and stir into creamed butter	
Spread a little of this on to	8 very small slices of
	French bread

Put remaining caviar butter into a piping
bag with a star nozzle, and pipe a circle

Avocado with prawns

each of the shells, and then place the
snails inside

Cream	50 g/2 oz softened
	butter
Peel and finely chop	½ onion
	1 clove of garlic
	2 shallots
and add to the butter, with	1 tbsp chopped
	parsley
Stir well, then season with	salt
	pepper

Spread over the filled snail shells, and
place them in flat ovenproof dishes
(filled with salt), or in snail dishes
Place these in a preheated oven
Electricity: 225° - 250° C/450° - 475° F
Gas: Mark 8 - 9
Cooking time: 10 - 15 minutes

Avocado with prawns

Wash, dry, and cut into half lengthways	2 ripe avocado pears
Remove stone, and scoop out, all but	
½ cm/¼ in of flesh and dice	
Sprinkle with	1 tbsp lemon juice

| *For the salad dressing* | |
| Melt | 1 tbsp butter |

Caviar slices

on to bread
Fill the circle with the remaining caviar,
and garnish with **lime slices**
onion rings
dill sprigs

Melon with chicken salad
(8 servings)

Wash, dry and cut in half lengthways **1 water melon**
Cut each half into 4 equal boat shapes
Using a spoon, scoop out the flesh,
leaving a 1 cm/$\frac{1}{2}$ in layer inside the skin
Remove pips, and cut flesh into small
pieces
Allow to drain well, and put the melon
boats in a cold place
Cut **250 g/8 oz cold**
cooked chicken

into small pieces
Clean and thinly slice **250 g/8 oz button**
mushrooms
Melt **tbsp butter**
and sauté the mushrooms in it for
about 10 minutes
Season with **salt**
pepper
lemon juice

and allow to cool
Mix melon, mushrooms and chicken
with **2 tbsp mayonnaise**
and spread mixture evenly on to the
chilled melon boats
Garnish with **parsley**
Variation:
Season ingredients with **a few drops of**

Melon with chicken salad

Worcester sauce or
tabasco

before mixing with mayonnaise

Smoked salmon Altona
(10 servings)

Whip	**250 ml/8 fl oz double cream**
until stiff and stir together with	**4 - 5 tbsp grated horseradish**
Season with	**lemon juice**
	salt
	sugar
Put into a piping bag Sprinkle	**10 thin slices smoked salmon**

with a little lemon juice if desired, and
roll into cone shapes
Fill cones with piped horseradish cream
Arrange on a serving dish and garnish
with **dill sprigs**
Serve with the remaining horseradish
cream

Greek button mushrooms

Clean and slice	**500 g/1lb button mushrooms**
Peel and dice	**1 onion**
Bring to the boil	**125 ml/4 fl oz water**
	4 tbsp olive oil
	1 bay leaf
	dried thyme
Add the mushrooms and onions, and season with	**salt**

Smoked salmon Altona

Greek button mushrooms

	pepper
	sugar
Cook until tender Add	**125 ml/4 fl oz white wine**
	1 - 2 tbsp tomato purée
Add salt and pepper to taste Allow to cool a little, and sprinkle with	**1 tbsp chopped parsley**
Cooking time: 8 - 10 minutes Serve with:	**French bread**

Italian style fennel
(8 servings)

Bring to the boil	**500 ml/1 pint salted water**
Clean and halve	**4 fennel bulbs**
Put them into the water, bring back to the boil, and cook until tender Arrange on a warm serving dish, and pour on	**50 g/2 oz melted browned butter**
Sprinkle with	**grated parmesan cheese**

and serve immediately
Cooking time: 20 - 30 minutes

Vegetables with avocado cream

Clean and wash	**250 g/8 oz button mushrooms**
Clean and peel the stalks	**375 g/12 oz broccoli**

Asparagus with whipped sauce

Remove any brown parts from Cut off the top end, wash the sticks, and cut into pieces 5 cm/2 in and $\frac{1}{2}$ cm/$\frac{1}{4}$ in thick	**4 - 6 sticks celery**
Halve, and wash and cut into pieces 5 cm/2 in long and $\frac{1}{2}$ cm/$\frac{1}{4}$ in thick	**2 - 3 medium leeks**
Scrape and wash and cut into pieces 5 cm/2 in long and $\frac{1}{2}$ cm/$\frac{1}{4}$ in thick	**2 large carrots**
Halve Remove the stalks, seeds and pith and cut into $\frac{1}{2}$ cm/$\frac{1}{4}$ in wide strips	**1 - 2 red peppers**
Cut into quarters, or if large into 6 pieces Remove any brown parts, and wash	**2 - 3 fennel bulbs**
Put each of the vegetables in turn into bringing it back to the boil each time, and removing vegetables when tender Renew the water once during this process, and when cooking the fennel, add	**boiling salted water**
	2 tbsp lemon juice
Allow vegetables to drain well, and lay them in a shallow dish Cooking time:	
for the mushrooms:	**about 1 minute**
for the broccoli:	**about 3 minutes, thick stems about 5 minutes**
for the celery:	**about 1 minute**

for the leeks:	**2 - 3 minutes**
for the carrots:	**3 - 5 minutes**
for the peppers:	**about 1 minute**
for the fennel:	**about 7 minutes**

For the marinade

Peel	**1 onion**
	1 - 2 cloves of garlic
Finely dice the onion, and crush the garlic	
Stir them with	**4 tbsp salad oil** **4 tbsp white wine vinegar**
Season with	**salt** **pepper** **sugar**

and pour over vegetables
Occasionally, allow the marinade to run into a corner of the dish and pour it over the vegetables again
Allow to marinate for several hours

For the avocado cream

Peel and halve Remove stone, and purée flesh with an electric mixer or with a fork	**1 ripe avocado**
Sprinkle with	**1 tbsp lemon juice**
Stir	**150 g/5 fl oz double cream**

and mix it well into avocado purée,

together with	**150 ml/5 fl oz yoghurt**
Peel and crush and add to avocado cream	**1 clove of garlic**
Stir in	**1 tbsp chopped parsley**
	1 tbsp chopped dill
	1 tbsp finely chopped chives
Add	**lemon juice**
	onion salt
	salt
	pepper
	sugar
to taste	
Arrange vegetables on a large serving dish, and garnish with	**parsley**
Serve with avocado cream and	**small bread rolls or French bread and butter**

Asparagus with whipped sauce

Drain	**300 g/10 oz cooked asparagus tips**
and keep warm	
Heat	**50 g/2 oz butter or margarine**
Brown	**4 slices thick white bread**
on both sides in butter	
For the whipped sauce	
Whip together	**2 egg yolks**
	3 tbsp lukewarm water
over hot water until mixture thickens (do not allow it to boil)	
Fold in	**2 stiffly whipped egg whites**
and season with	**salt**
	pepper
	lemon juice
Place toast slices on	**washed lettuce leaves**
and arrange asparagus tips on them	
Spread a little sauce over the asparagus, and serve remaining sauce separately	
Cut	**125 g/4 oz or cooked smoked ham**
into strips and scatter over toast slices	
Sprinkle with	**chopped parsley**

Milanese salami with wine onions

Peel	**250 g/8 oz small onions**
Heat	**2 tbsp olive oil**

and sauté the onions gently	
Season with	**salt**
	pepper
Sprinkle with	**sugar**
and brown lightly, stirring constantly	
Add	**125 ml/4 fl oz white wine**
	2 tbsp lemon juice
	1 tbsp tarragon vinegar
Allow the onions to cook gently for 10 - 15 minutes	
Allow them to cool in the liquid, then drain	
Arrange	**125 g/4 oz thinly sliced Milanese salami**
on 4 plates with the onions, and garnish with	**lemon balm**
	tomato wedges
Serve with:	**French bread**

Stuffed braised tomatoes

Cut tops off	**8 medium firm tomatoes**
Remove the pulp, and press through a sieve	
Make this up to 500 ml/1 pint with water	
Sprinkle the insides of the tomatoes with salt	
For the filling	
Clean, halve and slice	**250 g/8 oz mushrooms**
Peel and chop	**1 small onion**
Melt	**1 tbsp butter or margarine**

Stuffed braised tomatoes

25

and sauté mushrooms and onions
Stir in **1 egg**
**50 g/2 oz fine bread-
crumbs**
and season to taste with **salt**
pepper
Stir in **1 tbsp chopped
parsley**

and put mixture into tomatoes
Put lids of tomatoes on top of the filling
Melt **50 g/2 oz margarine**
and place tomatoes in it, side by side
Cover and cook until tender, arrange on
a serving dish and keep warm
Add **25 g/1 oz plain flour**
to the margarine and stir until it is light
yellow
Add tomato liquid and beat with an egg
whisk, being careful not to allow it to
become lumpy as it comes to the boil

Little celery tarts

Boil for 3 minutes, and season to taste
with salt, pepper, and **sugar**
Add **1 rounded tbsp
tomato purée**
and serve the tomatoes in the sauce
Cooking time: about 20 minutes

Fresh figs with pastrami
(Illustrated on pages 16-17)

Rinse **4 fresh figs**
under running cold water
Dry and halve them
Arrange them on a serving dish with **125 g/4 oz very thinly
sliced pastrami**
Serve with: **toast or white bread
and butter**

Little celery tarts

Drain **5 slices tinned
celeriac**

and cut them into 8 cm/3 in circles with
a round cutter or a glass, to make them
look even more appetizing
Lay them on a serving dish and sprinkle
with **lemon juice
salt**
Shell **1 hard-boiled egg**
and dice, together with **1 large pickled
gherkin
125 g/4 oz ham
125 g/4 oz tinned
celeriac (the rest of
the tin)**

For the mayonnaise
Beat until thick **1 egg yolk
1 - 2 tsp mustard
1 tbsp vinegar or
lemon juice
salt
1 tsp sugar**
Gradually beat in **125 ml/4 fl oz salad
oil**

and add the diced ingredients
Put this on top of the celery slices, and
arrange them on **washed lettuce leaves**
Garnish with **parsley**

Variation:
Instead of mayonnaise, make a salad
dressing from **3 tbsp salad oil
1 - 2 tbsp lemon juice
a little salt
a little sugar**

Farmer's trout appetiser

Farmer's trout appetiser
(1 serving)

Wash	**1 endive leaf**
	1 chicory leaf
and allow to drain	
Arrange them on a dessert plate with	**1 slice of orange**
Remove skin of	**1 smoked fillet of trout**
and lay it on salad leaves	
Sprinkle with	**1 tsp lemon juice**

Place	**1 tsp grated horse-radish**
beside trout	
Stir together	**1 tbsp double cream**
	1 tsp finely chopped dill
Season to taste with	**lemon juice**
	salt
	pepper
and pour this over trout fillet	
Serve with:	**toast**

SOUPS

Cold avocado cream soup
(Recipe on p.35)

Vichyssoise

Bring to the boil	**1 1/2 pints instant chicken stock**
Peel and dice	**500 g/1 lb potatoes**
Clean	**1 - 2 leeks**

thoroughly, and cut into rings
Wash again if necessary, then add both ingredients to the stock, bring to the boil, and cook for about 25 minutes
Purée with an electric mixer or blender

Stir in	**125 ml/4 fl oz cream**
Season with	**seasoning salt**
	pepper
Garnish with	**finely chopped chives**
Serve chilled	

Russian soup
(4 - 6 servings)

Mix	**375 ml/12 fl oz cucumber juice (freshly pressed from unpeeled cucumber)**
with	**450 ml/15 fl oz sour cream**
Wash	**½ cucumber**

Russian soup

Avocado soup with flaked almonds

Remove stalks, pips and pith from	**½ red pepper**
	½ green pepper
and wash	
Drain	**200 g/6 oz pickled beetroot**
Dice these 3 ingredients	
Shell and dice	**2 hard-boiled eggs**
Wash, pat dry, and chop	**2 bunches chives**
Stir everything into the cucumber cream and season with	**3 tbsp vodka**
	salt
	freshly ground pepper
Serve chilled	

Avocado soup with flaked almonds

Halve	**2 ripe avocado pears (about 250 g/8 oz)**
Remove stones and scoop out the flesh from the skin, and press through a sieve	
Immediately stir into pulp	**2 tbsp lemon juice**
Heat	**250 ml/8 fl oz instant chicken stock**
Add	**3 tbsp white wine**
	125 ml/4 fl oz cream
and heat together	
Stir in the avocado, but do not allow it to boil, and season with	**salt**
	freshly ground pepper
Pour the soup into 4 soup bowls, and sprinkle with	**blanched flaked almonds, toasted**

Cold wine soup with figs

Reserving the juice, drain Make the fig juice up to 500 ml/1 pint with water Bring the liquid to the boil, with	**250 g/8 oz tinned figs**
	2 slices of lemon (½ cm/¼ in thick) **1 stick cinnamon** **a little ground cardamon** **1 - 2 tbsp sugar**
Sprinkle on and allow to cook for about 15 minutes Remove the soup from heat, and take out the lemon slices and cinnamon Add	**25 g/1 oz sago** **500 ml/1 pint white wine**
Cut the figs into strips, add to the soup, and serve chilled	

Refreshing cold melon soup

Cut	**1 honeydew melon** (about 1.2 kg/2 ½ lb)
in half crossways and remove the seeds Using a large spoon, scoop out the flesh, and purée in a mixer	
Add	**250 ml/8 fl oz white wine** **1 - 2 tbsp sugar** **3 - 4 tbsp lemon juice**
Wash, halve, and remove pips from	**250 g/8 oz black grapes**
Add them to the ingredients and put into the melon shells Serve chilled	

Royal consommé

Beat together	**2 eggs** **4 tbsp cold milk** **salt** **ground nutmeg**
and pour it into a greased container Cover with baking foil, and place in boiling water Bring the water back to the boil, put the lid on the pan, and simmer (do not allow to boil again) When the mixture has set, turn out and cut into cubes Bring to the boil	**1 l/2 pints instant beef stock**

Cold wine soup with figs

Cut   **50 g/2 oz raw smoked ham**

into strips

and add to the soup, together with   **125 g/4 oz cooked peas**

and the egg cubes

Reheat, and sprinkle with   **finely chopped parsley**

Cooking time: about 30 minutes

Gazpacho

Soak   **2 slices white bread**

in cold water

Halve   **1 red and 1 green pepper**

Remove seeds and pith and wash

Gazpacho

Peel   **½ cucumber**

Dip   **3 tomatoes**

first into boiling water then into cold water, and skin

Cut all the ingredients into small pieces, and purée them in an electric mixer or blender, together with the well squeezed bread and   **2 peeled and crushed cloves of garlic**

Season with   **salt**
pepper

Gradually add   **3 tbsp salad oil**
and stir well

Add   **2 - 3 tbsp vinegar**
seasoning salt

to taste

Serve chilled

Spanish farmer's soup
(6 - 8 servings)

Wash and dry   **250 g/8 oz beef**
250 g/8 oz mutton

and cut into cubes, then heat   **3 - 4 tbsp cooking oil**

and fry meat on all sides

Peel and finely dice   **1 onion**

Add this to the meat and fry all together

Season with   **salt**
pepper
dried thyme
dried basil
garlic powder

Add   **2 l/5 pints instant beef stock**

Bring to the boil and cook for about 30 minutes

Peel and wash   **200 g/6 oz potatoes**

Spanish farmer's soup

Scrape and wash   **200 g/6 oz carrots**
Dice both ingredients
Clean   **2 leeks**
thoroughly, then cut into rings and wash
again if necessary
Add these 3 ingredients to the soup,
bring to the boil, and cook for about 30
minutes
About 10 minutes before the end of the
cooking time, add   **300 g/10 oz frozen peas**
Slice   **2 coarse smoked German sausages**
and cut into strips
Add both ingredients shortly before the
end of the cooking time, and heat in the
soup
Sprinkle with   **chopped parsley**
Cooking time: about $1\frac{1}{4}$ hours

French onion soup

Peel and slice   **375 g/12 oz onions**
Melt   **75 g/3 oz margarine**
Sauté the onions in the margarine
Add   **1 1/2 pints instant beef stock**
and cook until tender
Season with   **salt**
pepper
4 tbsp white wine

Cooking time: about 20 minutes
Variation:
Put the soup into ovenproof bowls, and
add   **small cubes of white bread browned in butter**
Sprinkle   **grated cheese**
on top and heat under the grill

Curry cream soup

Cut   **375 g/12 oz pork fillet**
into strips
Peel, halve, and slice   **375 g/12 oz onions**
Peel, quarter, and core   **250 g/8 oz apples**
and cut into pieces
Heat   **3 - 4 tbsp cooking oil**
and brown meat on all sides
Dust with   **1 tbsp plain flour**
Add onion slices and apple pieces, and
season with   **salt**
sugar
1 tsp sweet paprika
2 tsp curry powder
Pour in   **750 ml/1 $\frac{1}{4}$ pint instant chicken stock**

and cook until meat is tender
5 minutes before the end of the cooking

Bortsch

time, add   **25 g/1 oz washed raisins**
Stir in   **150 ml/5 fl oz double cream**
and season with salt and   **curry powder**
Sprinkle with   **blanched flaked almonds, toasted**

Cooking time: 20 - 25 minutes

Bortsch

Peel and dice   **1 kg/2 lb beetroot**
Sprinkle with   **salt**
and leave to stand for a while
Bring to the boil   **2 1/4 pints water**
Wash   **500 g/1 lb beef**
and add to the boiling water with   **250 g/8 oz streaky bacon**

Bring back to the boil, and cook for
about $1\frac{1}{2}$ hours
Peel   **125 g/4 oz onions**
Peel and wash   **250 g/8 oz potatoes**
250 g/8 oz celeriac
Finely dice all 3 ingredients
Clean   **250 g/8 oz savoy cabbage**
and cut into small strips
Clean   **1 leek**

thoroughly, halve and cut into strips, and wash again if necessary
Remove meat from stock after about $1\frac{1}{2}$ hours cooking
Dice meat finely, and add to stock again, together with the rest of the ingredients
Allow to cook for about another hour

Season with **salt**
pepper
monosodium glutamate
seasoning salt
2 - 3 tbsp vinegar

Stir **150 ml/5 fl oz double cream**

and add to the soup
If wished, sprinkle on **chopped parsley**
Cooking time: about $2\frac{1}{2}$ hours

Creamed vegetable soup

Peel and dice **2 medium onions**
Melt **50 g/2 oz margarine**
and sauté onions
Add **1 1/2 pints instant chicken stock**
250 ml/8 fl oz milk

Creamed vegetable soup

and bring to the boil
Add **750 g/1 $\frac{1}{2}$lb prepared vegetables (e.g. leeks, carrots, kohlrabi, celery)**

Season with **salt**
pepper
grated nutmeg

Bring to the boil again, and cook for 15 - 20 minutes
Press soup through a sieve or purée in an electric mixer
(Reserve some leek and celery to add later if wished)
Reheat soup
Beat together **2 egg yolks**
4 tbsp sherry

and stir into soup
Add finely sliced leek and celery, pour into soup bowls, and pour a little into each bowl **double cream**

Midnight soup
(8 - 10 servings)

Wash, dry, and dice **250 g/8 oz beef**
250 g /8 oz pork
Melt **50 g/2 oz pork dripping**

and brown meat well on all sides
Peel and halve **250 g/8 oz onions**
and add to the meat
Fry them gently together, and season with **salt**
pepper
sugar
hot paprika
tabasco
monosodium glutamate
chilli sauce
cayenne pepper
madeira
Add **1 1/2 pints instant beef stock**

and bring to the boil
Clean **1 leek**
Cut into small rings, and wash again if necessary
Quarter **1 red pepper**
Remove seeds, stalk, and pith
Clean, and wash **1 stick celery (about 125 g/4 oz)**

Scrape and wash **2 carrots**
Cut these 3 ingredients into strips, and add vegetables to the soup after it has been cooking for about 15 minutes
Cook until tender
5 minutes before the end of the cooking time, add **425 g/15 oz tinned**

Midnight soup

together with their liquids, and heat for a while
Add salt, pepper, sugar, tabasco, chilli sauce, cayenne pepper to taste
Cooking time: about 1 hour

	red kidney beans 425 g/15 oz tinned white haricot beans

Cold avocado cream soup
(Illustrated on pages 28-29)

Wash and dry	2 ripe avocado pears (about 500 g/1 lb)
Halve them lengthways and remove the stones	
Carefully scoop out the flesh, and cut it into small cubes	
Sprinkle with	1 tbsp lemon juice
Bring	750 ml/1 ¼ pint instant beef stock

to the boil	
Add the avocado pieces and bring back to the boil	
Cook for about 5 minutes, then rub through a fine sieve or purée in a liquidizer	
Season with	salt
	pepper
	white wine
and reheat for a short time	
Stir in	2 tbsp double cream
and allow to cool	
Serve the soup sprinkled with	½ tbsp finely chopped dill
	1 tsp chopped chilis

Note: This soup can also be served hot

Piquant party soup
(4 - 6 servings)

Wash, dry, and dice	250 g/8 oz beef
	250 g/8 oz pork
Heat	3 - 4 tbsp cooking oil
and fry meat on all sides	
Peel	250 g/8 oz shallots or spring onions
halve if necessary, and add to the meat	
Allow to cook together for a short while	
Add	2 tbsp tomato purée
Season with	salt
	pepper
	sugar
	monosodium glutamate
	sweet paprika
	dried oregano
Add	750 ml/1 ½ pint water
	250 ml/8 fl oz red wine
Bring to the boil, and allow to simmer	
Dip	2 - 3 tomatoes
first into boiling water, then into cold water	
Skin, core, and dice them	
Clean	1 leek
Cut into small rings and wash again if necessary	
15 minutes before the end of the cooking time, add leeks, tomatoes, and	300 g/10 oz tinned sweetcorn
to the soup and continue to simmer	
Cooking time: about 1 hour	

SALADS

Gourmet's salad dish
(Recipe on p.40)

Mushroom salad with basil mayonnaise

Mushroom salad with basil mayonnaise

Soak	**15 g/$\frac{1}{2}$ oz dried mush-rooms**
in	**125 ml/$\frac{1}{4}$ pint luke-warm water**
Wash, and drain	**250 g/8 oz button mushrooms**

(halve or slice the larger ones)

Heat and fry	**2 tbsp cooking oil** **200 g/6 oz chicken breasts**

on both sides for about 5 minutes until golden brown

Season with	**salt** **pepper**

Remove from the pan, allow to cool, and cut into strips
Add mushrooms to the pan, fry, and season with salt and pepper
Add dried mushrooms with their liquid and cook all together for about 5 minutes, then allow to cool

Clean	**1 bunch spring onions**

and cut into rings
Mix all the ingredients together and place them in a salad bowl

For the basil mayonnaise

Beat until thick	**1 egg yolk** **1 tsp mustard** **1 tbsp vinegar or lemon juice** **1 tsp sugar**
Gradually beat in	**125 ml/$\frac{1}{4}$ pint salad oil**
Stir in	**2 tbsp double cream** **2 bunches chopped**

Season with	**fresh basil or** **1 tbsp dried basil** **salt** **freshly ground black pepper**

Pour mayonnaise over the salad and allow it to absorb flavours

Salad platter
(4 - 6 servings)

Discard outer leaves of	**1 small head of lettuce**

Tear large leaves into pieces, but leave the small leaves whole
Wash and drain well

Quarter	**1 red and 1 green pepper**

Remove the stalk, seeds, and pith, then wash and cut into strips

Remove cores of and slice	**4 large tomatoes**
Peel	**3 - 4 onions or one large Spanish onion**
and cut into rings	
Thinly slice	**$\frac{1}{2}$ cucumber**
Drain	**300 g/10 oz tinned sweetcorn** **300 g/10 oz tinned tuna fish**

Arrange all the salad ingredients on a large plate

For the salad dressing

Combine	**300 ml/10 fl oz double cream** **2 - 3 tbsp tomato**

Celery salad with apple

Bulgarian zucchini salad

For the salad dressing	
Combine	**150 g/5 fl oz yoghurt**
	1 - 2 tbsp grated horseradish
	3 - 4 tbsp lemon juice
	2 - 3 tsp sugar
Season with	**salt**
Whip	**125 ml/4 fl oz cream**
until stiff and fold in	
Coarsely chop	**125 g/4 oz walnuts**

Reserve some for garnishing and stir in remainder
Mix celery and apple with the dressing and place in a salad bowl lined with the chicory leaves
Garnish with the reserved walnuts

Bulgarian zucchini salad

Slice	**250 g/8 oz courgettes**
Remove cores of and slice	**4 tomatoes**
Quarter	**2 green peppers**
Remove the stalks, seeds, and pith, then wash and cut into strips	
Finely slice	**1 onion, peeled**
	8 - 10 olives
For the salad dressing	
Combine	**4 tbsp salad oil**
	1 tsp vinegar essence
	2 tbsp water
	$\frac{1}{2}$ tsp mustard
Add	**salt**
	pepper
	sugar
to taste	
Stir in	**1 tbsp finely chopped chives**
	1 tbsp finely chopped dill

Mix all the salad ingredients with the dressing

Shell	**2 hard-boiled eggs**
and cut into eighths	
Crumble	**150 g/5 oz Bulgarian sheep's cheese**

Carefully mix half of the cheese and all of the eggs with the salad, and sprinkle the remaining cheese over the top
Serve with: **sesame seed bread**

Fish and rice salad

Boil	**750 ml/1 $\frac{1}{4}$ pint salted water**
and add	**75 g/3 oz long grain rice**

---

	ketchup
	2 - 3 tbsp milk
Add	**salt**
	pepper
	sugar

to taste and pour over the salad
Sprinkle with **chopped parsley**
chopped dill
finely chopped chives

Celery salad with apple
(4 - 6 servings)

Wash and drain	**$\frac{1}{2}$ head chicory**
Wash and finely slice	**500 g/1 lb celery**
Cut	**2 medium red apples**
into eighths, core, and cut into thin crosswise slices	

Fish and rice salad

Bring back to the boil, and simmer for about 20 minutes until tender
Transfer it to a colander, rinse with cold water, and drain well

Flake	**250 g/8 oz cooked fish**
Drain	**3 slices tinned celery**
Peel, quarter, and core	**1 apple**
Peel	**1 onion**
Finely dice the last 4 ingredients	**50 g/2 oz Gouda cheese**

For the salad dressing

Stir together	**3 tbsp salad oil**
	5 tbsp vinegar
Season with	**salt**
	curry powder

Carefully mix with all the salad ingredients, and allow it to the absorb flavours

Gourmet's salad dish
(Illustrated on pages 36-37)

Wash	**50 g/2 oz young spinach**
thoroughly 5 or 6 times, and drain	
Wash and drain	**¼ head curly lettuce**
and separate the leaves	
Wash and slice	**½ cucumber**
Wash and drain	**1 bunch radishes**
Cut into slices	
Cut	**1 sweet green pepper**
in half across	
Remove stalk, seeds, and pith	
Wash and cut into rings	
Peel and slice	**1 onion**
Clean and wash	**125 g/4 oz sugar peas (mangetout)**

Scrape, wash and slice	**2 carrots**
Wash and thinly slice	**125 g/4 oz button mushrooms**
Rub a salad bowl with	**1 peeled clove of garlic**
and arrange the ingredients in it	

For the salad dressing

Stir together	**6 - 8 tbsp olive oil**
	3 tbsp wine vinegar
Season with	**salt**
	sugar
	pepper
Stir in	**1 tbsp finely chopped chives**
	1 tbsp chopped chervil
and pour it over the salad	

Fisherman's style salad dish with dill cream

Pile	**250 g/8 oz prawns**
in the middle of a large flat dish	
Shell	**3 - 4 hard-boiled eggs**
Cut in half lengthways, chop egg whites coarsely, and press the yolks through a sieve	
Arrange whites and yolks on either side of the prawns, in a circle	
Spread	**1 box chopped, washed cress**
around the egg	
Drain	**300 g/10 oz pickled beetroot slices**
and lay them in another circle, around	

40

Fisherman's style salad dish with dill cream

the other ingredients

For the dill cream

Stir together	**150 - 225 ml/ 5 - 8 fl oz double cream**
	2 - 3 tbsp chopped dill
Add	**salt**
	pepper
	sugar
to taste	

Serve the dill cream separately

Serve with:	**German rye bread or toast and butter**

Button mushroom salad

Clean, wash, and quarter	**500 g/1 lb button mushrooms**
Cook until tender in	**a little water**
Season with	**salt**
	pepper
and allow to cool	
Cut	**250 g/8 oz cooked roast beef slices**
into strips	
Shell and dice	**2 hard-boiled eggs**

Mix all the ingredients together

For the salad dressing

Combine	**4 tbsp salad oil**
	2 tbsp herb vinegar
	1 - 2 tbsp tomato ketchup
	4 - 5 tbsp cream
	1 tsp brandy
	sweet paprika
Season with	**salt**

	pepper
	sugar
Stir in	**2 tbsp chopped parsley**

Mix with the salad and leave to stand in the refrigerator for about 20 minutes
Add salt, pepper and sugar to taste

Garnish with	**egg slices**
	parsley

Cooking time: about 10 minutes

Bean salad

Reserving the liquid, drain	**450 g/15 oz tinned haricot beans**
	450 g/15 oz tinned red kidney beans
	450 g/15 oz tinned green beans
Peel and dice	**2 - 3 onions, red if available**

For the salad dressing

Stir together	**4 - 5 tbsp salad oil**
	3 - 4 tbsp bean liquid
Season with	**salt**
	pepper

Bean salad

| | sugar |
| Stir in | **2 tbsp finely chopped chives**
a little chopped savory
a little chopped borage |

Mix the salad ingredients with the dressing, and allow it to absorb the flavours
Adjust seasoning

Iceberg lettuce and kiwifruit salad
(4 - 6 servings)

Discard any faded outer leaves from	**½ head iceberg lettuce**
Tear remaining leaves into bite-sized pieces, wash and drain	
Wash, and peel if necessary	**2 - 3 courgettes**
Peel	**3 kiwifruit**
Cut both ingredients into slices	
Clean, wash, and cut into pieces 3 cm /1 in thick	**250 g/8 oz celery**
Cut into strips	**125 g/4 oz raw smoked ham**
For the salad dressing	
Stir together	**3 tbsp salad oil** **4 tbsp lemon juice**
Add	**salt** **pepper** **sugar**
to taste	
Stir in	**1 tbsp chopped tarragon**
Mix the dressing with the salad ingredients and sprinkle with	**25 g/1 oz shelled pistachio nuts**

Iceberg lettuce and kiwifruit salad

Italian farmer's salad

Italian farmer's salad
(4 - 6 servings)

Drain	**250 g/8 oz tinned green beans** **250 g/8 oz tinned chick peas** **250 g/8 oz tinned haricot beans**
Peel, halve, and slice	**1 large Spanish onion**
Cut	**250 g/8 oz tomatoes**
into eighths and remove cores	
Cut	**150 g/5 oz salami slices**
into strips	
For the salad dressing	
Stir together	**6 tbsp salad oil** **3 tbsp wine vinegar** **1 tsp mustard**
Season with	**salt** **pepper** **sugar**
Stir in	**½ tsp dried tarragon**

Mix the dressing with the salad ingredients and allow them to absorb the flavours
Adjust seasoning

Sweetcorn salad

Dip	**250 g/8 oz tomatoes**
first into boiling water, then into cold water	
Skin and dice	
Drain	**275 g/9 oz tinned sweetcorn**

Sweetcorn salad

	250 g/8 oz fresh peeled prawns
For the salad dressing	
Peel and dice	**1 onion**
Add to	**3 tbsp salad oil**
	1 tsp vinegar
	4 tsp water
and stir together	
Season with	**salt**
	pepper
	sugar
Stir in	**1 bunch finely chopped parsley**
	1 bunch finely chopped chives

Mix the dressing with the salad ingredients and add salt, pepper and sugar to taste if necessary

Asparagus salad with herb dressing

Wash	**500 g/1 lb peeled asparagus**
under running cold water and cut into pieces 3 - 5 cm/1 $\frac{1}{2}$ - 2 in long	
Boil with	**250 ml/8 fl oz water**
	1 knob butter
	1 level tsp salt
	sugar

Add asparagus and bring back to the boil then simmer until tender
Drain, allow to cool, then arrange on washed lettuce leaves
For the herb dressing

Combine	**6 tbsp salad oil**
	3 tbsp vinegar

	salt
	pepper
	2 small peeled, diced onions
Add	**sugar**
to taste and stir in	**3 - 4 tbsp chopped mixed herbs**

Pour some of the dressing over the salad, and serve the rest separately

Shell and halve	**1 hard-boiled egg**

Press the yolk through a sieve, and sprinkle over the salad, together with

Garnish with:	**finely chopped chives**
	small washed lettuce leaves

Cooking time: about 30 minutes

Green pepper salad with sheep's cheese

Halve	**3 green peppers**
Remove stalks, seeds, and pith, wash, and cut into strips	
Dip	**400 g/14 oz tomatoes**
first into boiling water, then into cold water	
Skin and core them, then cut into eighths	
Peel, halve, and slice	**2 - 3 large Spanish onions**

Arrange all the ingredients in a salad bowl

Crumble	**250 g/8 oz sheep's cheese**

and sprinkle it over the salad

For the salad dressing	
Stir together	**3 tbsp salad oil**
	1 tsp vinegar
	4 tsp water
Season with	**salt**
	pepper

Pour the dressing over the salad and allow it to absorb the flavours

Before serving, sprinkle with	**2 tbsp finely chopped chives**

Savoury potato salad
(4 - 6 servings)

Boil	**750 g/1 $\frac{1}{2}$ lb potatoes**
in their skins until tender, then peel whilst still warm and cut into slices	
Dice	**250 g/8 oz cooked beef**
Cut	**1 leek**
in half lengthways, wash and finely slice	

Drain	**150 g/5 oz tinned button mushrooms**
Halve if necessary	
Dip	**3 - 4 tomatoes**
first into boiling water, then into cold water	
Skin and dice	
For the salad dressing	
Peel and dice	**1 large onion**
Add to	**6 tbsp salad oil**
	1 tbsp vinegar
	5 tbsp water
	1 tsp mustard
and stir together	
Season with	**salt**
	freshly ground black pepper

Mix the dressing and the salad ingredients together, and leave for about 1 hour, to absorb the flavours

White herring salad

Pour	**250 ml/8 fl oz mineral water**
over	**6 white herring fillets**
and leave to stand for 3 - 4 hours	

Drain and pat dry, and cut into pieces 3 - 4 cm/1 $\frac{1}{2}$ in long	
Peel and slice	**2 onions**
and separate the onion rings	
Slice	**2 - 3 pickled gherkins**
	150 g/5 oz sautéed button mushrooms
For the salad dressing	
Combine	**150 g/5 fl oz double cream**
	1 - 2 tbsp yoghurt
	2 tsp grated horse-radish

Mix the dressing with the other ingredients and arrange in small dishes

Mussel salad
(2 - 3 servings)

Wash and drain	**150 g/5 oz bottled or tinned mussels**
Dice	**125 g/4 oz pickled gherkins (mustard gherkins if available)**
Halve	**10 stuffed olives**
	10 silverskin (cocktail) onions

Savoury potato salad

White herring salad

Mussel salad

Dip	**2 tomatoes**

first into boiling water, then into cold water
Skin, halve, remove pips and cores, and dice

For the salad dressing

Mix	**150 ml/5 fl oz sour cream**
	1 tbsp dried chives
	salt
	pepper

Mix together the salad ingredients and leave to stand for about 30 minutes to absorb the flavours. Arrange on and serve with dressing **lettuce leaves**

Beautiful gardener's salad
(6 servings)

Boil	**1 1/2 pints salted water**
Add	**100 g/4 oz long grain rice**

Bring back to the boil, and simmer for about 20 minutes until tender
Transfer to a colander, rinse with cold water and drain well

Dip	**3 tomatoes**

first into boiling water, then into cold water
Skin, quarter, remove pips and cores and cut into strips

Halve	**2 avocados**

Remove stones and dice

Shell and dice	**2 hard-boiled eggs**
Clean and thinly slice	**100 g/4 oz button mushrooms**
Cut	**150 g/5 oz ham**

into strips
Rub the inside of a large salad bowl with 1 peeled clove of garlic

For the salad dressing

Combine	**3 tbsp salad oil**
	1 tbsp herb vinegar
	4 tbsp white wine
	3 tbsp cream
Season with	**salt**
	freshly ground white pepper
	curry powder

Mix together with the salad ingredients, and allow to stand for about 30 minutes, to absorb the flavours
Put into the salad bowl, and garnish with **tomato roses** **basil**

Beautiful gardener's salad

MEAT PIES,
TERRINES,
MOUSSES

Broccoli pie
(Recipe on p.55)

Chicken liver pie

Chicken liver pie

For the filling	
Peel and finely dice	**1 large onion**
Heat	**2 tbsp cooking oil**
and sauté onion	
Wash	**500 g/1 lb chicken livers**
Pat dry, add to the onion and fry well	
Add	**5 tbsp brandy or dry sherry**
	$\frac{1}{2}$ tsp freshly ground pepper
	2 pinches ground cloves
	2 pinches grated nutmeg
	1 pinch dried basil
	1 pinch celery salt
	1 pinch ground coriander
	1 tsp green peppercorns
	10 crushed juniper berries

Stir them all together, and fry the liver for about another minute, then allow to cool

Chop liver finely, and stir with	**1 kg/2 lb raw sausagemeat**
and the pan juices until creamy	
Season with	**salt**

Put the mixture into a pie dish, and press it well to remove all air bubbles (the dish must be no more than $\frac{3}{4}$ full)
Place in a preheated oven
Electricity: 150° - 175° C/300° - 325° F
Gas: Mark 2 - 3
Cooking time: 30 - 40 minutes

For the pastry	
Mix together	**1 pkt 370 g/12 oz bread mix**
	lukewarm water
following instructions on packet	
Dust the dough with	**plain flour**

and remove from the bowl
Knead for a short while, and roll out on a floured surface to a thickness of 1 cm/$\frac{1}{2}$ in
Cut out to the size and shape of the pie dish, and lay it over the cooked pie
(Decorate the pie as desired with the remaining dough, and use any remaining dough to make bread rolls, to be baked with the pie)
Cut a few small holes in the pastry (do not press) and brush with water
Bake in a preheated oven
Electricity: 200° - 225° C/400° - 425° F
Gas: Mark 6 - 7
Baking time: 30 - 35 minutes

Ham mousse

Finely mince	**500 g/1 lb cooked ham**
Cream	**125 g/4 oz butter**
Stir in the ham and	**125 ml/4 fl oz cream**
	2 level tbsp tomato purée
Season with	**salt**
	pepper
Sprinkle	**1 pkt gelatine**
on to	**5 tbsp cold water**
and leave to soak for 10 minutes	
Heat	**375 ml/12 fl oz meat stock made with stock cube**
Add gelatine and stir until dissolved	
Add	**3 tbsp port**

and season with salt and pepper
Allow to cool a little, and stir 6 tbsp of the liquid into the ham mixture
Rinse out a 30 × 11 cm/12 × 5 in loaf tin with water, and pour in the aspic liquid to a depth of about 1 cm/$\frac{1}{2}$ in
Leave in refrigerator to set

Garnish the aspic layer with **black olives, halved**
parsley

and carefully cover with a few spoonfuls
of the remaining aspic liquid
then allow to set
Shape the ham mixture to the size and
shape of the loaf tin, and put it on top
of the aspic layer
Carefully smooth surface with a knife
dipped in cold water, and leave in a cold
place
Pour the remaining aspic liquid on to a
flat plate, and allow to set, then cut into
cubes
Turn out the ham mixture, and garnish
it with the aspic cubes

Trout en croûte

Fillet and remove skins of **2 trout**
Wash under running cold water and pat
dry
Peel **1 onion**
and cut into rings
Layer the trout, onion rings, and **1 tbsp finely chopped**
chives

in a dish
Stir together **125 ml/4 fl oz white**
wine
5 tbsp cooking oil

and pour over the fillets
Cover, and leave to stand in a cool
place for 4 - 5 hours, or overnight
Sieve **300 g/10 oz plain four**
on to a pastry board
Make a hollow in the middle, and pour
in **1 egg**
$\frac{1}{2}$ egg yolk
$\frac{1}{2}$ egg white
1 tbsp cold water
$\frac{1}{2}$ tsp salt

Mix to a thick paste with some of the
flour
Cut into pieces, and add **125 g/4 oz cold pork**
dripping

Cover with flour, and working from the
middle outwards, quickly rub into a
smooth dough
Leave this dough in a cool place for 4 -
5 hours, or overnight
Thaw **500 g/1 lb frozen**
plaice fillets

at room temperature
and mince finely
Stir together with **2 eggs**
1 heaped tbsp
chopped dill
2 tbsp fine bread-
crumbs
grated rind of lemon
150 ml/5 fl oz double
cream

25 g/1 oz melted
butter
Season well with **salt**
pepper
Knead the dough again, and roll out $\frac{2}{3}$ of
it
Cut it out to fit the base and sides of a
30 × 11 cm (12 × 3 in) loaf tin
Grease the loaf tin with **soft margarine**
and lay the pastry base in it
Brush the sides of the tin with a little of
Brush the remaining pastry pieces with **$\frac{1}{2}$ beaten egg white**
the egg white, and use them to line the
sides of the tin
Seal the edges well by pressing together
Put $\frac{1}{2}$ of the fish mixture into the tin, remove the trout fillets from the mari-
nade, pat them dry, and lay them on the
mixture
Cover the fillets with the remaining fish

Trout en croûte

mixture, press lightly, and trim the pastry sides to about 1 cm/$\frac{1}{2}$ in above mixture
Roll out remaining pastry, and cut to fit the loaf tin
Cut out 2 - 3 holes (diameter 2 - 3 cm/$\frac{1}{2}$ - 1 in) in the pastry, and place it on top of the mixture to form a lid
Roll out pastry trimmings and cut out little shapes and fish scales, brushing the underneath with egg white, and arrange them on the top of the pie
Place pie in a preheated oven

Beat together | $\frac{1}{2}$ egg yolk
| $\frac{1}{2}$ tbsp milk

and brush over the pie after baking for 30 minutes
Electricity: 175° - 200° C/350° - 400° F
Gas: Mark 4 - 6
Baking time: about 1 $\frac{1}{4}$ hours
After baking, carefully loosen the pie from the sides of the tin, and allow it to cool slightly, then remove it from the tin, and allow it to cool thoroughly

If desired, pour over | wine aspic (page 125)
Wrap in baking foil, and leave it for 1 - 2 days in the refrigerator
Serve with: | remoulade sauce (page 90)
| green salad

Vol-au-vents with pea and ham ragout

For the filling
Peel and finely dice | 2 small onions
Melt | 1 tbsp butter
Stir the onion and | 1 heaped tbsp plain flour
in the butter until the flour is light yellow
Add | 250 ml/8 fl oz cream
and beat with an egg whisk, taking care that no lumps form while you bring it to the boil
Add | 300 g/10 oz frozen peas
and cook for about 6 minutes
Cut | 250 g/8 oz ham
into strips
and add, continuing to heat
Beat together | 2 egg yolks
| 3 tbsp white wine
and use to enrich the ragout
Season with | salt
| freshly ground pepper
Stir in | 2 tbsp chopped parsley

Vol-au-vents with pea and ham ragout

Place | 8 ready-made puff pastry vol-au-vents
on a baking tray together with their lids, and warm them in a preheated oven
Electricity: 200° - 225° C/400° - 425° F
Gas: Mark 6 - 7
Warming time: about 5 minutes
Put the hot filling into the cases and put the lids on gently
Garnish with | parsley
If desired, serve with: | herb mayonnaise
Tip: If wished, pour aspic (page 124) over cooled vol-au-vents

Cucumber mousse

Peel and grate | 1 cucumber
Sprinkle with | salt
and leave for a while to draw out the juices, then squeeze out in a tea towel
Sprinkle | 2 tsp gelatine
on to | 3 tbsp cold water
and leave to soak for 10 minutes
Warm, stirring constantly, until dissolved
Cream | 50 g/2 oz butter
and stir well with | 50 ml/2 fl oz yoghurt
| 2 tbsp vinegar
Stir in grated cucumber and gelatine
Beat until stiff, and fold in | 150 ml/5 fl oz cream
Stir in | 2 tbsp chopped herbs
Rinse out a mould with cold water, then fill with the mixture, and leave in refrigerator to set
Carefully loosen from sides of the mould with a knife, and turn out on to a serving dish
Garnish with | dill sprigs

Cucumber mousse

Serve with:	**parsley** **German rye bread or** **pumpernickel**

Chicken breast terrine

Wash and pat dry	**2 chicken breasts**
Heat	**1 - 2 tbsp margarine**
and fry chicken breasts a few minutes on each side	
Sprinkle with	**salt** **pepper** **sweet paprika**
Remove from the pan, and allow to cool	
Wash, and pat dry	**400 g/14 oz chicken livers** **300 g/10 oz pork belly** **300 g/10 oz fatty bacon** **50 g/2 oz white bread**
Cut into 1 cm/$\frac{1}{2}$ in cubes, together with	
Peel and coarsely chop	**2 onions**
Fry them in the margarine until transparent, then add to the diced ingredients	
Add	**4 tbsp cream** **1 egg** **2 tbsp brandy** **1 tsp dried thyme** **$\frac{1}{2}$ tsp dried rosemary** **2 tsp sweet paprika** **1 tsp white pepper** **about 2 tsp salt**
and stir well	

Chill thoroughly in freezing compartment of refrigerator
Finely mince this mixture twice
Brush inside of an ovenproof 1 $\frac{1}{2}$ l/

3 pint lidded terrine with	**cooking oil**

Put half of the liver mixture into terrine and press down lightly
Lay the chicken breasts on to this, and cover with the remaining liver mixture
Level surface with a knife
Put on the lid, and place it in a roasting tin in a preheated oven

Pour	**1 l/2 pints warm water**

into the roasting tin and, halfway through the cooking time, add another **750 ml/1 $\frac{1}{4}$ pint warm water**

Electricity: 200° - 225° C/400° - 425° F
Gas: Mark 6 - 7
Cooking time: about 1 $\frac{1}{4}$ hours

Allow to cool, and garnish with	**parsley**

Liver terrine

Wash	**1 kg/2 lb pig's liver**
Pat dry and finely mince with	**500 g/1 lb fresh bacon or fat pork belly**
Peel and finely dice	**1 onion**
Melt	**1 tbsp butter**
and sauté the onions	
Coarsely chop	**200 g/6 oz cooked**

Chicken breast terrine

and add to the onion
Cook together, and allow to cool
slightly
Add   **1 tbsp chopped parsley**

and mix with the minced meat
Season well with   **dried marjoram**
salt
pepper
grated nutmeg

Reserving a few rashers, line a
30 × 11 cm/12 × 3 in loaf tin with   **150 g/5 oz thin cut fatty bacon**

Add liver mixture, smooth surface with
a knife, and lay remaining bacon slices
on top
Put it in a preheated oven
Electricity: 175° - 200° C/350° - 400° F
Gas: Mark 4 - 6

Liver terrine

mushrooms

Cooking time: about 1 ¼ hours
Leave the cooked liver terrine in a cold
place for at least one day, then remove
it from the tin
Prepare   **wine aspic (page 125)**
and pour it over the terrine
Garnish with   **small lettuce leaves**

Truffled pheasant terrine

Wash and pat dry   **1 oven-ready pheasant (about 1 kg/2 lb)**

Remove legs, and lay breasts in a small
dish
Pour over them, cover, and leave to
marinate for 1 - 2 hours   **3 tbsp brandy**
Finely mince   **200 g/6 oz fatty bacon**

and purée with an electric mixer
Wash and pat dry   **400 g/14 oz lean pork**
Peel   **1 small onion**
1 clove of garlic

and put them through a fine mincer with
the pheasant and the pork
Remove the breasts from the brandy
marinade, and pat dry
Add the marinade and the minced meat
to the puréed bacon, and stir in   **3 tbsp port**
1 egg
150 ml/5 fl oz double cream
1 tsp seasoning salt
Season with   **salt**
pepper
Finely dice 2 of   **3 bottled truffles (25 g/1 oz)**

and stir into the mixture
Line an ovenproof (1 ¾ l/3 pint) lidded
terrine with   **250 - 300 g/8 - 10 oz fatty bacon rashers**

reserving some for later, and put half of
the meat mixture into it
Lay the breasts on this, and spread the
rest of the mixture over them
Smooth surface and cover with remaining bacon rashers
Put on the lid, and place in a roasting
tin in a preheated oven
Pour   **1 l/2 pints warm water**
into the roasting tin, and add another   **750 ml/1 ¼ pint warm water**

halfway through cooking
Electricity: 200° - 225° C/400° - 425° F
Gas: Mark 6 - 7
Cooking time: about 1 ¾ hours
Pour off liquid fat from the terrine,
weight it, and leave in a cold place for
at least one day

For the port aspic

Sprinkle **1 rounded tsp gelatine**

on to **1 tbsp cold water**

and leave to soak for 10 minutes

Make up to 125 ml/4 fl oz **100 ml/3 oz concentrated tinned truffle stock**

with **port**

Bring to the boil, and remove from heat

Add the gelatine, stirring continuously until dissolved

Cut the remaining truffle into slices

Garnish the terrine with **shelled pistachio nuts**

and the truffle slices

Pour the cooled aspic liquid over it, and leave to set

Pike-perch mousse with prawns

Wash **400 g/14 oz pike-perch (if available)**

under running cold water, and pat dry

Bring to the boil **750 ml (1 ½ pints) water**

1 level tsp salt

1 pinch pepper

4 lemon slices (each

½ cm/¼ in thick)

6 peppercorns

Add the pike-perch, bring back to the boil, and simmer without boiling until tender

Remove fish from water, and pour the liquid through a cloth

Allow it to cool, and measure out 125 ml/4 fl oz

Remove skin and bones from fish

Flake it, and mince it finely twice, or press it through a sieve, or purée it with an electric mixer

Stir it into **300 ml/10 fl oz double cream**

Sprinkle **1 pkt gelatine**

on to **5 tbsp cold water**

Stir, and leave to soak for 10 minutes

Heat **125 ml/4 fl oz fish liquid**

Remove from heat and add gelatine, stirring until dissolved

Allow to cool a little then stir into the fish mixture

Season with salt, pepper and **lemon juice**

Rinse out 4 moulds (e.g. coffee cups, wine glasses) with water, and fill with fish mixture, smoothing surfaces with a knife

Leave in refrigerator to set

Pike-perch mousse with prawns

Prepare	**wine aspic (page 125)**
and allow to cool	
Turn out the firm fish mousses on to a wire rack, and put a plate beneath them	
On each mousse place one of	**4 king prawns, halved**
Pour the almost cold wine aspic over each and leave in a cold place	
Repeat several times, until each mousse is completely covered with aspic	
(If necessary, gently rewarm the aspic that has dripped off)	
Arrange the mousses on a glass plate, and garnish with	**lemon slices** **thyme** **tomato wedges**
Cooking time: about 15 minutes	
Serve with:	**toast or bread rolls and butter**

Pork terrine

Heat	**1 tbsp vegetable oil**
Wash	**375 g/12 oz lean pork pieces**
Pat dry and sprinkle with	**salt** **pepper**
and fry on all sides for about 10 minutes	
Sprinkle with	**sweet paprika**
and allow to cool	
Dice pork pieces, together with	**375 g/12 oz pork belly**
and mince finely	**125 g/4 oz fatty facon**
Mix the minced pork and bacon with	**250 g/8 oz minced meat**
Dice	**150 g/5 oz salted tongue**
Clean and slice	**125 g/4 oz mushrooms**
Peel and finely dice	**1 onion**
Finely chop	**2 tbsp shelled pistachio nuts**
Mix all the ingredients together with	**2 tbsp chopped parsley**
and	**2 eggs** **150 ml/5 fl oz madeira** **150 ml/5 fl oz cream**
Season with salt and	**freshly ground white pepper** **dried sage** **dried thyme**
Line the bottom and sides of a 30 cm/12 in loaf tin with	**150 g/5 oz thin cut fatty bacon**

Put in half of the meat mixture, and press lightly
Spread the diced tongue on this, and cover with the remaining meat mixture
Press down firmly
Fold the overhanging bacon slices over

Pork terrine

the meat mixture, and cover with baking foil
Place in a roasting tin in a preheated oven

Pour	**1 l/2 pints warm water**
into the roasting tin, and add another	**750 ml/1 ½ pint warm water**

about half-way through the cooking time
Electricity: 200° - 225° C/400° - 425° F
Gas: Mark 6 - 7
Cooking time: about 1 ½ hours
Pour off the liquid fat from the cooked terrine, weight it, and leave it in a cold place for at least one day
Turn out just before serving

> *Tip:*
> *Weighting of terrines*
> A terrine can best be weighted by laying a double layer of cooking foil over the mixture, and standing a dish of water (which is about the same size as the terrine) on it

Broccoli pie
(Illustrated on pages 46-47)

Remove the leaves from **500 g/1 lb broccoli**
Cut florets and stems from stalks, and cut a cross into the stems to just below the florets
Wash them
Bring to the boil **500 ml/18 fl oz salted water**

and add the broccoli (reserve some for garnishing)
Cook for 15 - 20 minutes until tender
Remove the broccoli, drain well, and rub through a sieve or purée in a liquidizer
Stir together **2 level tsp gelatine**
2 tbsp cold water

and leave to soak for 10 minutes
Stir it into the hot purée, and continue to stir until dissolved
Allow to cool a little
Stir in **2 tbsp double cream**
2 egg whites

and beat well
Add **salt**
grated nutmeg

to taste
Peel, wash and chop **400 g/14 oz celeriac**
Put it into **125 ml/4 fl oz boiling salted water**

and bring back to the boil
Cook for 25 - 30 minutes until tender, then remove, drain well, and rub through a sieve or purée in a liquidizer
Stir together **2 level tsp gelatine**
2 tbsp cold water

and leave to soak for 10 minutes
Stir into the hot purée, and continue to stir until dissolved
Allow to cool a little

Stir in **2 tbsp double cream**
2 egg whites

and beat well
Season with salt and **pepper**
Scrape, wash and slice **400 g/14 oz carrots**
Put them into **125 ml/4 fl oz boiling salted water**

Bring back to the boil, and cook for 25 - 30 minutes until tender
Remove and drain well, then rub through a sieve or purée in a liquidizer
Stir together **2 level tsp gelatine**
2 tbsp cold water

and leave to soak for 10 minutes
Stir it into the hot carrot purée and continue to stir until dissolved
Allow to cool a little
Stir in **2 tbsp double cream**
2 egg whites

and beat well
Season with salt **sugar**
powdered ginger

Oil a terrine or loaf tin with **cooking oil**
and put in the celery purée, levelling surface with a knife
Put half of the broccoli purée on top, and lightly press in the reserved broccoli florets, stems upwards
Cover them with the rest of the broccoli purée, and level surface
Finally put the carrot purée over the top and level surface
Cover the container with a lid or seal with baking foil, stand it in a pan of boiling water, and cook
Cooking time: 45 - 55 minutes
Leave the pie in a cool place for some time
Dip it briefly in hot water, remove it from the container, and slice fairly thickly
Serve with: **crisp salads**

**FISH,
CRUSTACEANS
AND SHELLFISH**

Marinated trout with dill sauce
(Recipe on p.59)

Seafood platter

Seafood platter

Put	**1 kg/2 lb mussels**

into plenty of cold water
Allow them to stay in the water for some hours, changing the water now and again
Finally scrub them thoroughly, and remove the hairy 'beards' and discard
Rinse them until the water runs clear
Any mussels that have opened while being washed and scrubbed are inedible, and must be discarded

Peel and halve	**1 onion**

Chop one half, and slice the other half
Put the mussels in a pan, add the finely chopped onion, and

	1 bunch chopped parsley
Add	**125 ml/4 fl oz dry white wine**
Season with	**freshly ground white pepper**

Bring to the boil, and cook for about 15 minutes until they are thoroughly cooked
Any mussels which do not open after being cooked are inedible and must be discarded
Allow the mussels to cool in the liquid

Allow	**150 g/5 oz frozen squid**
	150 g/5 oz frozen scampi

to thaw according to the instructions on the packets, and drain both ingredients

Slice	**100 g/4 oz Spanish olives, stuffed with paprika**
Drain	**8 tinned sardines**

and cut into pieces

For the marinade

Stir together	**2 tbsp sherry vinegar**
	5 tbsp olive oil
Season with	**salt**
	pepper

If wished, stir in a few drops of the liquid in which the mussels were cooked

Peel and crush	**1 clove of garlic**

and add it to the marinade, together with the onion slices, and half of

	1 bunch chopped dill

Remove mussels from their shells, and mix with the squid, scampi, olives, sardines, and the marinade
Leave for about 10 minutes to absorb flavours and season to taste with salt and pepper

Remove stalks of	**100 g/4 oz lettuce**

and discard any faded leaves

Cut any large leaves in half
Wash thoroughly, then drain well
Tear up the leaves, and place them on a plate
Remove the seafood from the marinade, and arrange it on the lettuce

Add	**4 tsp double cream**
	2 tsp bottled caviar
Garnish with	**dill sprigs**
Serve with:	**toast or French bread and butter**

Marinated trout with dill sauce

(4 - 5 servings)(Illustrated on pages 56-57)

Rinse under running cold water	**1 kg/2 lb trout**
Pat dry, and divide lengthways	
Remove backbone and other bones	
Lay one half, skin side down, in a shallow dish, and sprinkle	**2 bunches coarsely chopped dill**
over it	
Mix together	**1 tbsp salt**
	1 tbsp sugar
	2 tbsp freshly ground white pepper
and spread over fish	
If wished, sprinkle with	**½ tsp brandy**

Lay the other half of the fish, skin side uppermost, on top of the first half
Cover with baking foil, lay a board (larger than the fish) over this, and weight it evenly, with
2 - 3 full tins of fruit
Leave in a cold place (refrigerator) for 2 - 3 days
Baste now and then with the juices which collect

Marinated trout with dill sauce

Remove the trout from the juices, and dab dry
Remove skin, and arrange fish on a serving dish

For the dill sauce	
Stir together	**4 tbsp hot mustard**
	1 tsp mustard powder
	3 tbsp sugar
	2 tbsp wine vinegar
Gradually beat in	**5 tbsp salad oil**
Stir in	**3 tbsp chopped dill**
Serve the sauce with the fish	
Serve with:	**toast, rye bread, or crispbread**

Mixed fish platter

Cover	**3 white herring fillets**
with water for 1 - 2 hours	
Drain well, pat dry if necessary, and roll them up	
Fill them with	**3 tbsp horseradish cream (page 90)**
Remove skin from	**4 smoked trout fillets**
Remove skin and bones from and fillet them	**250 g/8 oz smoked eel**
Cut off heads of	**500 g/1 lb smoked herrings**
Cut all the above ingredients into bite-sized pieces	
Arrange them with	**250 g/8 oz smoked ray**
	200 g/6 oz sliced smoked salmon
	250 g/8 oz sprats
	200 g/6 oz fresh peeled prawns
on	**washed lettuce leaves**

on a large serving platter, putting the prawns in the centre and the other fish around them

Garnish with	**slices of lemon**
	dill sprigs

Salmon with tartare sauce

Rinse	**4 salmon steaks (each about 250 g/8 oz)**
under running cold water and pat dry	
Sprinkle with	**lemon juice**
and leave to stand for about 15 minutes	
Season with	**salt**
	pepper
Brush 4 pieces of baking foil with	**butter**

and wrap a piece of fish in each one
Seal the foil pieces loosely but firmly
Lay them on a baking tray, and place it

Salmon with tartare sauce

in a preheated oven
Electricity: 225° - 250° C/425° - 475° F
Gas: Mark 7 - 9
Cooking time: 25 - 30 minutes
Remove the foil packets from the oven, and allow the cooked fish to cool
For the tartare sauce

Stir together	**3 heaped tbsp mayonnaise**
	3 heaped tbsp sour cream
Shell and finely chop	**2 hard-boiled eggs**
Stir them into the mayonnaise, with	**1 tbsp finely chopped chives**
	1 heaped tsp chopped parsley
	1 tsp chopped dill

Season to taste with salt and pepper

Brush the salmon slices lightly with	**salad oil**
Arrange them on	**washed lettuce leaves**
Garnish with	**parsley**
Serve with the sauce, and	**toast**

Gourmet salmon rolls

Beat together	**4 eggs**
	2 tbsp milk
	salt
	pepper

	1 bunch chives finely chopped
Melt in a steel pan	**1 tbsp butter or margarine**

Add the egg and milk mixture, and heat
Stroke mixture from pan bottom with a spoon, heating until it has all set, then remove it from the pan, and allow to cool

Spread the scrambled egg evenly over	**8 slices smoked salmon**
and roll them up	
Arrange them on	**washed lettuce leaves**
Garnish with	**cooked asparagus tips**
	sliced stuffed olives
	cress
Serve with:	**toast and butter**

Lobster

The lobster is a saltwater crustacean, which is grey-brown to green-black when alive
Living lobsters are very sensitive, and must be protected from heat and from cold
When you buy them the claws are tied up so that the animals do not injure each other
The tail of a living lobster must be drawn in and elastic
You do not have to make any special arrangements for the transport of dead lobsters

Hold the back of	**1 lobster (about 2 kg/4 lb)**
and scrub it thoroughly in cold water	
Clean, and chop	**1 leek**

Gourmet salmon rolls

Peel and quarter	**1 carrot** **1 turnip** **1 bunch parsley** **2 medium onions**
Bring	**4 - 5 l/8 - 10 pints water**

to the boil
with the vegetables and with **3 rounded tsp salt**
In order to kill the lobster as quickly as possible, put it head first into the boiling water
Bring the water back to the boil, and continue to boil until the lobster is fully cooked
Allow it to cool in the liquid, then re-move it, cut open, and remove the flesh
Arrange it on a serving dish, and serve hot
Cooking time: about 20 minutes

Serve with: **toast**
mayonnaise
butter
lemon wedges

Crispy coated plaice fillets

Sieve	**125 g/4 oz plain flour**
into a bowl and mix carefully with	**1 tsp dried yeast**
Add	**½ tsp sugar** **salt** **1 egg** **125 ml/4 oz luke-warm water**

and whisk to a batter with an electric mixer, first on the lowest, and then on the highest setting, for about 5 minutes

Cut	**125 g/4 oz streaky bacon**

into narrow strips

Crispy coated plaice fillets

Stir into the batter, together with **2 tbsp blanched chopped almonds**

Leave the batter in a warm place until it has risen to about twice its size, then whisk it well once more on the highest setting

Rinse	**4 plaice fillets (about 300 g/10 oz)**

Pat them dry, and sprinkle with **lemon juice**
Leave to stand for about 15 minutes, then pat dry
Season with salt, and **pepper**
Dip them in the batter, and fry in hot **cooking oil** for about 3 - 4 minutes until they are a light brown
Allow to drain and to cool on a wire tray

Prepare the	**remoulade sauce (page 90)**

Pour the sauce on a serving dish, and arrange the fillets on top, garnished with **slices of lemon**
washed lettuce leaves

If wished, sprinkle with **browned chopped almonds**
crispy fried bacon, crumbled

Pickled salmon with a sweet and sour mustard sauce

Scrape scales off	**1 kg/2 lb salmon piece (from the mid-dle or the tail end)**

Rinse under running cold water, and pat dry
Cut in half lengthways
Remove backbone and other bones, pulling out the very small bones with a pair of tweezers

Wash and dry	**3 bunches dill**

Chop coarsely (use the stalk as well)

Mix together	**1 tbsp sugar** **2 tbsp salt** **1 tbsp crushed white peppercorns** **1 tbsp crushed juni-per berries**

and rub into the pieces of fish
Lay one piece of fish, skin side down, in a china dish, and sprinkle it with the dill
Lay the other piece of fish on top, skin side uppermost, and cover with baking foil
Lay a plate or a board on top, and weight it evenly with 2 - 3 tins of fruit
Leave in a cold place (refrigerator) for 24 - 36 hours
Baste now and then with the juices that collect
Remove fish from the liquid, and pat

dry
Using a sharp knife, cut it into very thin
slices, and arrange on a serving dish

For the mustard sauce

Stir together	**5 tbsp mayonnaise**
	4 tbsp cream
	1 tbsp hot mustard
	1 bunch finely chopped dill
Bring to the boil	**2 tsp wine vinegar**
	2 tbsp sugar

Allow to boil a little, then stir into the
mustard mayonnaise

Serve the salmon with the sauce and	**toast and butter**

Crayfish with mustard sauce

Scrub thoroughly under running cold water	**4 - 6 large crayfish**
Clean	**1 leek**
	1 carrot
	1 turnip
	1 bunch parsley
Peel and quarter	**1 onion**
Bring to the boil with the vegetables and	**1½ l/3 pints water**
	2 tsp salt

Add the crayfish, head first, (they will
turn red), and cook them for about 25
minutes
Allow to cool in cooking liquid
Arrange on a serving dish, and garnish

with	**lemon wedges**
	dill sprigs

For the mustard sauce

Stir together	**4 tbsp mayonnaise**
	1 tbsp hot mustard
Season to taste with	**salt**
	pepper
	sugar

Serve the sauce with the crayfish, together with	**French bread or toast and butter**

Imperial oyster platter

Oysters must be closed when you buy
them; any open oysters are inedible and
must be discarded

Thoroughly wash	**12 oysters**

and open them with an oyster opener
To do this, take an oyster in the left
hand, domed side down, and place the
oyster opener between the shells
Move it gently up and down until the

Crayfish with mustard sauce

Imperial oyster platter

Shell the king prawns, and rinse under running cold water, then pat dry
Lay cooking foil on a wire grill rack and place the king prawns on it

Spread with half of	**25 g/1 oz melted butter**

and slide under a preheated grill
After about 2 ½ minutes under the grill, brush with the rest of the butter
Grilling time:
Electricity: about 7 ½ minutes
Gas: about 5 minutes
Serve with the cream mayonnaise

Prawns in Pernod cream

Rinse	**12 large prawns (about 1 ¼ kg/ 2 ½ lb)**
under running cold water	
Bring	**750 ml/1 ¼ pint water**
	1 level tsp salt
	pinch pepper
	1 tbsp aniseed seeds
to the boil	

Add prawns, and cook for about 10 minutes

Prawns in Pernod cream

upper shell becomes loose Rinse the opened oysters, which are not yet loosened, in	**lightly salted water**
to remove any splinters formed when opening	
Finally place the oysters on a plate covered with	**small pieces of ice**
Garnish with	**lemon**
Loosen the oysters from their shells, and sprinkle with	**lemon juice**
Season with	**freshly ground pepper**
Serve with	**brown bread or pumpernickel and butter**

King prawns with cream mayonnaise

Use	**500 g/1 lb fresh king prawns (unpeeled)**
or thaw	**375 g/12 oz frozen peeled king prawns**
at room temperature for 1 hour	
For the cream mayonnaise	
Whip	**125 ml/4 fl oz double cream**
until stiff	
Carefully beat in	**2 heaped tbsp mayonnaise**
	3 tbsp sherry
Season with	**salt**
	pepper
	sugar
	lemon juice

Drain, and remove from shells while
still warm

For the sauce
Stir together | **150 g/5 fl oz double cream**
1 liqueur glass Pernod
pinch ground ginger
Season to taste with | **salt**
Arrange prawns on | **washed lettuce leaves**
Sprinkle sauce with | **chopped pistachio nuts**
Serve prawns with sauce and: | **slices of white bread fried in butter**

Classic crab dish

Scrub | **2 kg/5 lb crabs**
thoroughly under running cold water
Bring | **5 l/10 pints water**
6 tbsp salt
½ tsp caraway seeds
2 tbsp dried dill tips
to the boil
Allow to cook for about 5 minutes, then
add 2 crabs, head first
Bring them back to the boil (they will
turn red)
Gradually add the other crabs two by
two, bringing the water back to the boil
each time
When all the crabs are in the liquid,
cook them for about 10 minutes
Spread out | **2 bunches washed dill**
in a large dish, and lay the hot crabs on
them

Layered caviar

Strain the cooking liquid over the crabs,
and allow to cool
Cover with foil, and leave in a cold
place for 10 - 12 hours
Before serving, warm the crabs in the
liquid again for a short time, then remove them from the liquid, and garnish
with | **dill sprigs**
Serve with: | **French bread or toast and butter**

Layered caviar

Put | **50 g/2 oz bottled salmon caviar**
into a sieve
and wash with | **mineral water**
until the eggs all separate
Drain well
Peel | **1 small onion**
Shell | **1 hard-boiled egg**
Finely dice both ingredients
Layer | **50 g/2 oz yellow bottled trout caviar**
and | **50 g/2 oz black bottled trout caviar**
with the salmon caviar, onion and egg in
4 glasses
Serve chilled

Royal lobster

Leave to cool in cooking liquid | **1 cooked lobster (750 g - 1 kg/ 1½ - 2 lb) (see recipe on page 60)**

Remove, and lay it on its back on a
work surface
Using a pair of scissors, cut shell open
to right and left
Pull off shell on breast, and carefully re-
move meat without breaking back shell
Cut meat into slices
Arrange meat on back shell, together
with | **slices of egg**
Garnish with | **cress**
Drain | **6 tinned artichoke hearts**
Stir the small left-over pieces of lobster
meat, and with the creamy substances of
the lobster, with | **2 tbsp mayonnaise**
Put this into the artichoke hearts
Lay | **cooked asparagus tips**
on them, and garnish with | **strips of paprika**
Arrange the artichoke hearts around the
lobster
Serve with: | **cocktail sauce**

Royal lobster

Tip: When you have cooked lobsters, crayfish (crawfish) or crabs, keep the red shells. Cut up into small pieces, they make an excellent seasoning for soups or sauces if cooked in the liquid together with the vegetables

Salted herrings in cream sauce

Take **4 salted herrings**
and leave them to soak in water for about 24 hours, changing the water now and again
Rinse herrings under running cold water to loosen scales
Remove gills and gill covers, and cut off heads

Peel off inner black skin, and wash them once again
Cut open lengthways along their backs, remove bones, and if wished, skins

For the cream sauce
Peel **4 - 5 onions**
2 medium gherkins
and cut both ingredients into slices
Stir together **375 ml/12 fl oz cream**
1 - 2 tbsp vinegar
a few mustard seeds
a few peppercorns
Add the gherkin and onion slices, and **1 bay leaf**
Lay herrings in this sauce, and leave for about 24 hours
Garnish with **parsley**
Serve with: **potatoes boiled in their skins**
toast or white bread

toast and butter

MEAT

Steak tartare
(Recipe on p.79)

Grand Chef roulade

Grand Chef roulade

Lay	**4 large thin slices of beef (750 g/ 1 lb 10 oz)**
out on a large baking tin so that they overlap each other	
Spread thinly with	**Dijon mustard**
Season with	**salt**
	pepper
Cut	**300 - 375 g/10 - 12 oz leeks**
into halves or quarters lengthways, wash them and put them into	**boiling salted water**
Bring back to the boil, and boil for 2 - 3 minutes	
Transfer to a colander, rinse with cold water and drain well	
Lay them side by side on the meat	

Arrange	**125 g/4 oz bacon rashers**
over the leeks	
Soak	**1 thick slice bread**
in cold water, then squeeze well, and mix with	**375/12 oz sausage meat**
	1 egg
	2 tbsp chopped parsley
	2 tsp pepper
Season with salt and pepper	
Spread this mixture over the bacon	
Scatter	**125 g/4 oz finely diced sautéed button mushrooms**
over the mixture	
Roll up the meat, and fasten with thread	
Sprinkle with salt and pepper	
In an ovenproof casserole, heat and seal the roll quickly in it on all sides	**3 tbsp cooking oil**
Add	**250 ml/8 fl oz red wine**
and cover the pan	
Cook in preheated oven	
Turn the roll now and again, replacing the evaporated liquid gradually with	**250 ml/8 fl oz red wine**
Electricity: 175° - 200° C/350° - 400° F	
Gas: Mark 4 - 5	
Cooking time: about 1 hour	
Place the cooked roll on to a plate, cover it with foil, and leave to cool	
Remove the string, and cut into slices	
Garnish with	**cress**
	radishes
Strain the liquid, allow to cool, and remove the fat	
Stir	**150 g/5 fl oz double cream**
with enough of the liquid to make a creamy sauce, and if necessary season with salt, pepper and	**sugar**
Serve the sauce with the meat, together with:	**French bread mixed salad**

Ham with a spicy honey glaze
(15 - 20 servings)

About 1 week before you wish to prepare it, order the ham from your butcher	
Ask him to score the rind in squares	
Wash and dry	**3½ kg/8 lb unsmoked gammon joint (with the rind tied around the outside)**
Bring	**1½ l/3 pints water**
	1 bottle dry white wine
to the boil	

Ham with a spicy honey glaze

Peel	**1 onion** **1 clove of garlic**
and add them to the water, together with the ham and	**5 cloves** **2 - 3 bay leaves** **peppercorns** **coriander seeds**

Bring back to the boil, and simmer gently for about 2 hours until tender
Turn the ham occasionally while it is cooking
Place the cooked ham in the roasting tin, and put into preheated oven
Strain the cooking liquid, and reheat meat juices
As soon as these begin to brown, add a little of the strained liquid and remove from·heat

Stir together	**2 tbsp honey** **2 tbsp mustard**
	pinch ground cloves **pinch ground coriander**

About 30 minutes before the end of the roasting time, brush this mixture over the ham, and continue to roast
7 - 10 minutes later, brush with the remaining mustard and honey mixture
Electricity: 225° - 250° C/425° - 475° F
Gas: Mark 8 - 9
Roasting time: $1\frac{3}{4}$ - 2 hours

Allow the ham to cool, garnish with and place on a plate	**rosemary sprigs**
Cut	**1 bunch spring onions**
in half lengthways and wash	
Put the meat juices into a pan, and add	**250 ml/8 fl oz red wine**

Bring to the boil, and add the spring onions

Cook until the liquid has evaporated a little
Remove the spring onions from liquid
Wash and halve | **7 fresh figs**
and arrange them on the plate with the ham and the spring onions
Either pour the liquid over the ham, or serve it separately

For the apple and apricot chutney

Peel, quarter, core, and dice | **250 g/8 oz apples**
Mix with | **250 g/8 oz dried apricots**
| **50 g/2 oz grapes**
| **75 g/3 oz unrefined sugar**
| **4 tbsp white wine vinegar**
| **ground cloves**
| **ground coriander**
Add to | **125 ml/4 fl oz boiling water**

Bring back to the boil, and cook for about 10 minutes
Allow to cool, and serve with the ham

Pork loin with dried fruit

(8 - 10 servings)

Bring | **250 ml/8 fl oz water**
| **125 ml/4 fl oz madeira**
| **1 stick cinnamon**
| **3 cloves**
to the boil and
Add | **500 g/1 lb mixed dried fruit**

Bring back to the boil, and cook for about 10 minutes
Allow to cool in the liquid, then strain

Pork loin with dried fruit

Wash and dry | **$1\frac{3}{4}$ - 2 kg/4 - 5 lb section pork loin, smoked or un-smoked, with pocket cut into it**
Rub with | **salt**
| **pepper**
| **sweet paprika**

Fill pocket with dried fruit, and sew up
Wrap in a large sheet of baking foil, seal, and place in a preheated oven
Electricity: 200° C/400° F
Gas: Mark 6
Cooking time: about $1\frac{3}{4}$ hours
Remove from the oven, and leave to stand for a short while
Open the foil, and allow to cool
Cut into slices, and arrange on a serving dish
If desired, garnish with any remaining dried fruit
Serve with: | **wholemeal bread and butter**

Pork chop in breadcrumbs

Wash and dry | **4 pork chops (each about 200 g - 6 oz)**
Beat them lightly
Sprinkle with | **salt**
| **pepper**
Dip the chops, on both sides, first in | **1 - 2 tbsp plain flour**
then in | **1 beaten egg**
and finally in | **50 g/2 oz fine breadcrumbs**
Heat | **50 g/2 oz vegetable oil**

and fry meat for about 15 minutes, turning the chops over frequently
Arrange on a dish, and serve hot or cold
Serve with: | **potato salad**

Roast pork

Wash and dry | **2 kg/5 lb joint pork with rind**

and score rind into diamond shapes
Peel and crush | **2 - 3 cloves of garlic**
Mix them with | **4 tbsp Dijon mustard**
Wash and chop | **3 - 4 bunches basil**
| **3 - 4 bunches parsley**

and mix them with the garlic mustard
Season with | **freshly ground pepper**
| **dried thyme**
| **dried marjoram**
| **ground rosemary**

Spread this mixture evenly over the meat, roll it up, and tie it with thread

Roast pork

Place in roasting tin in a preheated oven
After it has been cooking for about 2
hours, brush it with | **salted water**
then cook for a further 15 minutes
Electricity: 200° C/400° F
Gas: Mark 6
Roasting time: about $2\frac{1}{4}$ hours
Lay the roast pork on a plate, and cover
with foil
Allow to stand for about 10 minutes, re-
move string, then carve fairly thick
slices
Serve with: | **mixed salad**
wholemeal bread

Fillet of pork Giselle

Wash and pat dry | **750 g/1 $\frac{1}{2}$ lb**
pork fillet

Remove skin and sinews
Season with | **salt**
pepper
dried marjoram
Wrap | **250 g/8 oz streaky**
bacon rashers
around the meat
Lay in an ovenproof dish, and place in a
preheated oven

Electricity: 225° C/425° F
Gas: Mark 7
Cooking time: 30 - 35 minutes
Allow to cool, then carve slices, and ar-
range on a plate
Garnish with | **parsley**
tomato wedges

For the sauce
Beat until thick | **1 egg yolk**
1 tsp mustard
1 tsp vinegar
1 level tsp salt
pepper
Gradually beat in | **125 ml/4 fl oz salad**
oil
Stir in | **2 tbsp yoghurt**
Halve | **2 medium tomatoes**
Remove the pips and cores
Shell | **2 hard-boiled eggs**
Dice tomatoes, eggs and | **1 pickled gherkin**
Stir them into the sauce, with | **1 tbsp chopped mixed**
herbs

Season with salt and pepper
Serve with: | **toast**
green salad

Turkish marinated lamb

Remove any fat and skin from | **1 $\frac{3}{4}$ kg/4 lb boned leg**
of lamb
Cut it into $\frac{1}{2}$ cm/$\frac{1}{4}$ in thick slices

For the marinade
Peel and finely dice | **3 onions**
Peel and crush | **3 cloves of garlic**
Mix these 2 ingredients with | **8 tbsp olive oil**
3 tbsp lemon juice
2 tsp dried thyme
Season with | **salt**
pepper

Spread the marinade over the meat
slices and layer them in a bowl
Cover with foil, and leave to marinate
overnight
Remove the meat from the marinade,
and scrape off some of the onion mixture
Heat | **cooking oil**
in a frying pan
and lay some of the meat slices in it side
by side
Fry them on both sides for about 5 - 6
minutes
Put them into a bowl, sprinkle with pepper, and repeat with the rest of the meat
Add the marinade and the onion mix-
ture to the oil in the pan, with | **4 tbsp water**
4 tbsp white wine
and cook them gently together
Season to taste with | **sugar**
Pour over the meat, and allow to cool

Keep pouring the liquid over the meat
from time to time
Halve   **1 kg/2 lb large beef tomatoes**

Remove the pips and cores and cut the
flesh into cubes
Peel and finely crush   **2 - 3 cloves of garlic**
and mix with the tomato
Stir in   **2 - 3 tbsp olive oil**
   2 - 3 tbsp lemon juice
   dried tarragon

Season to taste with salt, pepper and
Allow to stand, adding more seasoning
if necessary, and pouring off some of
the liquid if there is too much
Remove meat from marinade, and arrange on a deep serving dish
Pour a little of the marinade over
Arrange the tomato cubes around the
meat

For the sauce
Stir together   **150 ml/5 fl oz double cream**
   150 ml/5 fl oz yoghurt

Season with salt, pepper and sugar, and
serve with the meat

Roast veal in aspic
(7 - 8 servings)

Season   **1 ¾ - 2 kg/4 - 5 lb boned lean leg of veal**
with   **salt**
   pepper
   ground rosemary

Lay it on a large sheet of baking foil and
sprinkle with   **2 - 3 tbsp cooking oil**
Wrap the foil around it, seal and place
in a preheated oven
Electricity: 200° C/400° F
Gas: Mark 6
Cooking time: about 2 hours
Remove from oven, and leave to stand
for a short time
Open the foil, and allow to cool
For the stuffing
Wash and drain   **300 g/10 oz button mushrooms**

Peel   **2 onions**
   2 - 3 cloves of garlic

Finely dice all 3 ingredients
Melt   **1 - 2 tbsp butter**
and sauté the onion and garlic until they
are transparent
Add the mushrooms, and cook until the
liquid has all evaporated
Season with salt and pepper
Stir in   **3 tbsp chopped parsley**

Roast veal in aspic

and allow to cool
Stir in   **200 g/6 oz calf's liver pâté**

Carve the roast veal into 8 - 10 slices,
and spread with the filling, then put all
the slices together again to form one
piece

For the aspic
Sprinkle   **2 pkts gelatine**
on to   **6 tbsp cold water**
and leave to soak for 10 minutes
Reduce   **1 1/2 pints veal stock (see meat stock for aspic, page 124)**

to 750 ml/1 ¼ pints by boiling
Reduce   **375 ml/12 fl oz cream**
to 250 ml/8 fl oz by boiling
Rub the cream through a sieve, add to
the meat stock, and bring to the boil

Arrange the roast on a serving dish and
leave in a cold place
Cut into slices, and serve with **French bread
salad**

Tip: Any aspic remaining can be used
for a cream soup

leaves of flat-leaved
parsley

Fillet of beef stuffed with herbs and Gorgonzola cream

(5 - 6 servings)

Wash, dry, and remove skin from	**1 kg/2 lb beef fillet (cut from the middle)**
Roast	**50 g/2 oz pine kernels**
in a pan without fat until they are golden brown	
Allow to cool, then grind	
Peel and finely dice	**1 onion**
	1 clove of garlic
Heat	**1 tbsp cooking oil**
and sauté the onion and garlic until transparent	
Mix them with the ground pine kernels, and stir in	**1 tbsp Provence herbs**
	2 tbsp chopped mixed herbs
	1 generous tbsp double cream
Season with	**salt**
	pepper

Cut pockets lengthways in the fillets,
and stuff with the herb mixture
Tie them with thread, and lay them in a
long ovenproof dish

Peel and crush	**1 clove of garlic**
Stir with	**1 tbsp Provence herbs**
	2 tbsp chopped mixed herbs
	3 tbsp salad oil
Season with	**salt**
	pepper

Spread this mixture all over the fillets,
cover them, and leave to stand for
about 2 hours
Remove the lid, and place in a preheated oven
Turn the meat 2 or 3 times during
cooking
Electricity: 225° - 250° C/425° - 475° F
Gas: Mark 8 - 9
Cooking time: about 40 minutes
Allow the meat to cool, remove the
string, carve slices, and arrange on a
serving dish

whilst stirring	
Blend	**25 g/1 oz cornflour**
with	**2 - 3 tbsp white wine**
and use to thicken the stock	
Stir in	**1 beaten egg yolk**

and remove from heat
Add gelatine and stir until dissolved
Season with salt and pepper and rub
through a sieve if necessary
Allow the aspic to cool, stirring occasionally
As soon as it begins to thicken, place
the roast veal on to a wire tray with a
pan beneath it, and pour the sauce over
it repeatedly

Slice	**1 large cooked carrot**

and cut the slices into shapes with a
small serrated cutter
Arrange these shapes to form flowers on
the roast, together with **washed stalks and**

Garnish with: **small tomatoes little bunches of herbs**

For the Gorgonzola cream

Beat **150 ml/5 fl oz double cream**

Rub **125 g/4 oz Gorgonzola cheese**

through a sieve

Stir cream and cheese together, using an electric mixer if you want it to be very smooth

Serve with: **toast or French bread**

Chops with fruit stuffing

Wash and dry **4 chops (each about 250 g/8 oz) with pockets cut into them**

Drain **4 small tinned slices of pineapple**

Wrap **4 slices raw smoked ham**

around the pineapple slices

Place one slice of pineapple and ham in the pocket of each chop, and fasten with wooden skewers

Heat **1- 2 tbsp butter**

and fry the chops on both sides for 15 - 18 minutes

Place the cooked chops on a serving dish, and garnish with **parsley**

Serve hot or cold

Peppered saddle of pork

Wash and dry **1 $\frac{1}{2}$ kg /3 lb pork loin**

Combine **3 tbsp salad oil 1 tsp hot mustard 2 tsp green pepper-corns 1 level tsp salt 1 tsp sweet paprika**

Spread this over meat

Wrap meat in a large sheet of baking foil, and seal

Leave it to stand for about 2 hours, then place in a preheated oven

Electricity: 200° C/400° F

Gas: Mark 6

Cooking time: about 1 $\frac{1}{4}$ hours

Remove from oven and leave to stand for a short time

Open the foil, and allow to cool

Remove the meat from the bone, carve

Chops with fruit stuffing

Roast beef with herbs

slices, and arrange on a serving dish

Garnish with	**radishes**
	herbs
Serve with:	**potato, noodle, or rice salad**

Roast beef with herbs

Wash and dry	**2 kg/4 lb topside of beef**
Score fat lightly and rub with	**salt**
	pepper
Peel and crush	**2 cloves of garlic**
Rub the garlic into the meat, with	**2 tbsp mustard**
Sprinkle thickly with	**Provence herbs**

Rinse out a roasting tin with water, lay a wire rack in it, and place the meat on this
Place it in a preheated oven
Turn the meat over now and again
Electricity: 225° - 250° C/425° - 475° F
Gas: Mark 8 - 9
Roasting time: 35 - 40 minutes
Allow the meat to cool, then carve and arrange on a plate

Serve with:	**remoulade sauce (page 90)**
	French bread

Meat balls, Syrian style

Wash, dry, and remove the fat from	**750 g/1 ½ lb lamb**
Finely mince with	**250 g/8 oz cooked carrots**
Peel and press	**1 - 2 cloves of garlic**
Add them to the meat mixture, with	**150 g/5 oz cooked rice**

Season with	**2 eggs**
	salt
	pepper
	curry powder

Make about 50 walnut-sized balls from the meat mixture

Roll half of them in	**10 tbsp sesame seeds**

Deep fry them a few at a time for 5 minutes and drain on kitchen paper
Serve hot or cold

For the sauce

Stir together	**150 ml/5 fl oz double cream**
	150 ml/5 fl oz yoghurt

Season with salt and pepper
Serve with meat balls

Spring platter with avocado cream (4 - 6 servings)

Wash and dry	**1 kg/2 lb pork loin**

If necessary, remove skin and fat

Season with	**salt**
	pepper

Wrap in a large sheet of baking foil, seal and place in a preheated oven

Meat balls, Syrian style

Spring platter with avocado cream

Electricity: 200° C/400° F
Gas: Mark 6
Cooking time: about 1½ hours

Clean	**4 sticks celery**
Halve	**2 medium leeks**

lengthways, clean, and cut celery and
leeks into pieces 5 cm/2 in long

Trim, wash and quarter into eighths or cut them	**2 fennel bulbs**
Clean and scrape	**2 large carrots**

Cut them into pieces 5 cm/2 in long and
½ cm/¼ in thick

Put each of the vegetables, one at a time, into	**boiling water**

and bring it back to the boil
Allow to boil for:
celery 1 - 2 minutes
leeks 2 - 3 minutes
fennel about 8 minutes
carrots about 5 minutes

Finally dip	**4 - 6 small tomatoes**

into boiling water then in cold water
Skin and core
Drain all the vegetables well, and put
them in a large shallow dish

For the marinade

Stir together	**3 tbsp salad oil**
	3 tbsp herb vinegar
	salt
	pepper
	sugar

Pour it over the vegetables
Now and again collect the marinade in
one corner of the dish, and pour it over
the vegetables again
Leave for 2 - 3 hours to absorb flavours,
then drain
Allow the cooked meat to cool, and
carve thinly
Arrange it on a serving plate with the

vegetables and garnish with	**parsley**

For the avocado cream

Halve and stone	**1 rìpe avocado**

Scoop flesh out of shells, and purée with
an electric mixer, or by mashing it with
a fork

Stir in	**1 tbsp lemon juice**
Peel, crush, and add	**1 clove of garlic**
Stir in	**125 ml/4 fl oz salad oil**

one spoonful at a time

Season with	**onion**
	salt
	pepper
	lemon juice

Pipe into the avocado shells

Garnish with	**parsley**
Serve with:	**wholemeal bread**

Tip: if possible, prepare the avocado sauce shortly before serving, as the oil may separate from the avocado if it has to stand for a long time

Onion chops with mustard cream

Wash and dry	**4 pork chops (each about 200 g/6 oz)**
Sprinkle them with	**salt**
	pepper
Spread them thinly with	**Dijon mustard**
Peel and finely dice	**4 onions**
	2 cloves of garlic
and sprinkle over the chops, pressing them in lightly	
Oil a baking tray with	**4 tbsp cooking oil**
and lay chops on it	
Put into a preheated oven	
Electricity: 225° - 250° C/425° - 475° F	
Gas: Mark 8 - 9	
Cooking time: 30 - 35 minutes	
Arrange the chops on a serving dish	
Garnish with	**parsley**
Serve hot or cold	
For the mustard cream	
Stir together	**150 g/5 fl oz double**

	cream
	1 ½ tsp Dijon mustard
Season to taste with	**salt**
	curry powder
Serve sauce with chops	

Tip: When cooking for large numbers, oven roasting is particularly recommended

Gourmet fillet steak

Wrap	**4 fillet steaks (each about 150 g/5 oz)**
individually with	**4 rashers streaky bacon**
and tie with thread	
Stir together	**3 tbsp salad oil**
	1 tsp sweet paprika
	black pepper
and spread over the steaks	
Cover, and leave to stand for about 30 minutes	
Heat	**2 tbsp cooking oil**
and fry steaks on both sides for 5 - 6 minutes	
Remove string and sprinkle with	**salt**
Lay one steak on each of	**4 slices of toasted white bread**

Onion chops with mustard cream

Top steaks with	**3 - 4 tbsp pickled fruits (if available)**
Arrange on a serving dish, and serve hot or cold	

Fillet of veal with walnut cream

Wash and dry	**1 veal fillet (600 g/ 1$\frac{1}{4}$ lb)**
Remove the skin and sinews	
Season with	**salt**
	pepper
and dust with	**about 1 tbsp plain flour**
Beat	**1 egg**
and brush it over the fillet	
Chop	**125 g/4 oz walnuts**
and press the meat into the nuts, turning it so that both sides are covered	
Heat	**50 g/2 oz butter**
and seal meat on all sides, turning it carefully with 2 forks	
Cover pan, and allow to cook for 15 - 20 minutes	
Allow to cool, carve slices, and arrange on a serving dish	
For the walnut cream	
Peel and crush	**1 small clove of garlic**

Fillet of veal with walnut cream

Stir into	**150 g/5 fl oz double cream**
Season with salt and pepper	
Chop	**50 g/2 oz walnuts**
and stir in	
Serve the cream with the meat, and with:	**broccoli salad**
	French bread

Plaited fillet of pork

Wash and dry	**4 long pork fillets (each about 250 g/ 8 oz)**
If necessary, remove the skin and sinews	
Cut each fillet twice lengthways, down from the thicker end, and leaving 1 - 2 cm/$\frac{1}{2}$ in uncut at that end	
Plait the fillets, and fasten the ends with wooden skewers	
Season them with	**salt**
	pepper
	sweet paprika
Heat	**3 tbsp butter**
and fry the meat plaits on all sides for about 30 minutes	
Allow to cool, then place on a serving dish	
Garnish with	**tomato wedges**
	parsley
For the Madagascar sauce	
Stir together	**150 g/5 fl oz double cream**
	3 tbsp tomato ketchup
	1 tsp crushed green peppercorns
Season to taste with salt and	**chilli powder**
Serve with:	**chicory and orange salad**
	wholemeal bread and butter

Almond medallions

Remove skin and fat from	**800 g/2 lb pork fillet**
Wash and dry, and cut into slices 1$\frac{1}{2}$ - 2 cm/$\frac{3}{4}$ - 1 in thick	
Season with	**salt**
	pepper
Dip first into	**1 egg, beaten**
then into	**100 g/4 oz flaked almonds**
pressing these firmly into medallions	
Heat	**50 g/2 oz butter**
Add meat slices, and fry for 5 - 7 minutes on each side	
Allow to cool, arrange on a serving dish, and garnish with	**watercress**

Almond medallions

For the sauce
Mix | **3 tbsp mayonnaise**
| **2 tbsp double cream**
| **2 tbsp yoghurt**
Dip | **2 tomatoes**
first into boiling water, then into cold water
Skin, remove pips and core, and dice
Dice | **1 gherkin**
Stir tomato and gherkin into sauce together with | **1 tbsp crushed green peppercorns**
| **1 tbsp chopped dill**

Serve in sauce-boat with meat

Italian roast

Score diamond shapes in rind of | **1½ kg/3 lb lean belly pork, with a pocket cut into it**

Wash and dry meat
Put | **300 g/10 oz frozen broccoli**
into | **125 ml/4 fl oz boiling salted water**

Bring back to the boil, and cook for 10 - 15 minutes
Drain, then purée with an electric mixer or rub through a sieve

Dice | **75 g/3 oz bacon**
Stir bacon and broccoli with | **2 tbsp fine bread-crumbs**
and season with | **salt**
| **pepper**
| **ground nutmeg**

Rub meat inside and out with salt, pepper and | **dried thyme**
Put the stuffing into the meat pocket and sew up
Wrap the meat in a large sheet of baking foil, seal it, and place in a preheated oven
Electricity: 200° C/400° F
Gas: Mark 6
Cooking time: 2¼ - 2½ hours
Remove meat from oven, and allow to stand for a short time
Open the foil, and allow to cool
Carve slices, and arrange on a serving dish
Garnish with | **rosemary**
Serve with: | **wholemeal bread**
| **mixed salad**

Steak tartare
(Illustrated on p. 66-67)

Peel and finely dice | **2 onions**
Stir them together with | **500 - 750 g/1 - 1½ lb tartare steak**
| **1 tbsp salad oil**
| **1 - 2 tsp mustard**
Add | **salt**
| **pepper**
| **sweet paprika**
| **vinegar**
to taste
Put the steak in serving portions on to a plate or in a dish, and garnish with | **marjoram**
Make a hollow in each portion, and in each place 1 - 2 egg yolks of | **6 - 8 egg yolks**
Put into small dishes | **onion rings**
| **coarsely ground pepper**
| **pickled gherkins**
| **chives**
| **sweet paprika**
| **anchovy fillets**
| **capers**
as accompaniments
Serve with: | **wholemeal bread**

GAME AND POULTRY

Dressed smoked goose breast
(Recipe on p.87)

Larded leg of venison

Larded leg of venison
(4 - 6 servings)

Wash, dry, and remove the skin from	**2 kg/4 lb leg of venison**
Cut	**150 g/5 oz fatty bacon**
into strips and leave them for a while in a cold place	
Then roll them in	**pepper**
and use them to lard the venison	
Rub the meat with pepper and	**salt**
	dried sage
Put	**125 g/4 oz fatty bacon rashers**
into a roasting tin that has been rinsed out with water and lay the venison on them	
Clean	**1 leek**
	1 carrot
	1 turnip
	1 bunch of parsley
Add them to the meat, and put the roasting tin in a preheated oven	
As soon as the juices in the bottom of the tin begin to brown, add as required	**hot water**
Electricity: 200° - 225° C/400° - 425° F	
Gas: Mark 6 - 7	

Cooking time: 50 - 60 minutes (the meat should be pink inside)	
Allow to cool, then carve slices and arrange on a serving dish	
Garnish with	**bottled cranberries mint**
Serve with:	**toast and butter Cumberland sauce (page 95)**

Tip: Meat from young deer need not be pickled or marinated, but it can be soaked in milk for 2 days, or wrapped in a cloth soaked in vinegar

Duck with figs

Wash and dry	**1 oven-ready duck (about 1½ kg/3 lb)**
Rub inside with	**salt**
Place it on its back on a wire tray in a roasting tin which has been rinsed out with water, and then put it on the lowest shelf of a preheated oven	
Prick the meat on the legs and under the wings now and again while it is cooking to allow the fat to roast sufficiently	
After about 30 minutes roasting, skim	

off the fat that has collected
As soon as the juices in the bottom of the tin begins to brown, add a little | **hot water**
Now and again baste the duck with the roasting juices, and replace the evaporated water as necessary
About 10 minutes before the roast is finished, brush the duck with | **cold salted water**
and turn the heat up high, so that the skin becomes crispy
Electricity: 200° - 225° C/400° - 425° F
Gas: Mark 6 - 7
Roasting time: about $1\frac{3}{4}$ hours
Allow the cooked duck to cool
Pour the roasting juices through a sieve and remove the fat
Sprinkle | **1 tsp gelatine**
on to | **1 tbsp cold water**
and allow to soak for 10 minutes
Stir it into the still hot roasting juices, and stir until dissolved
Season with salt and | **pepper**
Stir in | **1 tbsp port**
and leave in a cold place
Remove breast meat from the bone, carve slices, and lay it back on the carcass
Arrange on a serving dish
Garnish with | **lemon balm**
Wash and drain | **4 - 6 fresh figs**

Cut a cross into them, and bend them outwards so that they look like flowers
Place them around the duck
Cut the cooled, solidified roasting juices into cubes, and put them on the serving dish
Garnish with | **lemon balm**
Serve with: | **toast and butter salad**

Turkey with pistachio stuffing
(4 - 6 servings)

Wash and dry | **1 oven-ready young turkey (about $1\frac{1}{2}$ kg/3 lb)**

For the filling
Cut into small cubes | **2 slices toast**
Sprinkle them with | **3 tbsp port**
Wash | **150 g/5 oz chicken livers**

Pat dry, and purée with an electric mixer or liquidiser
Mix these ingredients, together with | **75 g/3 oz peeled and ground pistachio nuts**
75 g/3 oz minced beef

Duck with figs

Season to taste with	**2 small eggs** **salt** **pepper**

Fill the turkey with the stuffing and close the opening with wooden cocktail sticks, or sew it up with kitchen thread

Stir salt and pepper with	**2 tbsp cooking oil** **½ tsp sweet paprika** **pinch curry powder**

Brush this on to the turkey, and place it in a roasting tin which has been rinsed out with water
Place it in a preheated oven

As soon as the juices in the bottom of the tin begins to brown, add a little of	**125 ml/4 fl oz hot instant chicken stock**

Replace the evaporated liquid every now and then
Electricity: 200° - 225° C/400° - 425° F
Gas: Mark 6 - 7
Cooking time: about 50 minutes
Allow to cool, then remove the cocktail sticks or thread
Carve the turkey into serving pieces, and arrange on a dish

Garnish with	**shelled pistachio nuts**

Stuffed breast of goose

Wash and dry	**750 g/1 ½ lb breast of goose, boned**
Rub the inside with	**salt** **pepper**
Spread with	**1 tsp hot mustard**

For the filling

Peel and finely dice	**1 onion**
Skin	**125 g/4 oz calf's liver**
If necessary, wash, dry, and chop finely	
Heat	**1 - 2 tbsp butter or margarine**

and fry both ingredients for about 2 minutes

Pour on	**2 tbsp brandy**
and allow to cool	
Mix with	**1 tbsp chopped pistachio nuts** **125 g/4 oz sausage-meat**

Put mixture on to one half of goose breast, place other half on top, and fasten with a wooden skewer
Place on a wire rack in a roasting tin that has been rinsed out with water, and place on the middle shelf in a preheated oven

As soon as the juices in the bottom of the tin begin to brown, add a little	**hot water**

Baste breast now and again with the roasting juices, and replace evaporated water as necessary

10 minutes before end of cooking time, brush breast with	**cold salted water**

and turn heat up high, so that skin will be crispy
Electricity: 200° - 225° C/400° - 425° F
Gas: Mark 6 - 7
Roasting time: 2 - 2 ½ hours
Allow cooked breast to cool, remove skewer, and carve thin slices
Arrange on a serving dish

Garnish with	**orange slices** **parsley**
Serve with:	**bread and butter**

Turkey drumsticks with chive sauce

Allow	**1 frozen turkey drumstick (1 kg/2 lb)**
to thaw at room temperature	
Bring to the boil	**about 1 ½ l/ 3 pints salted water**
Wash	**1 bunch parsley**
and put into the water and add the turkey and	**6 peppercorns**
Bring back to the boil, then simmer	
Scrape and wash	**300 g/10 oz carrots**

Cut in half lengthways, quarter, and cut with a serrated knife into 3 cm/1 ½ in long pieces

Clean	**2 - 3 sticks celery**

leaving leaves on stalk, and cut them into 4 cm/2 in long pieces
After the turkey has been cooking for about 50 minutes, add vegetables, and boil all together

Thoroughly clean	**2 medium leeks**

Halve, cut into 4 cm/2 in long pieces, and wash again if necessary

Break	**1 cauliflower**

into florets
Wash thoroughly
After about another 10 minutes, add these 2 vegetables, and cook for about 15 minutes until tender
Allow to cool in the liquid

For the sauce

Shell	**2 hard-boiled eggs**
and rub through a sieve	
Stir together with	**2 tsp hot mustard**
Gradually stir in	**about 125 ml/4 fl oz salad oil**

(sauce must be fairly thick)

Season with	**vinegar** **salt** **pepper**
Stir in	**2 bunches finely chopped chives**

Turkey drumsticks with chive sauce

Remove turkey and vegetables from liquid, and drain well
Arrange vegetables on a serving dish, and pour sauce over them
Carve drumstick into slices, and arrange on top of vegetables
Garnish with **chives**
Serve with: **French bread**

Fillet of rabbit in puff pastry

For the filling
Remove back flesh and fillets from **1 rabbit or hare (about 600 g/ 1 $\frac{1}{4}$ lb)**

Carefully remove the skin, wash, pat dry, and place in a bowl
Sprinkle with **$\frac{1}{2}$ tsp dried thyme**
$\frac{1}{2}$ tsp dried rosemary
1 tbsp lemon juice
2 tbsp cooking oil

Cover, and leave in a cold place for about 24 hours, turning the meat now and then
Remove meat from the marinade, drain, and season with **salt**

pepper
Heat **25 g/1 oz butter**
and seal the meat quickly in it on all sides
Allow to cool
Wash, drain, and finely dice **10 stoned prunes**
Clean, and wash **10 button mushrooms**
Reserve 6, and finely chop the rest
Mix both these ingredients with **250 g/8 oz sausage-meat**
2 tbsp brandy
1 tbsp chopped pistachio nuts

For the pastry
Thaw **300 g/10 oz frozen puff pastry**

according to the instructions
Roll out to a rectangle 3 times bigger than the pieces of rabbit (if wished, leave some of the pastry on one side for decoration)
Put half of the sausagemeat mixture down the middle of the pastry, so that it is the same length as the larger pieces of meat
Lay the larger pieces on top of it, then the smaller pieces
Between the fillets, place the mush-rooms to form a 'backbone'
Cover the rabbit meat with the remain-

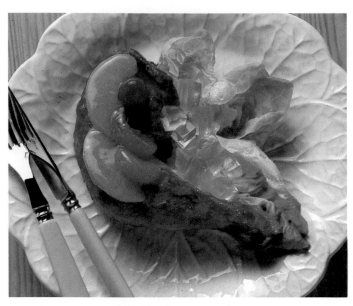

Dressed chicken drumsticks

ing sausagemeat
Fold the pastry over to enclose all the
meat, and lay it, smooth side uppermost, on a baking tray which has been
rinsed with water
Decorate with left-over pieces of pastry,
and make 2 - 3 small holes in the top

Beat   **½ egg yolk**
         1 tsp milk

and brush over the pastry
Place in a preheated oven
Electricity: 200° - 225° C/400° - 425° F
Gas: Mark 6 - 7
Cooking time: about 35 minutes
Remove from oven, and allow to cool
Cut into fairly thick slices, and arrange
on a serving dish

Garnish with   **prunes**
         shelled pistachio nuts

Rolled turkey joint

Dressed chicken drumsticks

Wash and dry	**4 chicken drumsticks (each about 250 g/8 oz)**
Stir together	**2 tbsp cooking oil** **½ tsp sweet paprika** **pinch curry powder** **salt** **pepper**

Brush this all over drumsticks
Lay on a wire rack in a roasting tin
which has been rinsed out with water,
and place on middle shelf of a preheated oven
As soon as the juices in the bottom of
the tin begin to brown, add a little of   **125 ml/4 fl oz hot water**

Baste drumsticks now and then with
roasting juices, and replace evaporated
water as necessary
Electricity: 200° - 225° C/425° - 450° F
Gas: Mark 6 - 7
Roasting time: 25 - 30 minutes
Allow drumsticks to cool, then place
them on a wire rack on a baking tray,
and garnish as desired with   **tinned pineapple slices, drained and halved**
tinned mandarin segments, drained
tinned peach slices, drained
cherries

Make up drained fruit juices with water
if necessary to 250 ml/8 fl oz
Sprinkle   **1 pkt gelatine**
on to   **3 tbsp white wine**
and leave to soak for 10 minutes
Heat, stirring constantly, until dissolved
Warm fruit juice, and stir gelatine into
it
Remove from heat, and as soon as it begins to thicken, spread it over drumsticks
Repeat until drumsticks are completely
covered with aspic
Allow remaining liquid to set, and cut
into cubes
Arrange drumsticks on a serving dish,
and garnish with the aspic cubes and   **lettuce hearts**

Rolled turkey joint

Wash and dry	**1 rolled turkey roast (about 1 kg/2 lb)**
Place on a spit or on a grilling rack	
Stir together	**1 tbsp cooking oil** **salt** **sweet paprika**

If wished, add **medium hot mustard**
Spread over the meat
While it is being grilled, brush the meat now and again with the fat that drips off into the grill pan
Grilling time:
Electricity: depending on the thickness of the roast, 45 - 60 minutes
Gas: depending on the thickness of the roast, about 50 minutes
Allow the cooked roast to cool, then carve slices
Serve with: **French bread and butter**
celery salad with apple (page 39)

Dressed smoked goose breast

(Illustrated on pages 80-81)

Wash **250 g/8 oz sour cherries**
and remove stalks and stones
Sprinkle them with **75 g/3 oz sugar**
½ level tsp ground ginger

As soon as the liquid has been drawn out of the cherries, stew them until soft
Allow to cool
Arrange **125 g/4 oz smoked goose breast slices**
on **washed lettuce leaves**
and garnish with the stewed fruit
Serve with: **toast and butter**

Chicken breasts in lime sauce

Wash and dab dry **4 chicken breasts (about 600 g/1 ¼ lb)**
Season with **salt**
pepper
Dip the chicken first in **plain flour**
then in **1 beaten egg**
and finally in **125 g/4 oz blanched chopped almonds**
Heat **50 g/2 oz butter or margarine**
and fry the meat on both sides for about 8 minutes
Allow to cool

For the sauce
Wash **2 limes**
with hot water: grate a little of the rind, cut limes in half, and squeeze juice

Chicken breasts in lime sauce

Stir together 4 tbsp of juice with the grated rind, and **300 ml/10 fl oz double cream**
2 tbsp finely chopped lemon balm
2 tbsp dry vermouth
Season with salt
Arrange chicken on **washed, finely shredded lettuce leaves**
Pour on half of the sauce, and sprinkle **2 tbsp green peppercorns**
over it
Garnish with **lemon balm**
lime slices
Serve with remaining sauce and: **toast and butter**

SAUCES, DIPS, BUTTERS AND SPREADS

Ham and quark
(Recipe on p.97)

Remoulade sauce, Herb dressing, Horseradish cream

Finely chop	**1 - 2 washed anchovies**
to taste	
Add all the ingredients with	**2 tbsp chopped mixed herbs**
	1 tsp pepper
to mayonnaise, together with the reserved hard-boiled egg white which has been finely diced	
Serve with:	**cooked meat and fish**

Herb dressing

Stir together	**150 ml/5 fl oz double cream**
	2 tbsp chopped mixed herbs
	3 tbsp tomato ketchup
Season with	**salt**
	pepper
	sugar
	sweet paprika
Serve with:	**lettuce salad**
	chicory salad
	vegetable salad
	cucumber
	as a dip with meat fondues

Horseradish cream

Whip	**250 ml/8 oz double cream**
until stiff and stir together with	**2 - 3 tbsp grated horseradish**
Season with	**salt**
	sugar
	lemon juice
Serve with:	**ham**
	hot sausages
	boiled beef

Remoulade sauce

Shell	**1 hard-boiled egg**
Reserve the white and rub the yolk through a sieve	
Stir together	**1 raw egg yolk**
	salt
	1 tsp sugar
Beat in, one drop at a time, half of	**125 ml/4 fl oz salad oil**
When the mixture is stiff enough, add	**2 tbsp vinegar or lemon juice**
	1 tsp mustard
Then add remaining oil	
Finely chop	**½ - 1 tbsp bottled capers**
Finely dice	**2 small pickled gherkins**

Aioli (Spanish garlic mayonnaise)

Peel and very finely crush	**4 - 5 cloves of garlic**
Stir together with	**125 ml/4 fl oz mayonnaise**
Season with	**salt**
	pepper
	cayenne pepper
	lemon juice
Serve with:	**grilled or barbequed meat**

Aioli (Spanish garlic mayonnaise)

Walnut sauce
(6 - 8 servings)

Stir together	**150 ml/5 fl oz double cream**
	125 ml/4 fl oz cream
Season with	**salt**
	freshly ground pepper
Coarsely chop	**50 g/2 oz walnuts**
Wash	**1 orange**
with hot water and dry	
Peel off some of rind very finely and cut into very fine strips	
Finely grate rest of the rind, and squeeze the juice	
Stir walnuts, orange peel and juice into sauce, with	**1 tbsp lemon juice**
Leave in a cold place	
Stir again, and season to taste before serving	
Serve with:	**grilled or barbequed meat**

Piquant mustard sauce
(6 - 8 servings)

Beat together	**2 egg yolks**
	2 tbsp Dijon mustard
	salt
	freshly ground pepper
	1 tbsp lemon juice
Beat in	**125 ml/4 fl oz salad oil**
one drop at a time at first, then in larger amounts	

Stir in	**4 tbsp cream**
Add more seasoning to taste	
Stir in	**2 bunches chopped parsley**
Serve with:	**grilled or barbequed meat**

Basil sauce
(6 - 8 servings)

Dip	**4 tomatoes (about 250 g/8 oz)**
first into boiling water, then into cold water	
Skin and quarter, remove pips, then purée	
Stir	**400 g/14 oz yoghurt salad cream**
	3 bunches chopped basil
	125 ml/4 fl oz cream
together with the tomato purée	
Season with	**freshly ground pepper**
Put sauce in a dish, and garnish with basil	
Serve with:	**grilled or barbequed meat**

Spicy vinaigrette

Stir together	**3 tbsp salad oil**
	2 - 3 tbsp wine vinegar
	1 tsp medium hot mustard

Walnut sauce, Piquant mustard sauce, Basil sauce

Spicy vinaigrette

	1 small peeled onion, diced
	2 hard-boiled eggs, chopped
	4 gherkins finely diced
	1 - 2 bunches chopped parsley
	a few chopped capers
Season with	salt
	pepper

Apricot sauce with curry

Stir	125 g/4 oz apricot jam
until smooth, then add	125 g/4 oz mayonnaise
	1 - 2 tsp curry powder

Ginger and curry dressing

Put	150 ml/5 fl oz yoghurt
into a sieve to drain	
Peel and grate	1 tsp fresh ginger root
Stir ginger together with	1 tsp curry powder
	½ tsp ground coriander
	1 tsp honey
	1 tsp Dijon mustard
	1 tsp ginger marmalade
	ground cinnamon
	salt

Stir in yoghurt	
Serve with:	salad
	grilled or barbequed meat
	fondue
Variation:	
Use 2 tsp ground ginger instead of fresh ginger	

Apricot sauce with curry

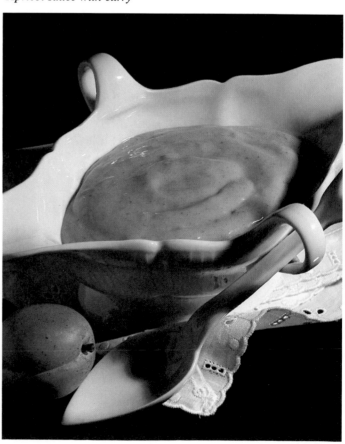

Almond and yoghurt dressing, Herb and yoghurt dressing, Ginger and curry dressing

Almond and yoghurt dressing
(6 - 8 servings)

Put	**450 ml/16 fl oz yoghurt**
into a sieve to drain	
Shell and finely chop	**3 hard-boiled eggs**
Stir	**2 tsp Dijon mustard**
into yoghurt, stir in eggs and	**50 g/2 oz lightly toasted ground almonds**
	2 tbsp olive oil
Season with	**salt**
	freshly ground pepper
	sugar

Herb and yoghurt dressing
(4 - 6 servings)

Put	**300 ml/10 fl oz yoghurt**
into a sieve to drain	
Peel and very finely dice	**2 large shallots or onions (about 50 g/2 oz)**

Peel and finely crush	**1 medium clove of garlic**
Stir	**1 bunch chopped dill**
	1 bunch chopped flat-leaved parsley
	1 bunch chopped basil
with	**3 tbsp lemon juice**
	3 tbsp olive oil
	salt
	freshly ground pepper
	sugar
then gradually stir in other ingredients	
Serve with:	**salads**
	grilled or barbequed meat
	fondue

Roquefort and cream sauce

Crush	**25 g/1 oz blue-veined cheese (e.g. roquefort)**
with a fork	
Gradually beat in, with an electric whisk	**125 ml/4 fl oz double cream**
Season with	**salt**
	freshly ground pepper
	about 1 tbsp lemon juice
Serve with:	**all salads with a slightly bitter flavour, such as spinach endive chicory**

Mustard and cream sauce

Whip	**125 ml/4 fl oz double cream**
Stir in	**2 tsp mustard**
Season with	**salt**
	pepper
Stir in	**1 tbsp lemon juice**
Serve with	**green salads such as lettuce, endive, or chicory, salads of raw vegetables with meat**

Sherry and cream sauce

Stir	**1 egg yolk**
until creamy, and	**1 rounded tbsp sugar**

add	**2 tbsp dry sherry**
	1 tbsp lemon juice
Fold in	**2 tbsp stiffly whipped cream**
Before serving, sprinkle	**1 tbsp blanched chopped almonds, toasted**
on to sauce	
Do not prepare sauce until just before serving	
Serve with:	**all fruit salads made from citric fruits**

Colourful quark dip

Stir together	**150 g/5 oz low fat quark (curd cheese)**
	4 tbsp buttermilk
Dip	**1 small tomato**
into boiling water then into cold water	
Skin, halve and remove pips	
Cut tomato and	**1 anchovy**
	2 olives
into very small pieces, and mix with	**2 tsp diced onion**
Stir them all into quark, and season with	**salt**
	freshly ground pepper
	thyme

Quark dip with cranberries

Stir together	**200 g/6 oz low fat quark (curd cheese)**
	5 tbsp milk
Stir in	**2 tbsp bottled cranberries**
	2 tsp mustard
Season with	**salt, sugar**
Serve with:	**Cold beef, cold poultry**

Quark dip with ham

Stir together	**125 g/4 oz low fat quark (curd cheese)**
	4 tbsp buttermilk
Cut	**125 g/4 oz raw smoked ham**
into small pieces	
Stir this into quark with	**1 tbsp chopped mixed herbs**

Quark dip with cranberries, Colourful quark dip, Quark dip with ham

Season with	**freshly ground pepper** **garlic salt**

Milanese dip

Peel	**1 medium onion**
Finely dice together with	**5 slices (about 50 g/2 oz salami)**
Stir with	**150 ml/5 fl oz double cream**
Season with	**salt** **sweet paprika**

Herb dip

Finely chop	**3 - 4 tbsp chopped mixed herbs** **3 anchovy fillets** **1 tbsp bottled capers** **10 stuffed Spanish olives**
Stir together	**3 egg yolks** **1 tsp hot mustard**

Milanese dip

Season with	**1 - 2 tbsp fruit vinegar** **salt** **freshly ground pepper**
Stir in	**5 tbsp salad oil**
Halve and remove the pips and cores from	**2 peeled tomatoes**
Dice them	
Stir all chopped ingredients and tomatoes into egg yolk mixture together with	**3 - 4 tbsp chopped mixed herbs**
Use this dip also as a filling for	**jacket potatoes baked in foil**

Cumberland sauce

Remove pith from and cut into very fine strips	**peel of 1 orange**
Boil for about 10 minutes in until soft	**3 tbsp red wine**
Remove from heat	
Stir	**250 g/8 oz redcurrant jelly**
well with	**1 - 2 tsp mustard**
Add the cooled orange peel and red wine	
Season with	**salt** **lemon juice**
Serve with:	**roast game** **meat pies** **cold roast meat**

Mustard cream with dill

Stir together	**1 - 2 tbsp mustard** **150 ml/5 fl oz sour cream** **4 tbsp finely chopped dill**
Season with	**salt** **pepper**
Stir in	**1 tsp gin (optional)**

Herb butter

Cream	**125 g/4 oz butter**
Add	**2 tsp finely chopped parsley** **1 tsp finely chopped onion** **4 finely chopped tarragon leaves** **1 peeled crushed clove of garlic** **1 tsp lemon juice** **white wine**

95

and stir together
Season with **salt**

4 dashes Worcester sauce

Put the butter in the middle of a piece of greaseproof paper, and fold one half of paper over it
Hold lower half of paper, and, using a knife to press and stroke the butter lengthways under upper half of paper, form the butter into a roll
Leave it in a cold place
Remove hardened butter from paper, and, with a knife dipped in hot water, cut into pencil thick slices
Serve with: **anything that is grilled or barbequed cheese bread Weinberg snails**

Paprika butter

Cream	**125 g/4 oz butter**
Add	**1 tbsp sweet paprika**
and stir in	
Season to taste with	**salt**

Lemon butter

Cream	**125 g/4 oz butter**
Wash in hot water, and dry	**1 - 2 lemons**

Peel very finely, and cut peel into very small cubes
Add to the butter, and stir in

Serve with:	**bread with cream cheese honey preserves**

Curry butter

Cream	**125 g/4 oz butter**
Add	**1 tbsp curry powder**
and stir in	
Season with	**salt**

Mustard butter

Cream	**125 g/4 oz butter**
Add	**2 tsp mustard**
and stir in	
Season with	**salt**

Curry butter, Paprika butter

Onion butter

Onion butter

Cream	**125 g/4 oz butter**
Add	**4 tbsp diced red onion (if available)**
and stir in	
Season with	**salt**
	white pepper

Ham and quark
(Illustrated on pages 88-89)

Stir together	**250 g/8 oz low fat quark (curd cheese)**
	4 - 5 tbsp milk
Stir in	**2 tbsp finely chopped basil**
	1 small finely chopped green chilli
Dice	**125 g/4 oz raw smoked ham**
and add	
Season with	**salt**
	pepper

Piquant chicken paste

Dice and fry	**125 g/4 oz streaky bacon**
Remove bacon from pan	
Stir fat from pan with	**200 g/6 oz tinned**

	liver paté for spreading
Remove skin from	**200 g/6 oz cooked chicken**
and mince or chop very finely	
Peel and crush	**1 - 2 cloves of garlic**
Add the garlic, minced chicken, bacon, and	**1 tbsp chopped parsley**
to the liver paté, and stir well	
Season with	**salt**
	pepper
Put the mixture into a small terrine, and leave in a cold place	
Serve with:	**toast**

Dill butter

Cream	**125 g/4 oz butter**
Add	**6 tbsp chopped dill**
and stir in	
Season with	**salt**
	white pepper
	thyme

Anchovy butter

Cream	**125 g/4 oz butter**
Add	**5 finely chopped anchovy fillets**
	5 g/$\frac{1}{2}$ oz anchovy paste
	2 tsp diced onion
and stir all together	

Chive butter

Cream	**125 g/4 oz butter**
Add	**6 tbsp finely chopped chives**
and stir in	
Season with	**salt**
	white pepper

Horseradish butter

Cream	**125 g/4 oz butter**
Add	**3 tbsp grated horseradish**
Season with	**salt**

SAVOURIES, SANDWICHES, CANAPES

Salmon on white bread
(Recipe on p.101)

Beer open sandwich

Beer open sandwich

Combine	**50 g/2 oz softened butter**
	1 tbsp mustard
	1 tbsp grated horse-radish
Spread this on to	**2 slices wholemeal bread**
Peel and finely dice	**1 onion**
Mix onion with	**125 g/4 oz cooked sausage meat**
	2 tbsp light beer
Season with	**salt**
	pepper
	few drops of onion juice

With wet hands, form the mixture into 2 small balls, and lay ball on each slice of bread

Place on top	**2 large slices of ham off the bone**
Slice into fan shapes	**2 pickled gherkins**
Clean	**4 radishes**
Peel and cut into rings	**1 onion**
Drain	**some cocktail onions**
	2 tinned baby corn-cobs
	2 pickled red peppers
Peel	**2 small white mouli radishes**

and cut them into spirals
Pull the spirals out a little
Garnish the slices of bread with the pickled gherkins, radishes, onion rings, cocktail onions, corncobs, red peppers, radish spirals, and **parsley**

Spring open sandwich

Clean and scrape	**2 - 3 carrots (about 200 g/6 oz)**
Peel, quarter, and core	**1 small apple**
Coarsely grate both ingredients and mix together	
Add	**lemon juice apple juice**
to taste	
Spread with	**1 slice bread butter**
Spread evenly with	**125 g/4 oz cottage cheese**
and arrange the carrot and apple salad on top	
Garnish with	**1 lemon slice cress**

Colourful open sandwich

Spread with	**1 slice bread butter**
Cover with	**washed lettuce leaves**
Lay on top	**1 slice ham**
Shell	**1 hard-boiled egg**
Remove core of	**1 tomato**

Stock exchange bites

Spring open sandwich, Colourful open sandwich, Quark open sandwich with radish

Clean	**3 radishes**
Slice all 3 ingredients and arrange them on the ham with	**4 slices gherkin**
Garnish with	**dill**
	chives

Quark open sandwich with radish

Clean	**1 bunch radishes**
Finely chop half of them, and thinly slice the others	
Stir together	**125 g/4 oz cream quark (curd cheese)**
	1 tbsp evaporated milk
	1 tbsp finely chopped chives
Season with	**salt**
	pepper
Stir in all of the chopped and $\frac{2}{3}$ of the sliced radishes	
Spread with	**1 slice bread**
	butter
Spread with the quark mixture	
Garnish with remaining radishes and	**finely chopped chives**

Stock exchange bites

Toast	**4 slices white bread**
Sprinkle them with	**a little brandy**
	garlic powder
Wash	**8 lettuce leaves**
Shake dry and place 2 lettuce leaves on each slice of bread	

Sprinkle with	**salt**
Remove the cores from	**4 small tomatoes**
and cut them into very thin slices	
Sprinkle with salt	
Drain and halve	**2 slices tinned pineapple**
Wrap each half slice in 1 of	**4 slices streaky bacon**
and fasten with a wooden cocktail stick	
Melt	**butter**
and fry the bacon and pineapple a little on both sides	
Lay one bacon and pineapple slice on each slice of bread, and sprinkle each with 1 tbsp of	**4 tbsp brandy**
Stick 1 of	**4 stuffed Spanish olives**
on the end of each cocktail stick	

Salmon on white bread
(Illustrated on pages 98-99)

Scrape and wash	**$\frac{1}{2}$ fresh horseradish root**
Peel off a few strips and reserve for garnishing	
Finely grate the rest of the horseradish	
Whip	**200 ml/8 fl oz double cream**
for $\frac{1}{2}$ minute	
Stir in the horseradish, and season to taste with	**salt**
Put it into a piping bag with a large star nozzle, and pipe it evenly on to	**8 large slices smoked salmon**
Roll them up	
Spread with	**4 slices white bread**
	dill butter (page 97)
Lay 2 salmon rolls on each slice of bread, and garnish with the strips of	

	horseradish and	**bottled salmon caviar**
		dill sprigs
		watercress

Spicy avocado open sandwich

Halve and peel	**1 ripe avocado**
Remove stone, and cut into small pieces	
Add	**75 g/3 oz roquefort cheese**
	75 g/3 oz softened butter
and purée the mixture with an electric mixer	
Add	**lemon juice**
	white pepper
to taste	
Spread	**4 slices German rye bread**
with some of the avocado cream	
Wash	**1 box cress**
and arrange it around the edges of the slices of bread	
Core and slice	**4 - 6 tomatoes**
Overlap slices inside the cress	
Put the rest of the avocado cream in a piping bag with a rosette nozzle, and pipe on to the tomato slices	
If wished, garnish with	**lemon slices**

Finch Island gourmet open sandwich

Spicy avocado open sandwich

Finch Island gourmet open sandwich
(8 servings)

Spread	**8 slices wholemeal bread**
with	**butter**
Beat together	**8 eggs**
	8 tbsp milk
	salt
Melt	**butter or margarine**
in a small pan and add the egg and milk	
Stir continuously, heating it until it has all set	
Allow the scrambled egg to cool, and then put equal amounts on each slice of bread	
Remove skin and bones from	**1 smoked eel**
and cut it into 16 pieces 4 - 5 cm/ $1\frac{1}{2}$ - 2 in long	
Place 1 of	**8 slices raw smoked ham**
on each portion, and lay a piece of eel on either side	
Peel	**2 - 3 onions**
and cut into rings	
Lay 3 onion rings on each portion	
Fill the middle onion ring with	**25 g/1 oz salmon caviar**

Whip until stiff	**125 ml/4 fl oz cream**
Add	**3 - 4 tbsp grated horseradish**
	lemon juice
	salt
to taste	
Spread thickly on	**8 slices smoked salmon**

Roll them up, and place 2 on each portion

Drain	**125 g/4 oz tinned palm hearts**
and cut into 8 slices	
Drain	**4 tinned artichoke hearts**

Place 2 palm hearts and 1 artichoke heart on to each portion

Put	**a little salmon caviar**
on top of the artichokes	
Garnish each portion with 1 of	**4 lemon slices**
	slices of stuffed Spanish olives
	cress

Prawn open sandwich with dill

Spread	**4 slices German rye bread**
with	**butter**
Wash	**4 lettuce leaves**

Shake dry and place 1 leaf in the middle of each slice of bread

| Divide | **200 g/6 oz fresh peeled prawns** |

and put them on top of the lettuce leaves

| Wash and slice | **½ cucumber** |
| Clean and slice | **4 radishes** |

Overlap the cucumber and radish slices

Gourmet open sandwich

| and the side rings with | **50 g/2 oz tinned caviar** |
| Garnish with | **chervil** |

Dainty mouthfuls

| Spread | **2 slices German rye bread** |
| with | **butter** |

and cut them into quarters

| Wash | **½ small cucumber** |

and cut it into 8 slices

Place 1 cucumber slice on each piece of bread

| Sprinkle with | **finely chopped dill** |
| Arrange | **150 g/5 oz prawns or scampi** |

on top of the cucumber slices

| Garnish with | **dill sprigs** |

Gourmet open sandwich

Toast	**4 slices white bread**
and cut off the crusts	
Wash	**4 lettuce leaves**

shake dry and lay one leaf on each slice of toast

Prawn open sandwich with dill, Spicy roast beef open sandwich, Gouda open sandwich with cucumber, Caviar open sandwich with egg yolk, Ham and kiwifruit open sandwich, Tomato open sandwich with scrambled egg

and cut into very fine strips	
Use this, together with	**1 tsp crisp fried onions**
to garnish the sandwiches	

Gouda open sandwich with cucumber

Spread	**4 slices German rye bread**
with	**butter**
Wash	**4 lettuce leaves**
Shake dry and lay 1 on each slice of bread	
For the cucumber salad	
Wash	**1 small cucumber**
and thinly slice	
Stir together	**2 tbsp salad oil**
	3 tbsp lemon juice
	salt
	pepper
Stir in	**1 bunch chopped dill**
and mix with the cucumber slices	
Put equal amounts of the cucumber salad on top of the lettuce leaves	
Cut	**200 g/6 oz Gouda cheese**
into 16 slices	
and place 4 slices of cheese on to each slice of bread	
Clean and wash	**4 radishes**
and cut them several times in a criss-cross fashion	
Garnish each slice of bread with one radish	

alternately, on either side of the prawns	
Sprinkle the prawns with	**chopped dill**

Spicy roast beef open sandwich

Spread	**4 slices German rye bread**
with	**butter**
Wash	**4 lettuce leaves**
Shake dry and lay 1 on each slice of bread	
Arrange	**200 g/6 oz cold roast beef**
on top of the lettuce	
Wash and slice	**½ small cucumber**
and arrange 3 slices on each slice of bread	
Peel	**1 small white mouli radish**

Caviar open sandwich with egg yolk

Spread	**4 slices German rye bread**
with	**butter**
Wash	**75 g/3 oz small lettuce leaves**
Shake dry and arrange on the slices of bread	
Arrange	**100 g/4 oz bottled caviar**
on the leaves	
Place 1 of	**4 egg yolks**
in half an egg shell on the caviar on each slice of bread	
Peel	**1 small onion (red if available)**
and cut into eighths and arrange on the sandwiches	

Ham and kiwifruit open sandwich

Spread	**4 slices German rye bread**
with	**butter**
Wash	**4 lettuce leaves**
Shake dry and place 1 on each slice of bread	
Peel and slice	**2 kiwifruit**
Arrange the kiwifruit with	**200 g/6 oz raw smoked ham slices (trimmed of any fat)**
on the slices of bread	

Tomato open sandwich with scrambled egg

Spread	**4 slices German rye bread**
with	**butter**
Wash	**4 lettuce leaves**
Shake dry and place 1 on each slice of bread	
Cut	**4 tomatoes**
into eighths, and remove the cores	
Arrange them on the lettuce leaves	
Beat together	**4 eggs** **4 tbsp milk** **salt**
Heat	**butter or margarine**
in a small pan and put in the egg mixture	
Stroke mixture from pan bottom with a spoon, heating until it has all set	
Put the scrambled egg on top of the portions	
Sprinkle with	**finely chopped chives**

Roast beef mouthfuls

Roast beef mouthfuls

Spread	**4 slices wholemeal bread**
with	**butter**
Halve	**8 slices cold roast beef**
fold together a little, and put 4 on each slice of bread	
Garnish with	**capers**

Garnished crackers

Drain liquid off	**250 g/6 oz quark (curd cheese)**
if necessary	

Garnished crackers

Stir together with	**150 ml/5 fl oz double cream**
Season with	**salt**
	sweet paprika
Stir in	**2 tsp chopped mixed herbs**
Put the cream into a piping bag with a rosette nozzle, and pipe on to	**about 25 crackers**
Garnish as desired with	**halved stuffed olives**
	capers
	pieces of radish
	onion rings (dipped in paprika)
	cucumber slices
	parsley
	cress
	dill tips

Orange and cheese mouthfuls

Peppered Swedish mouthfuls

Spread	**2 slices German rye bread**
with	**butter**
Crush	**1 bunch finely chopped chives**
and sprinkle over bread	
Drain	**about 125 g/4 oz Swedish smoked salmon**
Arrange them on top of the chives	
Peel	**2 onions**
Cut into rings and use to garnish the fish	
Sprinkle with	**freshly ground pepper**

Orange and cheese mouthfuls

Peel and thinly slice (8 slices)	**1 - 2 large oranges**
Cut	**8 small slices German rye bread**
to the same size as the oranges	
Spread them with	**butter**
and place 1 orange slice on each one	
On top of each, place 1 of	**8 pieces roquefort cheese**
With a knife, shave peel from	**1 orange**
and cut the peel into fine strips	
Use to garnish	

English sandwiches

Spread	**2 slices white tin loaf**
with	**butter**
Wash	**2 large lettuce leaves**
Shake dry and place 1 on 1 slice of bread	

Spread	**3 slices cold roast beef**
with	**3 tsp herb mayonnaise**
Arrange on them	**slices of pickled gherkin**
	tomato wedges
	onion rings
Roll them up, and place them on the bread with the lettuce leaf	
Cover them with the second lettuce leaf	
Dice finally	**$\frac{1}{4}$ red pepper**
	1 slice ham
and sprinkle on to the lettuce leaf	
Put the other slice of bread on top, and cut diagonally in half to make triangles	

Salmon canapés

Cut out 10 round shapes from using a 4 cm/1 $\frac{1}{2}$ in cutter	**slices of white bread**
Cream	**1 tbsp butter**
with	**$\frac{1}{2}$ - 1 tbsp lemon juice**
Add	**grated lemon rind**
	salt
	pepper
to taste, and spread on the bread	
Leave in a cold place	
Halve	**5 thin slices smoked salmon**
lengthways and make them into rolls the same size as the bread	
Lay them on the bread, and add	**a little grated horseradish**
Arrange the canapés on	**washed lettuce leaves**
Garnish with	**halved lemon slices**
	dill

Giant sandwich

Berlin style sandwich

Spread	**4 slices white bread**
with	**butter**
Wash	**4 lettuce leaves**
Shake dry and lay 1 on each slice of bread	
Cover with	**4 slices smoked salmon**
Spread them with	**3 tbsp grated horse-radish**
Sprinkle	**4 round apple slices, peeled and cored**
with	**lemon juice**
and lay a slice on each piece of bread	
Garnish with	**dill sprigs**
Spread	**4 slices white bread**
with butter, and lay them on top of the apple slices	
Cut the sandwiches diagonally in half to form triangles	

Giant sandwich

Cut	**1 roll**
in half and spread with	**butter**
Wash	**1 lettuce leaf**
Shake dry and lay it on the lower half of	

the roll
Spread on it	**1 level tbsp mayonnaise**
Roll up	**3 slices bierschinken (German sausage)**
and lay on top of the lettuce	
Clean	**3 radishes**
and thinly slice and place them, overlapping, on the meat	
Sprinkle with	**salt**
	pepper
	2 tbsp chopped fresh herbs
Cover with	**1 slice Emmenthal cheese**
Shell	**1 hard-boiled egg**
Cut it into slices, and lay them on the cheese	
Put on the top half of the roll	

Pastrami canapés

Cut out 10 round shapes from with a 4 cm /1 ½ in cutter	**white bread slices**
Melt	**butter**
in a frying pan and fry the bread on both sides until golden brown	
Put on to kitchen paper, and allow to cool	

Berlin style sandwich

Fold **10 slices pastrami (spiced cooked beef)**

together a little and put on to the bread

Shell and halve **1 hard-boiled egg**

Remove the yolk, and squeeze it through a garlic press on to the canapés

Parma ham and melon ball canapés

Cut out 10 round shapes from **white bread slices** with a 4 cm/1½ in cutter

Melt **butter**

in a frying pan and fry the bread on both sides until golden brown

Put them on to kitchen paper, and allow to cool

Halve **5 thin slices parma ham**

lenghtways and fold each one together a little

Lay them on the bread pieces

Remove seeds from **½ small melon**

Cut out 10 balls from the melon flesh, and place one on each of the ham slices

Sprinkle with **freshly ground pepper**

Game pâté and cranberry canapés

Cut out 10 round shapes from **white bread slices** with a 4 cm/1½ in cutter

Melt **butter**

in a frying pan and fry the bread on both sides until golden brown

Put them on to kitchen paper, and allow to cool

Stir together **75 g/3 oz tinned game pâté**

1 tsp brandy

and place in a cold place

Put into a piping bag with a rosette nozzle, and pipe on to the bread

Garnish with **cranberries**

Cream cheese and kiwifruit canapés

Cut out 10 round shapes from **white bread slices** with a 4 cm/1½ in cutter

Melt **butter**

in a frying pan and fry the bread on both sides until golden brown

Put them on to kitchen paper, and allow

Canapés

to cool	
Cream together	**150 g/5 oz full fat cream cheese**
	1 tbsp cream
Add	**grated rind**
	lemon
to taste	
Leave in a cold place	
Put into a piping bag with a plain nozzle, and pipe on to the bread	
Peel	**1 kiwifruit**
thinly and cut it in half lengthways	
Slice one half, and press each half-slice into the cream cheese	

Canapés with liver sausage and truffle strips

Cut out 10 round shapes from with a 4 cm/1 $\frac{1}{2}$ in cutter	**white bread slices**
Melt	**butter**
in a frying pan and fry the bread on both sides until golden brown	
Put them on to kitchen paper, and allow to cool	
Stir well	**75 g/3 oz tinned truffled liver pâté**
and put it in a cold place	
Put it in a piping bag with a rosette nozzle	
Wash	**10 very small lettuce leaves**
Shake dry and lay them on the bread	
Pipe the liver pâté on to them	
Cut	**1 tinned black truffle**
into very fine strips and use it to garnish	

Canapés with chicken breast and horseradish mayonnaise

Cut out 10 round shapes from with a 4 cm/1 $\frac{1}{2}$ in cutter	**slices of white bread**
Melt	**butter**
in a frying pan and fry the bread on both sides until golden brown	
Put on to kitchen paper, and allow to cool	
Wash and pat dry	**125 g/4 oz chicken**

	breasts
Sprinkle with	**salt**
	freshly ground pepper
Heat	**1 tbsp cooking oil**
and fry chicken breast on both sides until golden brown	
Put it on to kitchen paper, and allow to cool, then cut into small slices	
Add to	**1 tbsp mayonnaise**
	freshly grated, or bottled grated horseradish
to taste	
Make a piping bag with a very small hole from greaseproof paper	
Use this to pipe some of the mayonnaise on to the pieces of bread	
Lay a slice of the chicken breast on top of the mayonnaise, pipe on more mayonnaise, lay another slice of breast on top, and decorate with piped mayonnaise	
Garnish with	**shelled pistachio nuts**

Canapés with quark and radishes

Cut out 10 round shapes from with a 4 cm/1 $\frac{1}{2}$ in cutter	**slices of white bread**
Melt	**butter**
in a frying pan and fry bread on both sides until golden brown	
Lay on kitchen paper, and allow to cool	
Stir together	**150 g/5 oz quark (curd cheese)**
	2 tbsp cream
Peel and very finely dice and stir into the quark cream	**1 shallot**
Season with	**salt**
	freshly ground pepper
and leave for a short time in a cold place	
Put into a piping bag with a plain nozzle, and pipe on to the pieces of bread	
Clean and slice	**6 small radishes**
Cut the radish slices in half, and press 4 of these halves into the quark cream on each canapé	
Garnish with	**lemon balm**

LITTLE
DELICACIES

Caviar
(Recipe on p. 120)

Marinated sheep's cheese rolls

Marinated sheep's cheese rolls

For the filling	
Crumble	**175 g/6 oz sheep's cheese**
Stir it into	**150 ml/5 fl oz double cream**
Peel and crush	**1 glove of garlic**
Stir into the cream cheese, together with	**some fresh, washed basil leaves**
	or
	1 tsp dried basil
Wash	**15 large silverbeet (Swiss) leaves**
and put them in	**boiling salted water**
Boil for about 2 minutes	

Transfer to a colander, rinse with cold water and allow to drain well
Put about 1 tbsp of the cream cheese on to each silverbeet leaf, and roll them up
Lay them side by side in a shallow soufflé dish

For the sauce	
Stir together	**125 ml/4 fl oz olive oil**
	125 ml/4 fl oz white wine
	1 tbsp lemon juice
Season with	**salt**
	pepper
	sugar

Pour sauce over rolls, and leave overnight

Dip	**500 - 750 g/1 - 1 $\frac{1}{2}$ lb ripe tomatoes**

first into boiling water, then into cold water
Skin and halve, remove pips and cores, and dice flesh

Season with salt, pepper, sugar, and	**dried basil**
Peel and crush	**1 clove of garlic**
Stir it into	**1 - 2 tbsp olive oil**
and allow to stand for a short time	
Put into a bowl	
Arrange the rolls on a serving dish, and garnish with	**small basil leaves**
Serve with the diced tomato, the dressing, and:	**pitta bread or French bread**

Cheesy Scotch eggs

Bring	**125 ml/4 fl oz milk**
	1 tbsp butter
	salt
to the boil in a small pan	
Sieve	**50 g/2 oz plain flour**

Remove milk from heat, and add the flour all at once to the milk in the pan
Stir it until a smooth ball is formed and continue to stir while heating it for 1 minute
Then put it into a bowl, and gradually

stir in	**2 eggs**
	50 g/2 oz grated cheese
	grated nutmeg
Stir well	

Cheesy Scotch eggs

Shell **5 hard-boiled eggs**
Cover them first in the cheese dough,
then in **3 - 4 tbsp fine bread-crumbs**
Fry them until golden brown in hot **cooking oil**
Leave on kitchen paper to drain
Cut in half across, and arrange on a
large serving dish with **washed cress**
Serve with: **herb and yoghurt dressing (page 93)**

Stuffed tartlets

Clean, wash and thinly slice **300 g/10 oz button mushrooms**
Sprinkle them with **3 tbsp lemon juice**
Season with **salt**
pepper
Italian herbs

Allow to stand for several hours
Stir in **2 tbsp double cream**
and add salt and pepper to taste
Cut out **6 slices mortadella cheese**

with a 8 - 9 cm/3 - 3 $\frac{1}{2}$ in cutter
Cut them once, from the outer edge to
the centre, and form them into shallow
cones
Taking 6 of **12 pastry tartlet cases, baked blind**

put one cheese cone in each
Cut **6 slices salami**
in the same way and put them into the
remaining 6 cases
Shortly before serving, fill the tartlets
with the mushrooms
Garnish with **basil**
rosemary

Stuffed tartlets

Chicken on toast Alexandra

Chicken on toast Alexandra

Cut **2 chicken breasts**
into 4 fillets
Remove bone and fat, wash and pat dry
Season with **salt**
pepper
Heat **1 tbsp butter**
and fry the breast fillets on both sides
for about 10 minutes
About 3 minutes before the end of the
frying time add **8 thin rashers streaky bacon**
and fry them all together
Spread **4 slices toast**
with **butter**
Wash **4 lettuce leaves**
and drain on kitchen paper
Lay them on the toast slices
Remove cores from **4 tomatoes**
and slice
Arrange the tomato slices on the lettuce
so that they overlap
Sprinkle with salt, pepper, and **1 heaped tbsp finely chopped chives**

Arrange the breasts with the bacon on
top
Season **4 heaped tbsp double cream**
to taste with salt, pepper, and **lemon juice**
and put 1 tsp on to each serving
Sprinkle with **sweet paprika**
Garnish with **parsley**
and serve immediately
Tip: This can also be served cold
For this, drain the fried chicken breasts
and the bacon on kitchen paper, and allow to cool on a plate

113

Vegetable gardener's ring

Toast the bread shortly before serving, and top with the ingredients in the same order as given above

Vegetable gardener's ring

For the pastry	
Bring	**125 ml/4 fl oz water** **25 g/1 oz butter or margarine**
to the boil in a milk pan	
Sieve together	**75 g/3 oz plain flour** **25 g/1 oz cornflour**
Remove water from heat, and add flour mixture all at once	
Stir it until a smooth ball is formed, and continue stirring while heating for 1 minute	
Put the hot mixture into a bowl, and gradually stir in	**2 - 3 eggs**
Enough egg has been added when the pastry is shiny, and pulls away from the spoon when held up	
Stir	**½ level tsp baking powder**
into the cool pastry	

Put the pastry into a piping bag with a large star nozzle

Pipe a 20 cm/8 in diameter ring on to a greased, floured baking tray, and put into a preheated oven

Electricity: 200° - 225° C/400° - 425° F

Gas: Mark 6 - 7

Baking time: about 30 minutes

Do not open the oven door during the first 15 minutes of baking, or the ring will sink

Slice the ring into 2 layers immediately after baking

For the filling	
Cook	**300 g/10 oz frozen mixed vegetables**
according to instructions on packet	
Drain and chill them, and reserve some for garnishing	
Remove skin from	**125 g/4 oz cooked German sausage**
and dice it	
Mix with the vegetables and	**2 heaped tbsp mayonnaise**
Season with	**salt** **pepper**
and allow to stand	
If necessary, add more salt and pepper to taste	

Dressed poached eggs

Use some of the filling to make a sandwich of the two halves of the ring, and put the rest into the centre of the ring
Garnish this with the reserved vegetables and   **herbs**

Dressed poached eggs

Bring to the boil	**1 1/2 pints water** **2 tbsp vinegar**
Crack open	**4 eggs**
and slide them, one at a time, into a ladle	
Put them carefully into the boiling water, on a very low heat	
Remove the eggs after about 5 minutes with a perforated spoon	
Put them into cold water for a short time, and allow to cool	
Remove cores from and slice	**4 tomatoes**
Peel and slice	**300 g/10 oz cucumber**
Remove any brown parts from	**1 small fennel bulb (about 175 g/6 oz)**
Wash and quarter, and cut into slices	
Clean and slice	**125 g/4 oz button mushrooms**
Sprinkle the mushrooms with and then with	**1 tbsp lemon juice** **salt** **pepper**
and allow to stand for about 10 minutes	
Arrange the vegetables on 4 plates, and sprinkle with and	**1 - 2 tbsp lemon juice** **salt** **pepper** **2 tbsp finely chopped chives**
Wrap each egg in 1 of and place with the vegetable	**4 slices ham**

Remove rind from	**125 g/4 oz gorgonzola cheese**
and rub the cheese through a sieve	
Lightly whip	**150 ml/5 fl oz double cream**
Stir in the gorgonzola, and	**2 tbsp chopped mixed herbs**
Spread over the ham	
Serve with:	**wholemeal bread and butter**

Ham rolls with quark and horseradish

For the horseradish quark

Stir	**1 tsp gelatine** **2 tbsp cold water**
together in a small pan and leave to soak for 10 minutes	
Heat, stirring, until dissolved	
Stir together	**250 g/8 oz low fat quark (curd cheese)** **2 - 4 tbsp grated horseradish** **1 tbsp lemon juice**
Season with	**salt** **pepper** **sugar**
Whip	**250 ml/8 fl oz double cream**
until almost stiff and add lukewarm gelatine solution	
Whip until stiff, and carefully fold into the quark mixture	
If necessary, add more seasoning	
Put this on to and roll them up	**8 large slices ham**

Ham rolls with quark and horseradish

American scampi

Arrange the ham rolls on a plate, together with | **tomato quarters**
parsley
Serve with: | **toast**

American scampi
(1 - 2 servings)

Peel, and finely dice	**1 onion**
Peel and crush	**1 clove of garlic**
Dip	**4 tomatoes**
first into boiling water, then into cold water	
Skin, halve, remove pips and cores, and dice flesh	
Melt	**1 tbsp butter**
and sauté tomatoes, onion and garlic	
Sprinkle over them	**1 tsp plain flour**
Add	**125 ml/4 fl oz white wine**
and bring to the boil while stirring	
Cook for about 10 minutes	
Stir in	**150 ml/5 fl oz double cream**
	200 g/6 oz large scampi
and boil again	
Add	**salt**
	pepper
	cayenne pepper
	food flavouring
to taste	
Put into a dish, and garnish with	**dill sprigs**
Cooking time: 25 - 30 minutes	
Serve with:	**French bread**

Ham and leek rolls

Cut	**8 leeks (about 750 g/ 1½ lb)**
all to the same length	
Cut them lengthways, and wash	
Put them into	**boiling salted water**
and bring back to the boil	
Cook for about 7 minutes, then drain, and allow to cool	
Wrap 2 leeks in 1 of	**4 slices ham**
and arrange on a serving dish	
Whip	**150 ml/5 fl oz double cream**
Season with	**salt**
	pepper
	sweet paprika
	lemon juice
and spread it over the ham and leek rolls	
Halve	**2 tomatoes**
Remove pips and cores, and dice	
Shell and dice	**1 hard-boiled egg**
Spread the tomato and egg over the ham and leek rolls	
Sprinkle with	**1 tbsp chopped parsley**
Serve with:	**wholemeal bread and butter**

Meat in a herb marinade

Wash and dry	**375 g/12 oz pork fillet**
Remove skin if necessary	
Cut into ½ cm/¼ in slices	
Wash and dry	**375 g/12 oz beef (topside)**

Meat in a herb marinade

Remove fat if necessary	
Cut it into 3 pieces along the grain	
Cut these into $\frac{1}{2}$ cm/$\frac{1}{4}$ in slices against the grain	
Heat	**5 tbsp cooking oil**
and fry meat, in batches, on both sides for about 3 minutes	
Put the fried meat into a bowl, with the juices	
Sprinkle with	**salt**
	pepper

For the marinade

Stir together	**4 tbsp salad oil**
	3 - 4 tbsp red wine vinegar
	1 tsp Dijon mustard
Season with salt and pepper	
Add	**2 tbsp chopped parsley**
	1 - 2 tbsp chopped dill
	1 - 2 tbsp chopped chervil
	2 tbsp finely chopped chives

Mix marinade with meat, and allow to stand turning the meat now and again

Season again with salt, pepper and	**red wine vinegar**
Arrange meat on a serving plate with	

the marinade, and garnish with	**small bunches of herbs**
Serve with:	**French bread or roast potatoes salad**

Colourful meat platter

String	**375 g/12 oz green beans**
if necessary	
Wash and pat dry, and cut into pieces	
Put them into	**250 ml/8 fl oz boiling salted water**
Bring back to the boil, and cook for 10 - 15 minutes, then drain beans	
Halve	**375 g/12 oz tomatoes**
and remove pips and cores, then dice them	

For the salad dressing

Peel and finely dice	**1 onion**
Peel and crush	**1 clove of garlic**
Mix the 2 ingredients with	**2 tbsp olive oil**
	2 tbsp lemon juice
Season with	**salt**
	pepper
	sugar

Colourful meat platter

Apple halves with bacon

Mix the dressing with the beans, and allow to marinate
Stir in the tomato cubes, and add salt
and pepper to taste
Arrange on a large serving dish

Roll up	**8 large slices cold beef (about 300 g/10 oz)**
and arrange them on the salad	
Serve with:	**rye bread rolls and butter**

Apple halves with bacon

Peel, halve, and core	**4 medium apples**
Brush a grill tray with	**cooking oil**
and lay the apples, cut side down, on it	
Place under a preheated grill, and grill for about 4 minutes	
Remove the apple halves, turn them over, and in each hollow put 1 of	**8 tbsp sherry**
and lay on top of that 1 of	**8 thin rashers streaky bacon**
and then 1 of	**8 slices gouda cheese**
Put them back under the grill, and grill until the cheese begins to melt	
Arrange them on	**washed lettuce leaves**
and sprinkle with	**sweet paprika**
Garnish with	**parsley**

Chinese roast fillet of pork

Wash and dry	**2 pork fillets (each about 250 g/8 oz)**
Remove skin and sinews if necessary	
Clean, wash, and finely dice	**75 g/3 oz spring onions**
Peel and finely dice	**1 clove of garlic**

Stir the onions and garlic with **6 tsp soy sauce 2 tbsp medium sherry ground ginger salt**

Put meat in a small bowl, and pour
marinade over it
Cover with baking foil, and leave it
overnight

Warm	**2 tbsp honey 2 tbsp brown sugar**

stirring all the time until the sugar has
dissolved
Remove meat from marinade, pat it
dry, and spread with the honey mixture

Heat	**2 tbsp cooking oil**

in a roasting tin, and fry the fillets
quickly on all sides
Pour marinade over meat, and put the
tin in a preheated oven

During roasting, add if necessary	**3 - 4 tbsp water**

Electricity: 225° - 250° C/450° - 475° F
Gas: Mark 8 - 9
Roasting time: about 20 minutes
Remove cooked meat from oven, and
loosen the meat juices from the bottom
of the tin with 2 - 3 tbsp medium sherry
Pour this over the meat and allow it to
cool
Carve into very thin slices, and arrange
on a serving dish
Pour the juices over the meat

Garnish with	**herbs**
Serve with:	**French bread small washed lettuce leaves**

Emperor's asparagus

Peel	**1 kg/2 lb asparagus**
from top to bottom being careful to re-move all the skin and woody parts, but without damaging the tips	
Put into	**about 1 1/2 pints boil-ing salted water**
Add	**1 tbsp butter sugar**
and bring back to the boil	
Cook for about 25 minutes, then drain, and allow to cool	
Continuously beat	**125 ml/4 fl oz white wine 2 egg yolks 1 level tsp cornflour**
in a pan while heating, until mixture be-gins to bubble	
Remove from heat, and allow to cool whilst stirring	
Lightly whip	**150 ml/5 fl oz double cream**

Emperor's asparagus

and fold it into the wine cream
Season with salt and   **pepper**
Arrange asparagus on 4 plates, and
sprinkle with   **1 tbsp chopped parsley**
Arrange 2 of   **8 slices parma ham (about 175 g/6 oz)**

beside each portion of asparagus
Put some of the sauce over the aspara-
gus, and serve the rest separately
Garnish each portion with   **parsley**
Serve with: **French bread**

Roast meat rolls

Cut   **500 g/1 lb roast ham**
350 g/10 oz boiled ham

into very thin slices, the same size if
possible
Stir together   **150 g/5 oz fine liver pâté**
1 small glass brandy
Season with   **freshly ground pepper**

Spread the liver pâté thinly on to the
slices of roast ham, lay a slice of boiled

ham on top of each, and roll up
Cut the rolls in half, and fasten them
with wooden cocktail sticks

For the marinade
Peel and crush   **1 - 2 cloves of garlic**
Mix them with   **5 tbsp wine vinegar**
1 tsp salt
1 tbsp dried thyme
125 ml/4 fl oz cooking oil

Put the ham rolls into a deep dish, and
pour the marinade over them
Cover, and leave overnight
Shortly before serving, remove the rolls
from the marinade, drain, and place in a
dish with   **washed lettuce leaves**
Serve with: **French bread**
mixed salad

Roast meat rolls

Caviar
(1 serving) (Illustrated on pages 110-111)

Chill	**50 g/2 oz bottled caviar**
and arrange in a small dish	
Garnish with	**lemon slices or wedges slices of egg**
Serve with:	**toast and butter**

Smoked salmon on lemon beans with dill cream

If necessary, string	**500 g/1 lb dwarf beans**
Wash them, and put them into	**500 ml/16 fl oz boiling salted water**
Bring back to the boil, cook for about 15 minutes, and drain	
For the salad dressing	
Peel and dice	**1 small onion**
Stir it together with	**2 tbsp salad oil** **2 tbsp lemon juice**
Season with	**salt** **pepper** **sugar**
Mix with the beans, and allow to marinate	
Add salt, pepper, sugar and lemon juice to taste	
Divide the beans on to 4 plates, and arrange on each portion $\frac{1}{4}$ of	**200 g/8 oz smoked salmon slices**
Garnish with	**lemon slices**
Beat	**150 ml/5 fl oz double cream**
Stir in	**grated rind of $\frac{1}{2}$ lemon** **1 tbsp chopped dill**
Add salt and pepper to taste	
Put into a piping bag with a plain nozzle, and pipe on to the lemon slices	
Garnish the beans with	**dill sprigs**
Serve with:	**toast**

Veal medallions on toast with Hollandaise sauce

Cut out 4 rounds, 8 cm/2 $\frac{1}{2}$ in diameter, from	**4 slices thick white bread**
Heat	**butter**
in the base of a grill pan, dip bread in it, and grill on both sides	

Smoked salmon on lemon beans with dill cream

Gently pound	**4 slices veal fillet**
Heat	**margarine**
in the grill pan, and grill the meat in it on both sides for about 5 minutes, basting with the juices now and again, so that they remain moist	
Sprinkle with	**salt** **pepper**
Arrange on the slices of toast	
Garnish with	**herbs**
For the Hollandaise sauce	
Melt	**125 g/4 oz butter**
and allow to cool a little	
Beat	**2 egg yolks** **1 tsp tarragon vinegar** **2 tbsp water**
over hot water until thick	
Beat in the butter, and season to taste with	**salt** **pepper** **sugar** **lemon juice**
Keep it warm over the hot water until ready to serve, so that it does not coagulate	
Serve the medallions hot or cold with the sauce	
Heating time: about 6 minutes	
Serve with:	**green salad**

French stuffed eggs

French stuffed eggs

Carefully wash	**8 eggs**
Cut off $\frac{1}{3}$ from the pointed end of the shell, leaving the bottom $\frac{2}{3}$ whole	
For the chervil eggs	
Put the contents of 4 eggs into a bowl, and beat together with	**2 tbsp chopped chervil salt pepper**
Melt	**1 tbsp butter**

in a small pan and add the beaten egg
Stand the pan in boiling water, bring the water back to the boil, and stir the egg while it slowly sets
While it is still warm, put the cooked egg into 4 empty egg shells, and allow to cool

Garnish with	**black olive strips chervil leaves**

For the paprika eggs
Put the contents of the remaining 4 eggs into a bowl, and beat with salt, pepper,

and	**2 tbsp very fine strips of red peppers**
Melt	**1 tbsp butter**

in a small pan and add the beaten egg
Stand the pan in boiling water, bring the water back to the boil, and stir the egg while it slowly sets
While it is still warm, put the cooked egg into the remaining 4 empty egg shells, and allow to cool

Garnish with	**$\frac{1}{4}$ slices of lime olive slices bottled salmon caviar**

If desired, arrange the 8 filled egg shells

on a bed of	**coarse sea salt**

Cooking time: 5 - 6 minutes

Serve with:	**toast or wholemeal bread and butter**

BRAWN, ASPIC

Vegetable brawn
(Recipe on p. 129)

Aspic Jelly

Rules:
1. To make a jelly from 500 ml/1 pint liquid, use 1 pkt gelatine.

2. Sprinkle the gelatine on to cold water, stir and leave to soak for 10 minutes. If no other instructions are given in the recipe, warm it, stirring constantly, until it has dissolved. If necessary, put in a cold place. Stir it into the liquid that is to be set.

3. Liquids mixed with dissolved gelatine will only set when they have cooled sufficiently, and have stood for long enough.
If the room temperature is higher than 23° C/75° F the gelatine will not set. Thus you should prepare the aspic dish several hours before it is to be eaten, preferably the night before, and leave it in a cold place.

4. If the aspic dish is to be turned out, put it into a mould which has first been rinsed out with cold water. In order to turn the dish out, stand the mould for a moment in hot water, and loosen the aspic from the sides with a knife.

5. In order to get a clear stock, you can clarify it as follows:
Remove fat from cold stock.
Crush 1 egg shell, and beat it together with 1 egg white and 3 tbsp cold water. Add to the stock, and beat continuously while heating, until nearly boiling. The egg white will coagulate meanwhile and bind all the sediment together. Leave to stand in a cold place until it is clear.
Skim it, and pour through a clean cloth.

Basic aspic stock

Wash	**500 g/1 lb broken beef or calf bones**
	250 g/8 oz leg of beef (sliced)
	or
	500 g/1 lb broken chicken bones
	500 g/1 lb chicken pieces for soup
	or
	500 g/1 lb broken game bones

	250 g/8 oz game meat
	or
	500 g/1 lb fish bones
	250 g/8 oz fish
Put the ingredients into	**1 $\frac{1}{2}$ l/3 pints cold salted water**
and bring to the boil	
Skim	
Clean and chop	**$\frac{1}{2}$ stick celery**
	$\frac{1}{2}$ carrot
	$\frac{1}{2}$ turnip
	$\frac{1}{2}$ leek
and add them to the stock with	**1 parsley sprig**
	1 small bay leaf
	1 clove
	4 peppercorns

Bring to the boil, and allow to simmer
Remove bones and meat from stock
Sieve, allow to cool, and skim off the fat
Cooking time:
for meat broth 2 - 2 $\frac{1}{2}$ hours
for chicken broth about 1 $\frac{1}{2}$ hours
for game broth 2 - 2 $\frac{1}{2}$ hours
for fish broth 1 - 1 $\frac{1}{2}$ hours
Variation:
For a spicy meat stock, add 1 peeled and roasted medium onion, some bacon rind or salted smoked pork (Kasseler)bones
For a dark game stock, fry the bones and meat with 1 peeled onion in butter, and then add the salted water

Bulgarian brawn with yoghurt cream

Put	**600 g/1 $\frac{1}{4}$ lb mixed frozen vegetables (peas, red or green peppers, sweetcorn)**
into	**125 ml/4 fl oz boiling salted water**

Bring back to the boil, cook for about 5 minutes, then drain, and allow to cool

Sprinkle	**2 pkts gelatine**
	6 tbsp cold water
and leave to soak for 10 minutes	
Bring to the boil	**500 ml/1 pint strong meat stock, skimmed**
Remove from heat, add gelatine, and stir until dissolved	
Stir in	**250 ml/8 fl oz white wine**
	6 tbsp white wine vinegar
Season with	**salt**
	pepper
	Worcester sauce

Rinse out a 30 cm/12 in loaf tin with

Bulgarian brawn with yoghurt cream

cold water, and pour in enough of the stock to cover the bottom
Put it into refrigerator to set

Stir together	**300 g/10 oz Bulgarian sheep's cheese**
	50 g/2 oz softened butter
	3 tbsp cream
	1 tbsp pepper
Stir in	**dried basil**

With wet hands, form this into a roll, the same length as the loaf tin, on a board that has been rinsed in cold water

| Overlap | **10 - 12 large pickled vine leaves** |

to form a layer the same length as the loaf tin
Wrap the cheese roll in these

| Overlap 3 of | **6 slices boiled ham** |

in the bottom of loaf tin, on top of aspic
Wrap remaining 3 slices around the cheese roll
Lay this roll in the middle of the aspic layer, and spread the vegetables around it
Pour the rest of the stock over it, and leave in the refrigerator to set
Before serving, dip base of loaf tin briefly in hot water, and carefully loosen the brawn from the sides with a knife
Turn it out on to a serving dish

| Arrange | **3 - 4 quartered lemon slices** |

so that they overlap on top of the brawn, and garnish with **parsley**

For the yoghurt cream

Stir together	**150 g/5 fl oz yoghurt**
	150 g/5 fl oz double cream
	3 tbsp chopped mixed herbs
	1 tsp hot mustard
Season with	**salt**
	pepper
Serve with:	**rye rolls or rye bread and butter**

Madeira, wine or sherry aspic

Sprinkle	**1 pkt gelatine**
on to	**5 tbsp cold water**
and leave to soak for 10 minutes	
Measure out	**375 ml/12 fl oz basic aspic stock**

and bring it to the boil
Remove from heat, and add gelatine, stirring until dissolved

| Stir in | **4 - 8 tbsp madeira or** |

4 - 8 tbsp white wine
or
4 - 8 tbsp dry sherry

and allow to cool
This aspic can be used to pour over pastries and terrines, and for making cold meat, roast meat, poultry or fish in aspic

Trout fillets in aspic with horseradish sauce (6 servings)

Sprinkle	**1 pkt and 1 level tsp gelatine**
on to	**4 tbsp cold water**
Bring to the boil	**375 ml/12 fl oz strong meat stock, skimmed**
	4 juniper berries
	1 small onion peeled
	a few peppercorns
	pinch of saffron strands

and allow to simmer for about 5 minutes
Strain through a cloth, then bring to the boil again
Remove from heat and add gelatine, stirring until dissolved

Stir in	**250 ml/8 fl oz white wine**
	1 tbsp white wine vinegar
Season with	**salt**
	pepper
	tabasco
Drain	**150 g/5 oz cooked asparagus tips**
Shell and slice	**2 hard-boiled eggs**
Core and slice	**2 tomatoes**
Remove skin from	**6 smoked trout fillets**
Arrange ingredients on 6 plates and garnish with	**dill sprigs**

Pour the stock over them, and leave to set in the refrigerator
For the horseradish sauce

Stir together	**150 ml/5 fl oz double cream**
	1 - 2 tbsp grated horseradish
Season with	**lemon juice**
	salt
Serve with:	**toast**

Tomato aspic

Sprinkle	**1 pkt and 1 level tsp gelatine**
on to	**6 tbsp cold water**

and leave to soak for 10 minutes

Bring to the boil	**500 ml/1 pint tomato**

Trout fillets in aspic with horseradish sauce

	juice
Remove from heat, and add the gelatine	
Stir until dissolved	
Stir in	**2 - 3 tbsp lemon juice**
	6 tbsp vodka
Season with	**tabasco**
	celery salt
	garlic salt
	salt
	pepper

and leave to stand for a while

Dip	**2 tomatoes**

first into boiling water, then into cold water
Skin, halve and dice

Peel and finely dice	**1 small onion**
Stir the tomato, onion and	**2 tbsp finely chopped chives**

into the tomato liquid
Rinse out a round mould with cold water, put in the tomato liquid, and leave to set in refrigerator
Before serving, dip base of mould briefly in hot water and carefully loosen the aspic from the sides with a knife, then turn out on to a serving dish

Garnish with	**egg slices**
	cress

Serve tomato aspic as an accompaniment to cold meat

and remove from heat
Add the gelatine, and stir until dissolved

Stir in	**8 tbsp vinegar**
Season with	**salt**

Rinse out a 30 cm/12 in loaf tin with cold water, and pour in enough stock to cover the bottom
Leave it in the refrigerator to set

Remove the skin from	**250 g/8 oz cold cooked sausage, unsliced**
Core	**4 medium-sized tomatoes**
Dice both ingredients	
Finely chop	**4 medium pickled gherkins**
Shell	**6 hard-boiled eggs**

Finely chop 4 of them, and slice 2 of them for garnishing

Coarsely chop	**5 tbsp parsley**

Arrange the egg slices on the aspic layer, and spread half of the diced sausage over them
Pour about 125 ml/4 fl oz of the stock over it, and leave to set
Now fill tin with the following:
Half of the chopped gherkins, then about 125 ml/4 fl oz stock, and allow to set
Half of the tomato cubes with half of the chopped parsley sprinkled over them, and 125 ml/4 fl oz of the stock
Leave to set
The chopped egg and 125 ml/4 fl oz stock, and leave to set
The remaining tomato and parsley, then 125 ml/4 fl oz stock, and leave to set
The remaining meat, with 125 ml/4 fl oz and leave to set
Before serving, dip the base of the mould briefly in hot water, and loosen

Colourful brawn

Sprinkle	**2 pkts gelatine**
on to	**6 tbsp cold water**
and leave to soak for 10 minutes	
Bring to the boil	**1 1/2 pints strong meat stock, skimmed**

Tomato aspic

Colourful brawn

the aspic carefully from the sides with a
knife
Turn it out on to a serving dish
Serve with: **wholemeal bread and
butter**
or
fried potatoes

Chicken in sherry aspic

Wash **1 oven-ready chicken
(about 1 $\frac{1}{4}$ kg/2 $\frac{1}{2}$ lb)**

and put it into **1 $\frac{1}{2}$ l/3 pints boiling
water**

Bring back to the boil, and skim
Cook for about 45 minutes
Clean, wash, and chop **1 leek
1 stick celery
1 parsley sprig
1 turnip**

and add to the liquid
About 20 minutes before the end of the
cooking time, clean and scrape **2 medium sized
carrots**

Remove cooked chicken, and allow to
cool
Remove skin and bones, and dice meat
Slice carrots with a serrated knife
Strain stock through a cloth, and allow
to cool
Skim off fat, and measure out 750 ml/
1 $\frac{1}{4}$ pints of the liquid
Sprinkle **2 pkts gelatine**
on to **6 tbsp cold water**
and leave to soak for 10 minutes
Bring the measured stock to the boil,
remove from heat, and add gelatine
Stir until dissolved
Stir in **125 ml/4 fl oz dry
sherry
3 tbsp lemon juice**
Season with **salt
pepper
Worcester sauce**

Rinse out a 1 $\frac{1}{2}$ l/3 pint mould or dish
with cold water, and pour in enough
sherry stock to cover the bottom
Put in refrigerator to set
Clean **2 sticks celery**
and cut them across in strips
Put them into **boiling salted water**
Bring back to the boil, and cook for
about 1 minute
Rinse with cold water, and drain
Clean **125 g/4 oz button
mushrooms**

and add to the boiling salted water
Bring back to the boil, and cook for
about 1 minute
Rinse with cold water and drain

Quarter them
Cover the aspic layer with carrot slices
and **little sprays of
parsley**

Then put alternate layers of meat, carrots, celery, mushrooms, until all the ingredients have been used up
Pour the rest of the stock over and leave
to set in refrigerator
Shortly before serving, dip the base of
the mould briefly in hot water, carefully
loosen the aspic from the sides with a
knife, and turn out on to a serving dish
Garnish with **parsley
carrots
celery**

Ham in herb jelly
(6- 8 servings)

Wash **1 $\frac{1}{2}$ kg/3 lb salt bacon
(hock or fore leg)**
and put it into **750 ml/1 $\frac{1}{2}$ pint water**
with **250 ml/8 fl oz dry
white wine**
and bring to the boil
Scrape, and chop **1 carrot**
Peel **1 onion**
and stick it with **2 cloves**
Peel **1 clove of garlic**
Add these to the liquid, together with **4 coriander seeds
1 tsp allspice
1 bay leaf
3 sprigs parsley
1 sprig rosemary
2 sage leaves
1 sprig thyme**

Add the bacon, and bring to the boil
Turn it now and again, and cook for
about 1 $\frac{3}{4}$ hours
Allow to cool in the liquid, then remove
the meat, and cut into cubes
Pour the stock through a cloth, and allow to cool
Remove the fat, and measure out
750 ml/1 $\frac{1}{4}$ pints of the stock
Sprinkle **2 pkts gelatine**
on to 6 tbsp of the stock
Allow to soak for 10 minutes
Bring remaining broth to the boil, remove from heat, and add the gelatine,
stirring until dissolved
Stir in **2 tbsp brandy
5 tbsp port**
Season to taste with **salt
pepper**

Rinse out a 1 l/2 pint terrine with cold
water
Mix together **6 - 7 tbsp chopped
parsley**

	2 tbsp chopped chervil

Layer this mixture alternately with the meat cubes in the terrine
Pour the stock over them, and leave in refrigerator to set

Serve with	fried potatoes remoulade sauce (page 90) or wholemeal bread and butter

Vegetable brawn
(Illustrated on pages 122-123)

Rinse	250 g/8 oz chopped beef bones
under running cold water Wash	
Put both ingredients into	500 g/1 lb beef shin 1½ l/3 pints cold salted water

Bring to the boil, and skim
Wash and finely chop and add to the beef	2 bunches parsley

Allow to cook for about 2½ hours, then remove meat, and sieve liquid
Add to taste	seasoning salt

Allow to cool, remove fat, and clarify
Measure out 1 l/2 pints of the stock
Wash and drain	1 - 2 cleaned cauliflower florets 4 - 5 cleaned leek rings 3 - 4 cleaned broccoli florets 1 tbsp fresh peas

Put them into the broth, and bring slowly to the boil
Boil for a short time
Stir together	2 pkts gelatine 6 - 8 tbsp cold water

and allow to soak for 10 minutes
Stir into the hot broth, and continue to stir until dissolved
Put the vegetables and broth into a mould which has been rinsed with cold water, and allow to cool
Add	1 - 2 fresh basil tips dill sprigs

Put in refrigerator to set
When firm enough to cut, carefully loosen the edges with a knife, after dip-

ping it briefly in hot water
Turn out on to a plate
Serve with:	cold roast meat

Spicy orange brawn

Wash	1 kg/2 lb oven-ready chicken
and put it into	2 l/4 pints boiling salted water
Bring to the boil and skim Clean, chop, and add	1 turnip 1 carrot 1 stick celery 1 leek 1 parsley sprig

Cook for about 45 minutes, then remove the chicken
Remove skin and bones, and dice flesh
Pour stock through a cloth, and allow to cool
Skim off fat, and measure out 500 ml 1 pint of liquid
Sprinkle on to	1 pkt + 1 tsp gelatine 5 tbsp cold water

and leave to soak for 10 minutes
Bring the measured stock to the boil, then remove from heat
Add the gelatine, and stir until dissolved
Add	250 ml/8 fl oz orange juice (from 3 - 4 oranges)
Season strongly with	salt pepper sugar

Rinse out a 1¼ l/2½ pint mould with cold water, and pour in enough stock to cover the bottom
Put it in refrigerator to set
Drain	250 g/8 oz cooked asparagus pieces
Shell and slice	2 hard-boiled eggs

Garnish the aspic layer with some of the asparagus pieces and egg slices, then put in alternate layers of chicken cubes, and asparagus and egg
Pour the remaining stock over and leave in the refrigerator to set
Before serving, dip base of the mould briefly in hot water and carefully loosen the aspic from the sides with a knife
Turn it out on to a serving dish and garnish with

	halved orange slices parsley

DESSERTS

Fruit sorbet
(Recipe on p. 145)

Spicy berry salad

Wash and drain · **750 g/1 ½ lb berry fruit (e.g. strawberries, redcurrants blackcurrants gooseberries raspberries blackberries bilberries grapes)**

(just clean the raspberries, do not wash) Remove stalks
Halve grapes if necessary, and remove pips
Mix the prepared fruit, put into a dish, and dust with · **a little icing sugar**

For the salad sauce
To · **150 ml/5 fl oz double cream**
add · **1 - 2 tbsp mustard about 1 tbsp lemon juice 1 - 2 tbsp sugar salt pepper**

to taste
Spread the sauce over the fruit

Melon salad

Quarter · **1 honeydew melon (about 500 g/1 lb)**

Remove seeds and skin
Peel, quarter and core · **2 apples (about 150 g/5 oz)**

Cut both ingredients into fine strips
Peel and slice · **2 bananas (about 150 g/5 oz)**
Mix all the fruit together with · **150 g/5 oz mandarin segments**
Stir in · **2 - 3 tbsp lemon juice 2 tbsp honey**
Put into a glass dish, and sprinkle with · **chopped hazelnuts**

Viennese cold berry dish
(4 - 6 servings)

Wash and drain · **750 g/1 ½ lb berry fruit (e.g. strawberries redcurrants blackcurrants raspberries bilberries blackberries)**

Viennese cold berry dish

(Just clean the raspberries, do not wash)
Remove stalks
Carefully mix the prepared fruit with · **150 g/5 oz sieved icing sugar 2 tbsp lemon juice 1 tbsp Grand Marnier pinch ground cinnamon**

Cover and leave for 30 minutes
Stir in · **1 1/2 pints yoghurt**
Put into glass dishes, and add · **vanilla ice cream**

Macedonian fruit

Peel, quarter, and core · **2 apples**
Peel · **2 oranges**
· **1 kiwifruit**

Cut all the ingredients into small pieces | 1 banana
Wash, drain, and remove stalks from | 125 g/4 oz straw-berries

Wash, halve, and remove pips from | 250 g/8 oz grapes
Mix all the fruit with | 2 heaped tbsp sugar
and put into glass dishes

For the sauce
Stir together | 150 ml/5 fl oz double cream
| 2 tbsp orange liqueur

and put over the fruit
Slice and sprinkle on the top | 25 g/1 oz hazelnuts

Small sherry Charlotte

Stir | 2 heaped tsp gelatine
| 3 tbsp cold water

together in a small pan and leave to soak for 10 minutes
Warm, while stirring, until dissolved
Lay | 16 sponge fingers
on a plate and sprinkle with | 4 tbsp cream sherry
Cover, and leave to stand
Put | 3 egg yolks
| 125 g/4 oz (5 heaped tbsp) sugar
| 1 pkt vanilla sugar or

Small sherry Charlotte

few drops vanilla essence
1 tbsp orange juice

into a bowl and beat until frothy over hot water
Remove from heat, and put it in a cold place
Whip | 375 ml/12 fl oz cream
until stiff and reserve some for decoration
Stir the whipped cream, with | 4 tbsp cream sherry
and the lukewarm gelatine solution into the egg yolk mixture
Stand in a cold place
Stand 4 sponge fingers in each of 4 stemmed glasses, and fill with the cream
Decorate with the reserved whipped cream and with 1 of 4 maraschino (cocktail) cherries

Red wine cream

Boil | 250 ml/8 fl oz water
Mix together | 1 pkt raspberry jelly crystals
| 125 g/4 oz (4 heaped tbsp) sugar
and stir into | 250 ml/8 fl oz red wine

Remove water from heat, and stir in red wine mixture
Bring back to the boil and when crystals have dissolved, stand in a cold place, stirring occasionally
Whip | 250 ml/8 fl oz cream
until stiff
Reserve some for decoration, and fold the rest into the cooled mixture
Put the red wine cream into a glass bowl or stemmed dishes, and decorate with reserved whipped cream

Bilberry bavarois
(4 - 6 servings)

Stir | 2 pkts gelatine
| 8 tbsp cold water

together in a small pan and leave to soak for 10 minutes
Clean, wash, and drain | 750 g/1 ½ lb bilberries
Purée in a mixer a generous half of the berries with half of | 200 g/6 oz icing sugar
and | a little lemon juice
Warm the gelatine, whilst stirring, until dissolved
Stir the lukewarm gelatine into the bilberry pulp
Beat | 6 egg yolks

133

Bilberry bavarois

	2 tbsp lukewarm water
until foamy	
Gradually beat in the rest of the icing sugar, and then stir it into the bilberry pulp	
Whip	500 ml/18 fl oz double cream
until stiff	
As soon as the bilberry pulp begins to thicken, fold in the whipped cream	
Rinse a pudding mould with cold water, and put in the mixture	
Leave it in a cold place to set	
Turn out on to a dish, and decorate, as wished, with	whipped cream
and reserved bilberries	

Black Forest cherry cream

Stir	2 rounded tsp gelatine
	4 tbsp cold water
together and leave to soak for 10 minutes	
Bring	750 ml/1 ½ pint milk
to the boil	
Mix together	1 pkt vanilla blancmange
	75 g/3 oz (3 heaped tbsp) sugar
with	6 tbsp cold milk
Remove milk from heat, and stir in the blancmange mixture	
Bring back to the boil	
Add the gelatine, and stir until dissolved	
Leave to stand in a cold place, and stir occasionally	

Stir	2 tbsp kirsch (cherry liqueur)
into the cooled but not fully set mixture	
Stir together	250 ml/8 fl oz double cream
	1 pkt vanilla sugar or few drops vanilla essence
and whip until stiff	
Reserve some for decoration, and fold the rest into the cherry mixture	
Drain well	375 g/12 oz stoned bottled sour cherries
Reserve some for decoration, and put the rest into stemmed glass dishes in alternating layers with the cream, finishing with a layer of cream	
Decorate with the reserved whipped cream, cherries and	chocolate curls

Black Forest cherry cream

Walnut and orange cream

Stir	**1 pkt gelatine** **4 tbsp cold water**
together in a small pan and leave to soak for 10 minutes Warm, whilst stirring, until dissolved	
Whip	**2 egg yolks** **2 tbsp warm water**
until frothy	
Gradually beat in	**75 g/3 oz (3 heaped tbsp) sugar**
until creamy	
Beat in	**250 ml/8 fl oz orange juice** **125 ml/4 fl oz milk** **2 tbsp orange liqueur**
and the lukewarm gelatine solution Leave to stand in a cold place	
Whip	**2 egg whites** **250 ml/8 fl oz double cream**
separately until stiff As soon as the orange mixture begins to thicken, fold in the egg white and the whipped cream (Reserve some of the whipped cream for decoration)	
Very finely chop	**75 g/3 oz walnuts**
(leaving some nuts whole for decoration) and stir them in	
Add	**orange liqueur**
to taste Put into a glass bowl or dishes and leave in a cold place Decorate with the whipped cream and the walnuts	

Sweet crispy (krokant) ring

Sweet crispy (krokant) ring

For the krokant (crispy almond coating)	
Heat together, stirring	**1 $\frac{1}{2}$ tbsp butter** **60 g/2 $\frac{1}{2}$ oz sugar**
until sugar is lightly browned	
Stir in	**125 g/4 oz blanched chopped almonds**
and heat, while stirring, until sufficiently browned Put on to an oiled plate, and allow to cool If necessary, crush into small pieces	
Stir together	**2 pkts vanilla blancmange** **75 g/3 oz (4 rounded tbsp) sugar** **125 ml/4 fl oz cold milk**
and prepare, according to the instruc-	

tions on the packet, using	**1 1/2 pints cold milk**
Rinse out a ring mould with cold water, and pour in the blancmange Leave in a cold place Turn out the set blancmange on to a serving dish, and sprinkle with the krokant (crispy almond coating)	
Drain	**250 g/8 oz tinned apricots**
and collect the juice and measure out 250 ml/8 fl oz Put apricots into the middle of the ring, and decorate with	**whipped cream**
For the apricot sauce	
Wash and dry	**$\frac{1}{2}$ orange**
Peel thinly, and cut the peel into very fine strips Boil for a short time with the measured apricot juice	
Stir in	**1 - 2 tbsp orange liqueur**
and allow to cool Serve with the krokant ring	

Chocolate mousse

Break	**150 g/5 oz plain chocolate**

Chocolate mousse

into small pieces and stir it until smooth
in a small pan over hot water

Put	**3 egg yolks**
	1 egg
	50 g/2 oz (2 heaped tbsp) sugar
	2 tbsp coffee liqueur
	1 tsp instant coffee powder

into a bowl and beat with an electric
mixer over steam for 5 - 7 minutes, until
frothy
Remove bowl from heat and whip mixture for about 5 minutes, until stiff

Whip	**3 egg whites**
	150 ml/5 fl oz double cream

until stiff and stir into the mixture, together with the melted chocolate and

Put the pudding into stemmed glass
dishes and serve well-chilled

Orange cream

Halve	**2 large oranges**

and squeeze the juice
Measure out 10 tbsp
Clean the insides of the orange 'shells' if
necessary, and put them into a freezing

compartment

Stir	**1 pkt gelatine**
	6 tbsp cold water

together in a small pan and leave to
soak for 10 minutes
Warm, whilst stirring, until dissolved

Beat	**3 egg yolks**
	4 tbsp warm water

until frothy

Gradually add $\frac{2}{3}$ of	**125 g/4 oz sugar**

and beat until creamy

Beat in the measured orange juice	**1 tbsp lemon juice**

and the lukewarm gelatine solution
Leave in a cold place

Whip	**3 egg whites**

until stiff and beat in the remaining
sugar

Whip	**125 ml/4 fl oz cream**

until stiff
Fold both ingredients into the thick egg
cream
Put into a piping bag with a plain nozzle, and pipe into the orange shells

Garnish with	**flaked almonds (dipped in melted chocolate if wished)**

Serve the rest of the cream separately

Coconut rum crêpes
(6 servings)

Mix together	**75 g/3 oz plain flour**
	1 heaped tbsp sugar
Gradually stir in	**2 eggs**
	125 ml/4 fl oz milk
Melt	**1 tbsp butter**

and stir in

Orange cream

Coconut rum crêpes

Grease a small pan with **butter** and put in a thin layer of batter
Cook it on both sides until golden brown and keep warm
Use the rest of the batter to make thin crêpes in the same way
Sprinkle the crêpes with **grated coconut** and roll them around ice-cream rolls
made from **1 block vanilla ice-cream**

Just before serving, pour **125 ml/4 fl oz rum** over them and ignite

Banana feast

Peel and slice **2 - 3 bananas**
Put the banana slices on to 4 dessert plates
Sprinkle with **lemon juice**
Cut into 8 slices **1 block chocolate and malaga ice-cream**

and put 2 slices on each plate
Decorate as desired with **whipped cream
chocolate curls
cherries
lemon mint
lychees**

Strawberry and quark sweet

Wash and drain well **175 g - 250 g/6 - 8 oz fresh strawberries**

Remove the stalks, and purée with an electric mixer or a liquidizer
Beat in **500 g/1 lb quark**

Banana feast

Strawberry and quark sweet

Fruit jelly with raspberries

(curd cheese)
200 ml/6 fl oz milk
50 g/2 oz (2 heaped tbsp) sugar

Put the sweet into stemmed glass dishes
Variation:
Use 2 tbsp strawberry syrup instead of strawberries

Aphrodite ice-cream dream

Wash and dry	**1 mango**
Halve it and remove the stone	
Scoop the flesh out of the skin, cutting it into small pieces	
Sprinkle with	**2 tbsp Grand Marnier**
Cut into small cubes	**½ block pistachio ice-cream**
and put into the mango shells	
Mix the mango with the ice-cream and	
Decorate with	**whipped cream**

Fruit jelly with raspberries

Thaw at room temperature	**300 g/10 oz frozen raspberries**
Prepare according to instructions on packet, using	**1 pkt raspberry jelly**
	125 g/4 oz (4 heaped tbsp) sugar
	500 ml/1 pint water
Stir in the raspberries, put into stemmed glass dishes and allow to cool	
Serve chilled with	**whipped cream**

Forest delight ice-cream

Clean, wash and drain well	**375 - 500 g/12 oz - 1 lb fresh blackberries**
Mix them with	**75 g/3 oz sugar**
and leave, to stand to draw out the juice	
Put into 4 chilled tall glasses	
Make 16 ice-cream balls out of	**2 blocks vanilla ice-cream**
using an ice-cream scoop	
Divide them among the glasses, and decorate with	**whipped cream blackberries**
Variation:	
Bottled or tinned blackberries can be used instead of fresh	

Forest delight ice-cream

Special strawberry ice-cream

Wash and drain well	**375 g - 500 g/12 oz - 1 lb fresh strawberries**
Remove stalks, and halve if necessary Sprinkle with	**2 - 3 heaped tbsp sugar** **3 - 4 tbsp Grand Marnier**
Leave to stand to draw out the juice, then put them into 4 chilled tall glasses Using an ice-cream scoop, make 12 balls from	**1 block strawberry ice-cream**
Divide them among the glasses, and Decorate with	**whipped cream halved strawberries pistachio nuts waffle rolls**

Fruit salad

Cut up	**750 g/1 $\frac{1}{2}$ lb prepared fruit (e.g. mangoes strawberries bananas**

Special strawberry ice-cream

Fruit salad

	grapes redcurrants oranges)
and mix Sprinkle with	**a little sugar a little lemon juice**
Put into stemmed glass dishes	

Mona Lisa ice-cream

Scoop out 12 balls of ice-cream from	**1 block almond and caramel ice-cream**
Put them on to 4 chilled dessert dishes Pour on	**chocolate sauce for ice-cream**
Decorate with	**whipped cream chocolate curls**

Aladdin's magic lamp
(6 servings)

Make 6 rolls from	**1 block strawberry ice-cream**
place them on 6 small plates, and put in the freezer	

Aladdin's magic lamp

cream in a circle
Garnish with   **blackcurrants**
Serve the remaining whipped cream
separately

Fruit garden ice-cream
(1 serving)

Scoop 1 ball from each of   **lemon sorbet
cherry ice-cream
cassis (blackcurrant)
sorbet
vanilla ice-cream**

and put in a chilled stemmed glass dish
Decorate with   **whipped cream
chocolate curls
waffle rolls
fruit (e.g. pineapple**

Fruit garden ice-cream

For the frothy wine cream
Put   **1 egg
1 heaped tbsp sugar
1 level tsp cornflour
125 ml/4 fl oz white
wine**

into a bowl
Put bowl over hot water, and whip it
with an electric mixer until a large bub-
ble rises to the surface (do not allow it
to boil)
Take the ice-cream rolls out of the
freezer, and pour the wine cream over
them
Garnish with   **halved strawberries**

Summer dream ice-cream

Turn out on to an oval glass plate   **1 block cassis (blackcurrant) sorbet**
Mix together   **250 ml/8 fl oz double
cream
1 pkt vanilla sugar or
few drops vanilla
essence**

Whip until stiff
Pipe the whipped cream around the ice-

kiwifruit
cherries
mandarin oranges)

Black Forest paradise

Put on to 4 dessert plates	**4 slices marble cake**
Cut into 8 slices	**1 block Black Forest cherry ice-cream**
and lay 2 slices on each plate	
Decorate with	**whipped cream caramellized flaked almonds cherries**
Serve with	**sour cherry compôte, thickened with corn-flour, and with Amaretto liqueur stirred into it**

Rheingold ice-cream

Wash and halve	**375 - 500 g/12 oz - 1 lb black grapes**
Remove pips	
Cut into cubes	**½ block chocolate and**

	malaga ice-cream ½ block chocolate ice-cream
Arrange ice-cream cubes and grapes in 4 chilled stemmed glass dishes	
Decorate with	**whipped cream chopped hazelnuts ice-cream waffles**

Exotic magic
(6 servings)

Peel and slice	**6 kiwifruit**
Form 6 rolls from	**1 block hazelnut ice-cream**
Cut into thick slices and arrange alternately with the kiwifruit on 6 chilled glass plates	
Whip	**125 ml/4 fl oz double cream**
with	**1 pkt vanilla sugar or few drops vanilla essence**
until stiff	
Use to decorate the servings, and sprinkle with	**dessicated coconut, toasted**

Exotic magic

Banana ice-cream with ginger strips

Peel and mash well with a fork	**3 bananas**
Whip	**2 egg yolks**
	2 tbsp honey
	5 - 6 tbsp lemon juice
until frothy	
Cut	**5 pieces of preserved ginger**
into strips and stir in	
Whip	**250 ml/8 fl oz double cream**
until stiff and fold in	
Put the mixture into 2 freezer trays and freeze	
Cut the frozen ice-cream into cubes and put into chilled stemmed glass dishes	
Serve immediately with:	**chocolate sauce**

Alberto ice-cream

Peel	**1 mango**
Remove the stone, and cut the flesh into pieces	
Scoop out 8 ice-cream balls from each of	**1 block almond and caramel ice-cream**
	1 block lemon sorbet
and arrange in 4 stemmed glass dishes together with the mango pieces	
Sprinkle with	**2 - 3 tbsp rum**
	blanched chopped almonds, browned
Decorate with	**waffle rolls**

Sweet cherry ice-cream

Ice-cream fondue

Sweet cherry ice-cream

Scoop out of	**1 block cherry ice-cream**
ice-cream balls, and put them into 4 chilled stemmed glass dishes	
Decorate with	**whipped cream**
	orange slices
	cherries
	pistachio nuts

Caprice (Italian ice-cream)

Put on to 4 chilled stemmed glass dishes	**4 tbsp chocolate sauce for ice-cream**
Scoop out 12 ice-cream balls from	**1 block almond and caramel ice-cream**

into little dishes and arrange around the ice-cream

Ice-cream Alexandra

Scoop out ice-cream balls froms **1 block walnut ice-cream**

and arrange them in a chilled glass dish Put a ring of around the ice-cream and decorate with

4 - 6 tbsp egg nog

whipped cream

Caprice (Italian ice-cream)

ing (krokant - p 135)
chocolate chips
sauces for ice-creams
egg nog
whipped cream
grated chocolate
hundreds and thou-
sands

and put 3 balls in each glass
Decorate with **whipped cream**
almonds
waffle rolls

Ice-cream fondue

Form rolls from **strawberry**
vanilla
hazelnut
chocolate ice cream

then cut into slices
Arrange them on a chilled plate, and put into the freezer until ready to serve Before serving, put the plate of ice-cream rolls on top of a dish filled with **ice cubes**
Put **crispy almond coat-**

Autumn fruit salad

Clean and wash	**50 g/2 oz cranberries**
Bring	**200 g/6 oz redcurrant jelly**
to the boil and add cranberries	

Cook them for about 2 minutes, then remove with a perforated spoon, and put in a cold place
Boil jelly until syrupy, and allow to cool a little

Add	**2 tbsp slivovitz**
and put in a cold place	
Wash, halve, and stone	**500 g/1 lb prunes**
Wash, halve, and remove pips from	**500 g/1 lb grapes**
Mix fruit with	**2 tbsp sieved icing sugar**
	ground cinnamon
	2 tbsp slivovitz

and leave in a cold place
For the salad sauce

Whip	**2 egg yolks**
	125 g/4 oz sieved icing sugar
until frothy	
Stir in	**150 ml/5 fl oz yoghurt**
Whip	**125 ml/4 fl oz double cream**

until stiff and fold in

Autumn fruit salad

Dreams

Mix the cranberries into the salad	
Garnish with	**halved walnuts**
Serve with the sauce and with the redcurrant syrup	

Dreams

Cut into 8 slices	**1 block peach ice-cream**
Place 1 slice on each of 4 dessert plates	
Peel and slice	**4 - 6 kiwifruit**
and lay them on top of the ice-cream	
Sprinkle them with	**honey**
	crispy almond coating (krokant - p 135)
	chopped hazelnuts
Put another slice of ice-cream on top of each portion	
Decorate with	**whipped cream**
	waffle rolls

Cardinal's peaches

Scoop out 12 balls from	**1 block almond and caramel ice-cream**
using an ice-cream scoop, and arrange in 4 chilled stemmed glass dishes	
Decorate with	**whipped cream**
Drain	**4 tinned peach halves**
and lay them on top of the ice-cream	
Pour	**raspberry sauce for ice-cream**
over them and garnish with	**browned flaked almonds**
	ice-cream waffles

Petits fours ice-cream sweets

Trip in paradise

Put on to 4 chilled dessert plates	**6 - 8 tbsp strawberry sauce for ice-cream**
Cut	**1 block neapolitan ice-cream**
into pieces and put them on top of the sauce	
Decorate with	**fruit threaded on wooden toothpicks (e.g. cherries mandarin segments banana slices pieces of melon)**

Petit fours ice-cream sweets
(4 - 6 servings)

Break	**125 - 150 g/4 - 5 oz plain chocolate**
into small pieces and put with	**50 ml/2 fl oz coconut oil**
into a small pan over hot water	
Stir them over low heat until smooth	
Make 6 rolls from	**1 block ice-cream**
and slice in various thicknesses	
Dip them into the liquid chocolate	

(It is best to use a wooden skewer for this)
Put them into little moulds or glass dishes, and leave them in the freezer until ready to serve

Shortly before serving, decorate with	**whipped cream blackberries walnuts pistachios coffee beans cocoa powder maraschino (cocktail) cherries hazelnuts redcurrants**
according to taste	

Fruit sorbet
(1 serving) (Illustrated on pages 130-131)

Using an ice-cream scoop, scoop out 1 ball each of and	**lemon sorbet cassis (blackcurrant liqueur) sorbet**
Put them in a chilled stemmed glass or a small glass dish and add as wished	**iced fruit berries**

WAYS WITH CHEESE
Fried camembert and almonds
(Recipe on p. 153)

Pickled sheep's cheese

Pickled sheep's cheese

Cut	**300 g/10 oz sheep's cheese**
into large cubes	
Peel	**2 red onions (if available)**
	2 yellow onions
and cut into rings	
Peel	**1 clove of garlic**
	125 g/4 oz black olives
	2 bay leaves
	3 chillis
	1 tsp dried oregano
Put all the ingredients into a large jar with	**salt**
	pepper
	monosodium

	glutamate
Cover with	**250 ml/8 fl oz olive oil**
Cover, and leave in a cold place for about 7 days	

Colourful cheese triangles

Cream	**125 g/4 oz butter**
Stir in	**300 g/10 oz full fat cream cheese**
	3 tbsp cream
Season with	**salt**
	pepper
Stir	**2 - 3 tbsp chopped mixed herbs**
into ⅓ of mixture	
Stir	**1 - 2 tbsp tomato purée**
into ½ of remaining cream and add, to taste	**sweet paprika**
Season remaining cream again with salt and pepper to taste	
Spread	**12 slices German rye bread or pumpernickel**

with the 3 colours of cream, and stack slices in threes so that there is, in each case, 1 green, 1 red, and 1 white layer
Weight sandwiches, and leave in a cold place (best overnight)
Cut into triangles

Chive balls

Stir together	**200 g/6 oz full fat cream cheese**
	200 g/6 oz French cream cheese
Season with	**salt**
	pepper
Form about 12 balls from mixture (best with an ice cream scoop)	
Roll in	**2 bunches finely chopped chives**

Arrange on a glass dish, and leave in a cold place until ready to serve

Cheese ring

Cut through	**1 ring (about 750 g/1½ lb) brie cheese**
horizontally	
Spread bottom half with	**2 - 3 tbsp bottled cranberries**
Stir	**250 g/8 oz full fat cream cheese**
Whip	**125 ml/4 fl oz double**

Cheese ring

until stiff and fold into cream cheese

Season with **cream**

salt
pepper

Put ⅔ of cream into a piping bag with a rosette nozzle, and spread rest over cranberries

Cover with **50 g/2 oz walnut halves**

so that they can be seen on the edges
Put on the top half of the ring, and press down well
Decorate with piped cream

Garnish with **bottled cranberries**

Basil cheese
(4 - 6 servings)

Rub **200 g/6 oz sheep's cheese**

through a sieve

Cream it with **150 g/5 oz softened butter**
25 g/1 oz grated parmesan cheese
125 ml/4 fl oz cream
2 bunches basil

Wash
Pat dry, pull off leaves from stems, and chop coarsely

Stir basil and **25 g/1 oz ground pine kernels**

into mixture
Press mixture into a bowl which has been rinsed out in cold water, and smooth the surface
Leave for 3 - 4 hours in refrigerator
Stand bowl in hot water for a short time, if necessary, then turn out on to a serving dish

Roast **50 g/2 oz pine kernels**

in a pan until they are golden yellow, and allow to cool
Sprinkle them over basil cheese

Serve with: **wholemeal bread**
pumpernickel

Cheese and fruit kebabs

Cut **200 g/6 oz unsliced gouda cheese**

into 1 cm/½ in cubes

Drain **4 slices tinned pine-apple**

and cut into little pieces
Put the cheese and pineapple pieces alternately on to 4 metal kebabs sticks to-

Basil cheese

gether with	**2 - 3 tbsp mandarine segments or bottled sour cherries**
Brush with	**a little egg white**

Cover a grill rack with baking foil, and lay the kebabs on it
Put under a preheated grill, and grill them first on one side, then on the other
Grilling time:
Electricity: each side about $2\frac{1}{2}$ minutes
Gas: each side about 2 minutes

Tomato quark

Stir together	**250 g/8 oz quark (curd cheese) 4 tbsp milk 2 rounded tbsp tomato purée**
season with	**salt sugar**

and stir until frothy

Peel and very finely dice and stir it in	**1 small onion**
Variation: Stir in	**2 tbsp chopped herbs**

Tomato quark, Herb quark, Caraway seed quark

(e.g. parsley, chives, pimpernel, tarragon, cress, lemon balm)

Herb quark

Stir together	**250 g/8 oz quark (curd cheese) 2 tbsp milk 3 rounded tbsp double cream**
Season to taste with and stir until smooth	**salt**
Stir in	**2 tbsp finely chopped chives or 2 tbsp chopped mixed herbs**

Caraway seed quark

Stir together	**250 g/8 oz quark (curd cheese) 4 tbsp cream 1 heaped tsp caraway seeds**
Season to taste with and stir until smooth	**salt**

Variation:
Instead of caraway seeds, you can use, according to taste,

**grated onion
grated beetroot
chopped prawns
finely minced smoked fish
finely minced ham**

Cream cheese and crackers

Stir together	**125 g/4 oz quark 125 g/4 oz full fat cream cheese $\frac{1}{2}$ tsp salt celery salt 1 tsp lemon juice 3 drops tabasco**
Shell and halve	**1 hard-boiled egg**

Rub egg yolk through a sieve, and stir into mixture

Stir in	**1 tbsp milk**

If necessary, put into a piping bag with a rosette nozzle, and pipe on to

	about 15 crackers
Garnish with	**slices of carrot parsley olives caviar truffle strips**

Cream cheese and crackers

	cream cheese
	2 egg yolks
Season with	**salt**
	1 level tsp Mexican pepper (spiced pepper)
Whip	**125 ml/4 fl oz double cream**
until stiff and fold in	
Put ⅟₄ of the cream cheese into a piping bag with a rosette nozzle	
Stir	**2 hard-boiled eggs, cut up small**
into ⅟₃ of the remaining cream	
Stir	**2 tbsp chopped herbs**
Stir	**75 g/3 oz finely diced ham**
into the remaining cream	
Season all 3 fillings to taste with	**salt**
	pepper

Spread the bottom pastry base with the ham cream cheese
Cover with the second layer of pastry carefully press into place, and spread with the herb cream cheese
Cover with the third layer of pastry and spread with the egg cream cheese
Cover with the fourth layer of pastry and decorate with the piped cream cheese

Garnish with	**herbs**

	small pickled gherkins (cornichons) finely chopped red and green peppers

Savoury puff pastry cheese slice

For the dough	
Cover	**300 g/10 oz frozen puff pastry**

with a cloth, and leave to thaw
Divide into 3, roll out each slab individually, and cut out 22 cm/8 ½ in wide bases
Roll out the dough trimmings and cut out a fourth base the same size
In each case, lay 2 bases on to a baking tray which has been rinsed with cold water, and prick several times with a fork
Leave to stand for about 15 minutes, then put into a preheated oven
Electricity: 200° - 225° C/400° - 425° F
Gas: Mark 6 - 7
Baking time: about 10 minutes

For the filling	
Stir together	**400 g/14 oz full fat**

Cheese salad in tomatoes

Peel, quarter, and core	**1 apple**
Cut	**300 g/10 oz emmenthal cheese (cut into 3 mm/⅟₄ in thick slices)**
and apple into strips	
Mix these ingredients with	**50 - 75 g/2 - 3 oz blanched flaked almonds**
For the mayonnaise	
Beat until thick	**1 egg yolk**
	1 - 2 tsp mustard
	1 tbsp vinegar or lemon juice
	salt
	1 tsp sugar
Gradually beat in	**125 ml/4 fl oz salad oil**
Stir in	**2 tbsp yoghurt**
	40 g/1 ½ oz blanched chopped almonds
Add	**white wine**
to taste	
Mix sauce with salad	
Cut off the tops of	**8 - 10 tomatoes**

and remove pulp (this can be used for soup or sauces)

Fill the tomatoes with the salad, and replace lids

Serve remaining salad on a plate with tomatoes

Arrange the tomatoes on **washed lettuce leaves**

Cheese and sweet pepper slices

Wash   **2 - 4 green and yellow peppers (according to size)**

and pat dry

Cut off the top part with the stalk and core

Using a spoon, remove the seeds and the pith from the walls, taking care not to damage the sides

For the filling

Shell   **3 hard-boiled eggs**

and rub through a sieve

Cream   **125 g/4 oz butter**

Stir   **250 g/8 oz full fat cream cheese**

into the butter

Stir in the egg and   **150 ml/5 fl oz double**

   cream

Season with   **salt**

   pepper

   sweet paprika

   mustard

to taste

Put filling into peppers, and leave in a cold place (best overnight)

Shortly before serving, cut into 1 cm/ $\frac{1}{2}$ in thick slices

Serve with: **German rye bread or pumpernickel**

Fried camembert

Quarter   **1 camembert (not too ripe, well chilled)**

or cut into eighths

Dip in   **1 beaten egg**

and then in   **fine breadcrumbs**

Repeat once more, then, with the help of a wooden skewer, put them into hot and fry until golden yellow (Do not allow the cheese to become runny)   **cooking oil**

Serve with: **jacket potatoes baked in foil**

   apples, cranberries

Cheese and sweet pepper slices

Fried camembert and almonds
(Illustrated on pages 146-147)

Cover	**2 camembert halves (not too ripe, well-chilled)**
first in	**1 beaten egg**
and then in	**blanched chopped almonds**

Press almonds on firmly, then dip again in egg and again in almonds

Fry to a golden yellow in hot	**cooking oil**

and allow to drain on kitchen paper

Wash	**1 bunch parsley**

dry thoroughly and quickly dip it in the hot oil

Clean and wash	**250 g/8 oz large cranberries**
and stew them with	**125 ml/4 fl oz water**
	50 g/2 oz sugar

Allow to cool, and add **sugar** to taste

Arrange the camembert on a plate with the parsley and cranberries

Serve with:	**toast**

Roquefort balls

Cream	**50 g/2 oz butter**
Mash	**125 g/4 oz roquefort cheese**

with a fork and stir it into the butter

Add	**1 tsp minced capers**
	1 tsp brandy
Season to taste with	**pepper**

Leave in a cold place

With wet hands, form little balls from mixture

Roll first in	**finely grated pumpernickel**
and then in	**chopped parsley**

Leave in a cold place until ready to serve

Cheesy potato slices

Peel and wash	**1kg/2 lb medium potatoes**
Cook in	**boiling salted water**

for 10 minutes, drain, and slice

Overlap potato slices in a flat ovenproof dish and sprinkle with	**salt**
	pepper
	25 g/1 oz breadcrumbs
Dot with	**50 g/2 oz butter**
Scatter	**emmenthal cheese**

over potatoes, then put into a preheated oven

Electricity: 200° - 225° C/400° - 425° F

Gas: Mark 6 - 7

Cooking time: about 20 minutes

Satziki

Stir together	**125 g/4 oz quark (curd cheese)**
	150 ml/5 fl oz double cream
Peel and crush	**1 - 4 cloves of garlic (according to taste)**
Peel and finely dice	**1 piece of cucumber (about 200 g/6 oz)**

Stir both ingredients into quark mixture

Season with	**salt**
	pepper

Leave in a cold place

Arrange on	**washed lettuce leaves**
Garnish with	**black olives**
Sprinkle with	**olive or salad oil**

Peaches with cream cheese
(6 servings)

Drain	**6 stewed peach halves**
Stir	**125 g/4 oz full fat cream cheese**
Whip	**125 ml/4 fl oz double cream**

until stiff and fold in

Season with	**salt**
	pepper
	sugar
and add	**peach juice**

if desired

Put cream into a piping bag with a rosette nozzle, and pipe on to peach halves

Spread 1 tsp of	**raspberry sauce**

over cream cheese on each peach

BREAD SPECIALITIES

French bread (baguette) feast
(Recipe on p. 165)

Sauerkraut roll

Sauerkraut roll

For the filling

Melt	**1 tbsp margarine**
Loosen	**500 g/1 lb sauerkraut**

with a fork so that it is less dense, and cook gently in margarine

Peel	**1 onion**
Stick	**1 bay leaf**
	5 cloves

into the onion and add to the sauerkraut
Cook them gently together for about 15 minutes, then remove onion, and put sauerkraut in a cold place

For the dough

Prepare	**1 pkt bread mix (375 g/12 oz)**

according to instructions on packet,

adding	**1 - 2 tbsp caraway seeds**
and using	**250 ml/8 fl oz luke-warm water**

Towards the end of kneading, knead in **1 tbsp lightly warmed margarine**

Allow dough to rise
Dust with **plain flour**
and remove from bowl
Knead for a *short* time

Put dough on to a floured surface, and roll out to a rectangle about 35 × 25 cm/14 × 10 in
Put half of sauerkraut down centre (lengthways) of the dough, and lay **4 frankfurter sausages** 2 either side, lengthways along the sides of the sauerkraut
Spread the remaining sauerkraut over and around them
Fold first one side of the pastry over this, and brush with water, then fold the other side of the pastry over, and press firmly
Press the end of the roll firmly together
Lay on a greased baking tray, and leave in a warm place to rise again
Brush with water, and place in a pre-heated oven
Electricity: 200° - 225° C/400° - 425° F
Gas: Mark 6 - 7
Baking time: about 50 minutes

White tin loaf

Sieve	**500 g/1 lb strong plain flour**

into a mixing bowl and carefully mix

with	**1 pkt dried yeast**
Add	**1 level tsp sugar**
	1 rounded tsp salt
	2 eggs
	1 egg yolk
	about 125 ml/4 fl oz lukewarm milk
	150 ml/5 fl oz double cream

Mix with dough hook of an electric mixer, first on the lowest setting, then

White tin loaf

on the highest setting, for about 5 minutes, until a smooth dough is formed
Leave in a warm place to rise until doubled in size
Put dough into a greased 30 × 11 cm/ 12 × 4 in loaf tin dusted with fine breadcrumbs
Leave in a warm place again to rise
Make 1 cm/½ in incision along top of loaf, without pressing down
Brush with water, and put into a preheated oven
Electricity: 175° - 200° C/350° - 400° F
Gas: Mark 4 - 6
Baking time: 40 - 50 minutes

Rye bread with salami

In a large bowl, carefully mix	250 g/8 oz stone-ground rye flour
	250 g/8 oz strong plain flour
	1 pkt dried yeast
Add	1 tsp sugar
	1 tsp salt
	a little monosodium glutamate
	250 ml/8 fl oz lukewarm water

Using dough hook of an electric mixer, mix ingredients first on the lowest setting, then on the highest setting, for about 5 minutes, to form a smooth dough
Towards the end of kneading, knead in **150 g/5 oz finely chopped salami**

Leave dough in a warm place until it has visibly risen, then remove it from bowl, and knead *well*

Form 2 longish loaves of bread from the dough, and lay them on a greased baking tray
Leave in a warm place to rise again
Brush the upper side of the dough with water, and dust with flour
Put into a preheated oven
Electricity: 200° C/400° F
Gas: Mark 6
Baking time: about 40 minutes

Sesame seed rolls

In a large bowl, carefully mix	375 g/12 oz strong plain flour
Add	1 pkt dried yeast
	1 level tsp sugar
	1 rounded tsp salt
	50 g/2 oz melted lukewarm margarine
	200 ml/7 fl oz lukewarm water

Using the dough hook of an electric mixer, mix ingredients first on the lowest, and then on the highest setting for 5 minutes, to a smooth dough
Leave in a warm place until it has doubled in size
Form about 24 oval-shaped bread rolls from the dough, and lay them on a greased baking tray
Leave in a warm place to rise again
Brush the rolls with water, sprinkle them with **sesame seeds** and place them in a preheated oven
Electricity: 175° - 200° C/350° - 400° F
Gas: Mark 4 - 6
Baking time: about 30 minutes

Rye bread with salami

Stuffed French bread 'Doris'

Cut	**1 French loaf (about 50 cm/20 in long and 8 cm/3 in wide)**

in half across, and remove the centre, reserving the bread pieces

For the filling

Cream	**250 g/8 oz butter**
Dice	**125 g/4 oz ham**
	125 g/4 oz corned beef
Shell and chop	**2 hard-boiled eggs**

Stir these ingredients into the butter to-gether with

1 heaped tsp green peppercorns
1 - 2 tsp capers
a few stuffed olives

Season with	**salt, pepper**
	Worcester sauce

Mix the filling with the broken bread pieces removed from the centre of the loaf, and use to fill the hollow
Cover the loaf with baking foil, and leave in a cold place
Cut the bread into slices, garnish with

olives
peppercorns
small lettuce leaves

Stuffed French bread 'Doris'

Ham in bread jacket

Ham in a bread jacket

Prepare	**1 pkt (375 g/12 oz) bread mix**

according to instructions on packet

using	**250 ml/8 fl oz luke-warm water**

Allow dough to rise, then dust with plain flour
Remove from bowl, and knead for a *short* time

If wished, reserve some of the dough	**on a floured pastry board**

for garnishing, and roll out the rest to twice the size of the ham

Place	**1 kg/2 lb piece of cooked ham**

on the dough, and brush the edges of the dough with water
Fold the dough over the ham, and then lay it, smooth side down, on a greased baking tray
Decorate with the reserved dough, and, without pressing down, cut out 3 small round holes in the top of the dough
Leave in a warm place again to rise

Cheese bread

Brush with water, and place in a pre-
heated oven
Electricity: 200° C/400° F
Gas: Mark 6
Baking time: 40 - 50 minutes

Cheese bread

In a large bowl, carefully mix	**500 g/1 lb strong plain flour**
	1 pkt dried yeast
Add	**1 tsp sugar**
	1 tsp salt
	a little pepper
	a little monosodium glutamate
	3 tbsp cooking oil
	250 ml/8 fl oz luke-warm water

Using the dough hook of an electric
mixer, mix ingredients first on the lowest and then on the highest setting for 5
minutes, to a smooth dough
Put in a warm place until it has doubled
in size
Remove dough from bowl

| Cut | **175 g/6 oz emmenthal cheese** |

into fairly small cubes and add them to
the dough
Knead in well, and then place dough in
a greased soufflé dish (about 20 cm/8 in
diameter)

| Cut | **75 g/3 oz emmenthal cheese** |

into small wedges and press them into
the dough
Leave in a warm place to rise again

| Beat together | **1 egg yolk** |
| | **1 tbsp water** |

and brush it over the dough, then place
it in a preheated oven
Electricity: 200° C/400° F
Gas: Mark 6
Baking time: about 50 minutes
Remove the cheese bread from the dish,
and serve warm or cold

Sesame seed bread

In a large bowl, carefully mix	**500 g/1 lb strong plain flour**
	1 pkt dried yeast
Add	**1 tsp sugar**
	1 good tsp salt

Sesame seed bread

a little monosodium
glutamate
250 ml/8 fl oz luke-
warm water

Using the dough hook of an electric
mixer, first mix on the lowest setting,
then on the highest for 5 minutes
Towards the end of kneading, knead in   **3 tbsp toasted sesame
seeds**

Leave dough in a warm place until dou-
bled in size, then remove from bowl,
and knead *well*
Put the dough into a greased loaf tin,
and leave in a warm place to rise again
Brush with   **milk**
and sprinkle with   **sesame seeds**
Put into a preheated oven
Electricity: 200° C/400° F
Gas: Mark 6
Baking time: about 45 minutes

Ham croissants

Prepare   **1 pkt (375 g/12 oz)
bread mix**

according to instructions on packet
with   **250 ml/8 fl oz luke-
warm water**

and allow to rise
Dust the dough with   **plain flour**
and remove from bowl
Knead it for a *short* time
Put dough on to a pastry board dusted
with flour, and roll out to a 40 cm/16 in
diameter circle
Using a pastry cutting wheel, cut it into
12 segments as if cutting a cake
Put a little   **125 g/4 oz finely
chopped raw smoked
ham**

on to each piece of dough
Pull out curved side of segments a little,
and roll them in towards the point, then
bend ends round a little
Lay the croissants, pointed side under-
neath, on a greased baking tray, and
leave in a warm place to rise
Brush with water and dust lightly with
flour, then put into a preheated oven
Electricity: 200° - 225° C/400° - 425° F
Gas: Mark 6 - 7
Baking time: about 25 minutes

Bread with a savoury stuffing

For the dough
Prepare   **1 pkt (375 g/12 oz)
bread mix**

according to the instructions on the
packet

Wholemeal wheaten bread

using   **250 ml/8 fl oz luke-
warm water**
and allow to rise
For the filling
Soak   **1 bread roll (muffin)**
in cold water
Peel and dice   **1 onion**
Heat   **1 tbsp cooking oil**
and sauté onion and   **1 bunch chopped
parsley**

for a short time
Remove from heat, and add   **500 g/1 lb minced
meat (half beef and
half pork)**
1 egg
Squeeze out the bread roll and add   **125 g/4 oz sautéed
mushroom slices**
Season with   **salt**
pepper
1 tsp mustard
1 tsp tomato purée

Dust the risen dough with plain flour
Remove from bowl, and knead for a
short time
Set some of the dough to one side for
garnishing
Put the dough on to a pastry board
dusted with flour, and roll it out to a
30 cm/12 in diameter circle
Form the meat mixture into a ball
(about 15 cm/6 in diameter), and lay it

and remove it from bowl
Knead for a *short* time
Form 10 round bread rolls from the dough, and lay them in a ring on a greased baking tray
Leave in a warm place again to rise
Brush rolls with water, and sprinkle with **sesame seeds**
caraway seeds
poppy seeds
rye or barley flakes
grated cheese

and put into a preheated oven
Electricity: 175° - 200° C/350° - 400° F
Gas: Mark 4 - 6
Baking time: 30 - 35 minutes

Wholemeal wheaten bread
(with Provence herbs)

In a large bowl, carefully mix **175 g/6 oz granary flour**
250 g/8 oz strong plain flour
1 pkt dried yeast
Add **1 tsp powdered sugar**
just on 2 level tsp salt
3 tbsp cooking oil
200 ml/7 fl oz luke-warm water

Using the dough hook of an electric mixer, mix ingredients first on the lowest setting and then on the highest setting for 5 minutes, to a smooth dough
Towards the end of kneading, knead in **2 tbsp Provence herbs**

Leave dough in a warm place until it has visibly risen, then remove from bowl, and knead *well*
Form into a round loaf and lay it on a greased baking tray
Leave it in a warm place again to rise
Make several 1 cm/$\frac{1}{2}$ in deep cuts in the top of the loaf (do not press), and brush with water
Place in a preheated oven, and brush occasionally with water during baking to produce a good crust
Electricity: 200° C/400° F
Gas: Mark 6
Baking time: about 50 minutes

Herb rolls

In a large bowl, carefully mix **500 g/1 lb strong plain flour**
1 pkt dried yeast
Add **1 tsp sugar**
2 tsp salt

on the dough
Cut **75 g/3 oz cheese (e.g. edam)**

into small cubes and scatter over the meat
Bring the dough up over the meat and press it firmly together
Place it on a greased baking tray, and garnish with the reserved dough
Leave in a warm place to rise again
Make cuts in the top of the dough, about 1 cm/$\frac{1}{2}$ in long and 3 cm/1 $\frac{1}{2}$ in deep
Brush it with water, and dust with flour, then place in a preheated oven
Electricity: 200° - 225° C/400° - 450° F
Gas: Mark 6 - 7
Baking time: about 1 hour

Bread roll ring

Prepare **1 pkt (375 g/12 oz) bread mix**

according to instructions given on packet
with **250 ml/8 fl oz luke-warm water**
and allow to rise
Dust dough with **plain flour**

Herb rolls

Leave in a warm place to rise again
Cut a 1 cm/$\frac{1}{2}$ in deep cross in the top of each roll (do not press down)

Beat together | **1 egg yolk**
1 tbsp water

and brush over the rolls
Place them in a preheated oven
Electricity: 175° - 200° C/350° - 400° F
Gas: Mark 4 - 6
Baking time: about 25 minutes

Cheese rolls

In a large bowl, carefully mix | **425 g/15 oz strong plain flour**
1 pkt dried yeast

Add | **1 tsp sugar**
1 tsp salt
a little pepper
250 ml/8 fl oz luke-warm water

Using the dough hook of an electric mixer, mix ingredients first on the lowest setting, then on the highest setting for about 5 minutes, to a smooth dough

Towards the end of kneading, knead in | **150 g/5 oz coarsely grated gouda cheese**

Leave dough in a warm place until it has doubled its size
Remove from the bowl, and knead *well*
Form 10 smooth oval rolls from the dough, and lay them on a greased baking tray
Leave them in a warm place to rise again

Beat together | **1 egg yolk**
1 tbsp water

and brush over the rolls

Cheese rolls

freshly ground pepper
3 tbsp cooking oil
250 ml/8 fl oz luke-warm water

Using the dough hook of an electric mixer, mix ingredients first on the lowest setting and then on the highest setting for about 5 minutes, to a smooth dough

Towards the end of kneading, knead in | **2 tbsp chopped parsley**
2 tbsp finely chopped chives
1 tbsp chopped dill

Leave the dough in a warm place until it has doubled in size, then remove from bowl and knead *well*
Form 12 round rolls from the dough, and lay them on a greased baking tray

162

Sprinkle with **50 g/2 oz coarsely grated gouda cheese**

and put into a preheated oven
Electricity: 175° - 200° C/350° - 400° F
Gas: Mark 6 - 8
Baking time: about 25 minutes

Stoneground rye bread

In a large bowl, carefully mix **250 g/8 oz strong plain flour
125 g/4 oz granary flour
200 g/6 oz stoneground rye flour**
Add **1 pkt dried yeast
1 tsp sugar
1 - 2 tsp salt
300 ml/10 fl oz lukewarm water**

Using the dough hook on an electric mixer, mix first on the lowest setting, then on the highest setting
Add **200 g/6 oz sour dough
(ordinary dough kept for 3 - 4 days, which allows it to ferment)**

and mix for about 5 minutes to a smooth dough
Leave in a warm place until it has visibly risen
Remove from bowl, and knead *well*
Form an oval loaf from the dough, and put on to a greased baking tray
Leave in a warm place to rise again
Brush with water, and put into a preheated oven
To obtain a good crust, brush occasionally with water during baking
Electricity: 200° C/400° F
Gas: Mark 6
Baking time: 50 - 60 minutes

Party bread
(7 - 8 servings)

Grate the crust of **1 loaf of white bread (500 g/1 lb)**

Cut off the top of the loaf, and hollow out the inside

For the filling
Halve **1 sweet pepper**
Remove stalk, seeds and pith, then wash it
Dip **1 - 2 tomatoes**

into boiling water, then into cold water
Skin them, and remove cores and pulp
Cut tomatoes and pepper into cubes, and mix with **1 tbsp chopped parsley
750 g/1 $\frac{1}{2}$ lb pork sausagemeat**

Put the filling into the bread, put the top back on, and fasten with 2 wooden skewers
Place the bread on to a large piece of baking foil, and brush with **50 g/2 oz melted butter**

Wrap the baking foil round it, seal, and place in the middle of a preheated oven
Electricity: 200° C/400° F
Gas: Mark 6
Baking time: about 1 $\frac{1}{4}$ hours

Bacon bread

Dice **150 g/5 oz streaky bacon**

and heat it in a frying pan to remove the fat
Leave in a cool place
Prepare **1 pkt (375 g/12 oz) onion bread mix**

according to instructions on packet,

Party bread

using | **250 ml/8 fl oz luke-warm water**

Towards the end of kneading, knead in the bacon
Allow to rise
Dust with | **plain flour**
Remove from bowl and knead for a *short* time
Form a round loaf out of the dough, and lay on a greased baking tray
Leave in a warm place to rise again
Make several 1 cm/$\frac{1}{2}$ in deep cuts in the top of the dough (do not press down)
Brush with water, dust with flour, and place in a preheated oven
Electricity: 200° - 225° C/400° - 425° F
Gas: Mark 6 - 7
Baking time: 40 - 50 minutes

Herb and cheese bread

For the dough
In a large bowl, carefully mix | **500 g/1 lb strong plain flour**
1 pkt dried yeast
Add | **1 tsp sugar**
1 tsp salt

freshly ground pepper
250 ml/8 fl oz luke-warm water

Using the dough hook of an electric mixer, mix ingredients first on the lowest setting and then on the highest setting for about 5 minutes
Leave in a warm place until it has doubled in size

For the filling
Peel and dice | **2 - 3 onions**
Melt | **1 tbsp margarine**
and sauté onions in it, then remove from heat
Stir in | **1 egg**
125 g/4 oz grated gouda cheese
5 - 6 tbsp chopped mixed herbs

Remove risen dough from bowl and knead *well*
Roll it out on a floured pastry board to a 30 × 40 cm/12 × 16 in rectangle, and spread with | **1 tbsp soft margarine**
Spread the filling evenly over it
Fold the longest sides of the dough over a little, and roll up the shorter sides of the dough to meet in the middle

Herb and cheese bread

Put into a greased loaf tin (30 × 11 cm/12 × 4 in) and leave in a warm place to rise again

Cut a 1 cm/$\frac{1}{2}$ in deep zig-zag into the upper sides of both rolls (do not press down)

Beat together | **1 egg yolk**
1 tbsp water

and brush over the dough
Place in a preheated oven
Electricity: 175° - 200° C/350° - 400° F
Gas: Mark 4- 6
Baking time: 40 - 50 minutes

French bread (baguette) feast
(Illustrated on pages 154-155)

Cut | **1 French loaf (about 25 cm/10 in long)**

in half lengthways and spread the cut surface with | **butter**
Cover the lower half with | **washed iceberg lettuce leaves**
Lay | **2 slices ham**
| **tomato slices**
| **gherkin slices**
| **radish slices**
| **green pepper rings**
| **green pepper strips**
| **onion rings**
| **hard-boiled egg quarters**

on the lettuce
Sprinkle with | **chopped herbs**
Replace top half of bread and serve

Plaited bread

Prepare | **2 pkts (each 375 g/ 12 oz) bread mix**

according to instructions on packet using | **500 ml/16 fl oz lukewarm water**

and allow to rise
Dust the dough with | **plain flour**
Remove from bowl, and knead for a *short* time
Use about $\frac{2}{3}$ of the dough to form 3 rolls about 40 cm/16 in long
Plait them, and lay the plait on to a greased baking tray
Flatten it lengthways with a rolling pin
Cut the rest of the dough into 3 equal pieces, and form these into 35 cm/14 in long rolls, then plait them
Lay the second plait on top of the first one, and leave in a warm place again to rise

Plaited bread

Brush with water, dust with flour, and place in a preheated oven
Electricity: 200° - 225° C/400° - 425° F
Gas: Mark 6- 7
Baking time: about 50 minutes

Smoked pork in a bread jacket

Prepare | **1 pkt (375 g/12 oz) bread mix**

according to instructions on packet using | **250 ml/8 fl oz lukewarm water**

and allow to rise
Dust dough with | **plain flour**
remove from bowl, and knead for a *short* time
If wished, reserve some of the dough for garnishing
Roll out dough on a floured pastry board to a rectangular shape twice as big as the smoked pork
Place | **1 kg/2 lb piece of boneless smoked pork**

on the dough
Brush the edges of the dough with water, and fold it over the meat
Lay it (smooth side uppermost) on a greased baking tray, and decorate with the reserved dough
Without pressing down, cut out small round holes in the top of the dough, and leave in a warm place to rise again
Brush with water, and place in a preheated oven
Electricity: 200° C/400° F
Gas: Mark 6
Baking time: 40 - 50 minutes

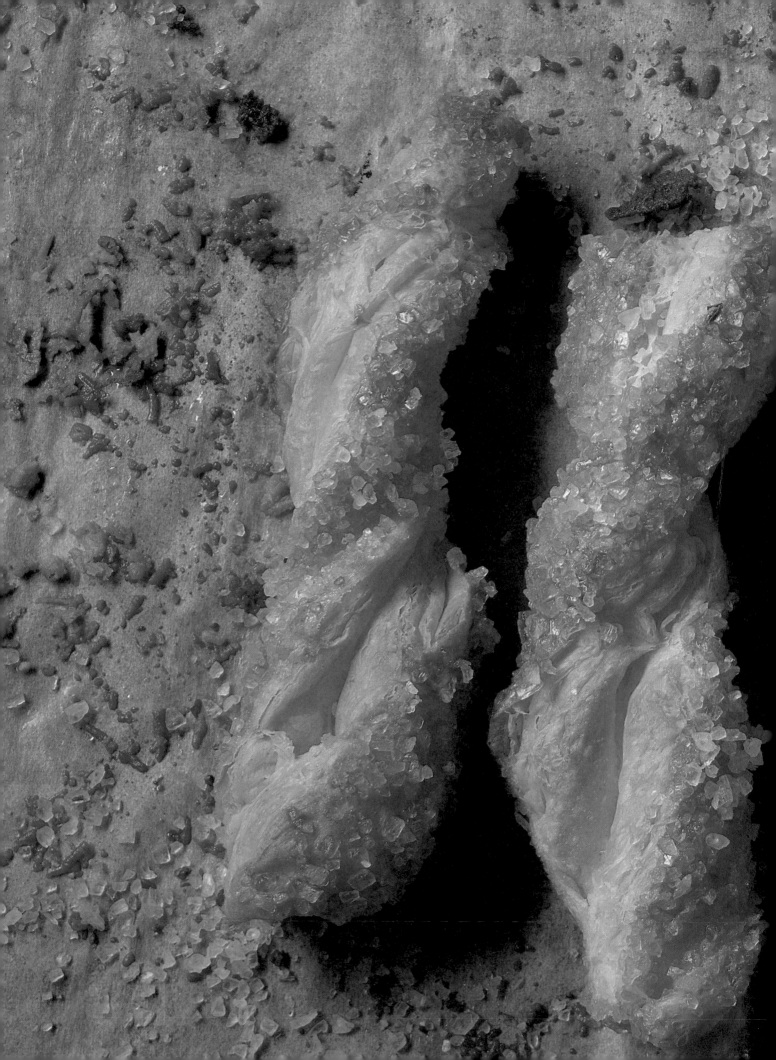

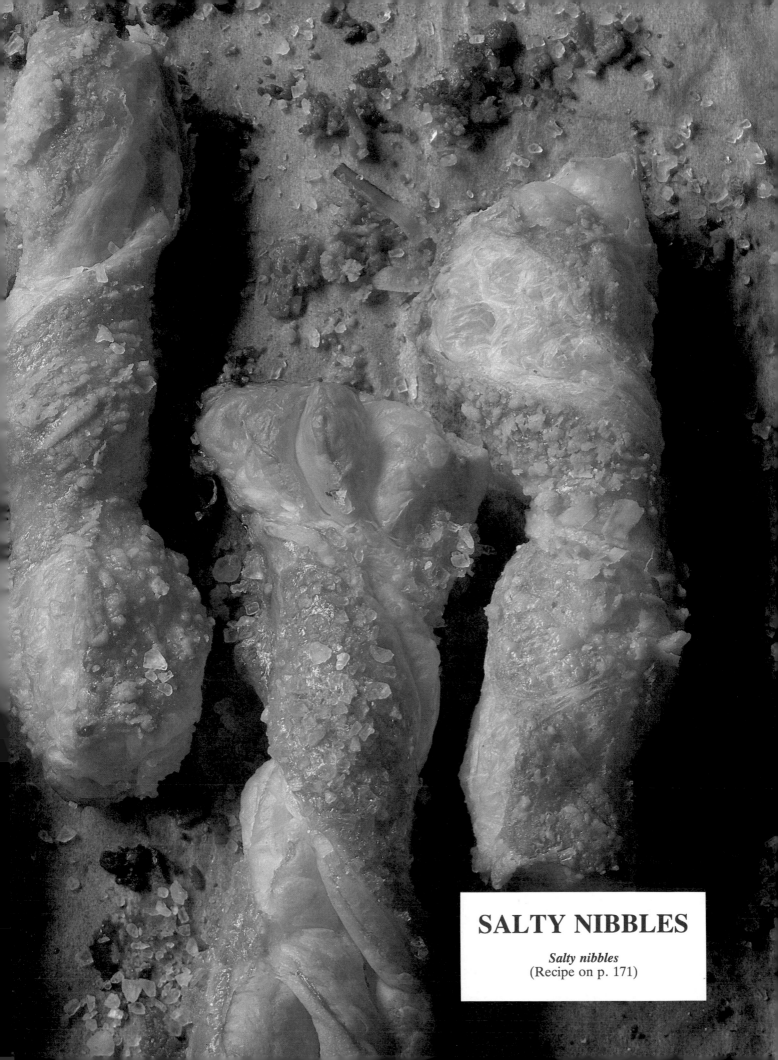

SALTY NIBBLES

Salty nibbles
(Recipe on p. 171)

Caraway seed diamonds

Allow	**300 g/10 oz frozen puff pastry**

to thaw according to instructions on packet, and divide into 3 portions

Beat	**1 egg**

Brush some of it on to each portion of pastry (do not allow the egg to run over the edges)

Sprinkle one of the portions with	**salt** **pepper** **sweet paprika** **a little caraway seed**
and $\frac{1}{3}$ of	**125 g/4 oz grated gouda cheese**

Lay the second portion, egg side down, on top of the first, and brush it with beaten egg
Sprinkle it with salt, pepper, paprika, caraway seed and $\frac{1}{2}$ of the remaining cheese
Lay the third portion on top, egg side down
Carefully roll out the pastry to a 32 cm/12 in square, and cut it into 4 cm/2 in squares
Brush them with beaten egg, and sprinkle with the caraway seeds and cheese
Lay the squares on to a baking tray

Caraway seed diamonds

Cheesy snails

which has been rinsed with cold water
Put into a preheated oven
Electricity: 200° - 225° C/400° - 425° F
Gas: Mark 6 - 7
Baking time: about 20 minutes

Cheesy snails

Mix together	**150 g/5 oz plain flour** **1 level tsp baking powder**
and sieve on to a pastry board	
Make a hollow in the middle and put	**125 g/4 oz grated stale Swiss or Dutch cheese** **1 egg white** **$\frac{1}{2}$ egg yolk**
into it	

Mix to a thick paste with some of the flour

Cut	**125 g/4 oz cold butter or margarine**
into pieces and add to the paste with	**50 g/2 oz blanched ground almonds**

Cover with flour, and quickly knead to a smooth dough, working from the middle outwards
If it becomes sticky, leave it for a while in a cold place

Divide the dough into 2 equal portions and roll them out to 28 × 24 cm/11 × 9½ in rectangles

Beat together	½ **egg yolk** **1 tsp milk**

and brush over the 2 dough portions

Sprinkle each with ½ of	**15 g/½ oz grated parmesan cheese**

Roll each of them up tightly from the longer side, and leave the rolls in a cold place until they are firm enough to slice
Cut them into ½ cm/¼ in thick slices, and lay them on a greased baking tray
Put into a preheated oven
Electricity: 175° - 200° C/350° - 400° F
Gas: Mark 4 - 6
Baking time: about 12 minutes

Parmesan crescents

Mix together	**125 g/4 oz plain flour** **2 level tsp baking powder**

and sieve on to a pastry board
Make a hollow in the middle and drop into it

	1 egg

Mix to a thick paste with some of the flour

Cut	**125 g/4 oz cold butter**
into pieces and add to the paste with	**125 g/4 oz grated parmesan cheese**

Cover with flour and quickly knead to a smooth dough, working from the middle outwards
If it becomes sticky, leave it for a while in a cold place
Form thumb-thick rolls out of the dough, and cut these into 2 cm/1 in long pieces
Form these into rolls about 5 cm/2½ in long, and roll the ends a little thinner
Lay these as crescents on a baking tray, and put into a preheated oven
Electricity: 175° - 200° C/350° - 400° F
Gas: Mark 4 - 6
Baking time: about 10 minutes

Salted almonds

Put	**250 g/8 oz un-blanched almonds**
into	**boiling salted water**

and remove pan from heat
Allow the almonds to soak for 2 - 3 minutes and then drain
Rinse with cold water, then skin and dry them well

Stir	½ **egg white**

until smooth and add the almonds, stir-

Salted almonds

ring until they are all covered with egg white

Sprinkle lightly with	**salt**

and stir again for a short time
Lay the almonds on a baking tray and dry them in a preheated oven, lightly browning them
Electricity: 110° - 130° C/225° - 250° F
Gas: Mark ¼ - ½
Drying time: 15 - 25 minutes

Cheese sticks

Cream	**125 g/4 oz butter or margarine**
Grate	**125 g/4 oz stale gouda or Swiss cheese**

Sieve **125 g/4 oz plain flour**
good pinch baking
powder

together
Gradually stir the ingredients into the
butter, and add **salt**
sweet paprika

to taste
Put into a piping bag with a rosette noz-
zle, and pipe 10 cm/4 in lengths on to a
baking tray
Put into a preheated oven
Electricity: 175° - 200° C/350° - 400 F
Gas: Mark 4 - 6
Baking time: 10 - 15 minutes

Herb balls

Herb balls

Sieve **250 g/8 oz plain flour**
into a large bowl and carefully mix with **1 pkt dried yeast**
Add **1 level tsp sugar**
$\frac{1}{2}$ level tsp salt
50 g/2 oz melted
butter
125 ml/4 fl oz luke-
warm milk

Using the dough hook of an electric
mixer, mix ingredients first on the lowest setting, and then on the highest setting, for 5 minutes
Knead in **1 heaped tsp**
Provence herbs

Leave the dough in a warm place until
doubled in size, then knead it well again
on the highest setting
Form long rolls about 1 cm/$\frac{1}{2}$ in thick
from the dough, and cut them into $\frac{3}{4}$ in
lengths
Roll these into balls, and lay them on a
greased baking tray
Leave in a warm place until the balls
have doubled their size
Brush them with **evaporated milk**
and sprinkle with **coarse salt**
Put into a preheated oven
Electricity: 175° - 200° C/350° - 400° F
Gas: Mark 4 - 6
Baking time: about 15 minutes

Cheese rings, cream puffs and éclairs

For the choux pastry
Bring **125 ml/4 fl oz water**
salt
25 g/1 oz butter or

to the boil in a milk pan **margarine**
Remove from heat
Sieve together **25 g/1 oz cornflour**
75 g/3 oz plain flour

Tip it all at once into the water, and stir
it to a smooth ball
Heat for about 1 minute whilst stirring
Put the hot dough ball immediately into
a bowl, and gradually stir in **2 - 3 eggs**
Enough egg has been added when the
dough is very shiny and pulls away from
the spoon when held up
Shortly before this consistency has been
attained, add **1 $\frac{1}{2}$ g/$\frac{1}{4}$ level tsp**
baking powder

to the cooled dough
Remove $\frac{1}{3}$ of the dough, as the dough
for the cheese rings has to be deep-fried
and needs to be somewhat firmer
Add sufficient egg to the remaining
dough to bring it to the right consistency

For the cheese rings
Put the firmer dough into a piping bag
with a narrow rosette nozzle, and pipe
rings (about 4 cm/2 in diameter) on to
greased greaseproof paper
Deep fry immediately in hot **oil**
until they are light brown on both sides
Remove them with a small wooden
skewer, allow them to drain well, and
slice in half

For the cream puffs
Put half of the softer dough into a piping bag with a narrow rosette nozzle,
and pipe walnut-sized amounts on to a

Cheese rings, Cream puffs and éclairs

greased, floured baking tray
Put into a preheated oven
Electricity: 200° - 225° C/400° - 425° F
Gas: Mark 6 - 7
Baking time: about 20 minutes
Cut a small lid off each cream puff immediately after baking

For the éclairs
Put the remaining dough into a piping bag with a narrow rosette nozzle, and for each éclair pipe two 6 cm/2 $\frac{1}{2}$ in long strips close together on to a greased, floured baking tray, and pipe a third strip on top of the first two
Baking time: about 20 minutes (temperature settings as for cream puffs)
Slice the éclairs open immediately after baking

For the filling

Cream	**125 g/4 oz butter**
Mash	**125 g/4 oz roquefort cheese**

with a fork and stir into butter

Whip	**125 ml/4 fl oz double cream**

until stiff
Fold into the butter-cheese mixture
Fill the cheese rings, the cream puffs, and the éclairs with the cream cheese, spread the cream cheese thinly on to all the lids, and sprinkle with **chopped parsley**
caraway seeds
poppy seeds
sweet paprika

and place them on the corresponding pastries

Salty nibbles (Illustrated on pages 166-167)

Allow	**1 pkt (300 g/10 oz) frozen puff pastry**

to thaw according to instructions given on packet
Roll out, and cut it into
12 × 2 cm/5 × $\frac{1}{2}$ in strips

Beat together	**1 egg yolk** **1 tbsp evaporated milk**

and brush over the pastry strips

Sprinkle with	**coarse salt**

Twist the strips into spirals (by twisting one end to the right and the other end to the left)
Lay them on a baking tray which has been rinsed with cold water and put in a preheated oven
Electricity: 200° - 225° C/400° - 425° F
Gas: Mark 6 - 7
Baking time: about 10 minutes

Viennese bacon cookies

into it
Mix with some of the flour to a thick
paste
Add the cooled fat, onion and bacon,
cover with flour, and quickly knead to a
smooth dough, working from the middle
outwards
Form the dough into 3 cm/1 $\frac{1}{2}$ in thick
rolls and leave them in a cold place until
they have become firm enough to slice
Cut them into $\frac{1}{2}$ cm/$\frac{1}{4}$ in thick slices and
lay them on a baking tray

Beat together	**1 egg yolk**
	1 tbsp milk

and brush over the cookies

Sprinkle them with	**caraway seeds**
	coarse salt
	grated cheese

and put them in a preheated oven
Electricity: 175° - 200° C/350° - 400° F
Gas: Mark 4 - 6
Baking time: 10 - 12 minutes

Sesame seed cheese sticks

Stir together	**125 g/4 oz quark**
	(curd cheese)
	3 tbsp milk

Sesame seed cheese sticks

Viennese bacon cookies

Finely dice	**125 g/4 oz fatty bacon**

and heat in a frying pan until fat begins
to run

Peel and finely dice	**1 small onion**

and add to the bacon
Fry until onions are golden yellow, then
remove from heat

Sieve	**250 g/8 oz plain flour**
	50 g/2 oz cornflour
	1 level tsp baking powder

together on to a pastry board
Make a hollow in the middle and put

**just about 1 level tsp
salt**
1 egg white
3 tbsp water

Sieve together — 1 egg / 1 egg white / 3 tbsp cooking oil / 1 level tsp salt / 250 g/8 oz plain flour / 1 pkt baking powder

Stir half of it into the quark, and knead in the rest

Knead in — 50 g/2 oz toasted sesame seeds / 25 g/1 oz grated parmesan cheese

Roll out dough to $\frac{1}{2}$ cm/$\frac{1}{4}$ in thickness, and cut it into strips $1\frac{1}{2}$ cm/$\frac{3}{4}$ in wide and 12 cm/4 $\frac{1}{2}$ in long

Beat together — 1 egg yolk / 1 tsp milk

and brush over dough strips
Lay them on a greased baking tray, and put into a preheated oven
Electricity: 175° - 200° C/350° - 400° F
Gas: Mark 4 - 6
Baking time: 10 - 15 minutes

Cheese triangles

Cheese triangles

Sieve — 150 g/5 oz plain flour

on to a pastry board
Make a hollow in the middle and put — 75 g/3 oz grated parmesan or Swiss cheese / $\frac{1}{2}$ tsp salt / pepper / sweet paprika / 1 egg / 3 tbsp milk

into it
Mix with some of the flour to a thick paste

Cut — 125 g/4 oz cold butter or margarine

into pieces and add
Cover with flour and quickly knead to a smooth dough, working from the middle outwards
If it becomes sticky, leave it for a while in a cold place
Roll out thinly, and cut out into 5 cm/ 2 $\frac{1}{2}$ in squares
Cut the squares diagonally in half to make triangles
Lay them on a greased baking tray, and brush with — evaporated milk
Sprinkle with paprika if desired, and place in a preheated oven
Electricity: 175° - 200° C/350° - 400° F
Gas: Mark 4 - 6
Baking time: about 10 minutes

Salted nuts

Shell — 250 g/8 oz peanuts (groundnuts)
Stir — $\frac{1}{2}$ egg white
until smooth
Put peanuts into egg white and stir until they are all evenly covered
Sprinkle lightly with — salt
and stir again for a short time
Lay them on a baking tray, and dry them in a preheated oven lightly browning them
Electricity: 110° - 130° C/225° - 250° F
Gas: Mark $\frac{1}{4}$ - $\frac{1}{2}$
Drying time: about 15 minutes

DRINKS

Juanito's drink
(Recipe on p. 177)

Aperitive Kir

Aperitive Kir
(1 serving)

Put	**125 ml/4 fl oz dry white wine**
into a glass	
Stir in	**2 tbsp crème de cassis (blackcurrant liqueur)**
Serve well-chilled	

Green grass (champagne mix)

For the cucumber ice cubes	
Peel	**1 small cucumber**
and cut into large cubes	
Purée in a mixer or a liquidizer	
Season with	**pepper**
	celery salt
Stir in	**chopped mixed herbs**
Put it into an ice cube tray, and freeze in freezing compartment of refrigerator	
For the drink	
Put one cucumber ice cube into each champagne glass, and fill with	**chilled champagne**

Blue angel (champagne mix)
(1 serving)

Put	**1 - 2 tbsp blue curaçao**
into a champagne glass and fill with	**chilled champagne**

Soft blossom (champagne mix)
(1 serving)

Put	**1 - 2 tbsp apricot liqueur**
into a champagne glass and fill with	**chilled champagne**
Add	**dash of Angostura bitters**
if desired	

Schwyz (champagne mix)
(1 serving)

Put	**1 tsp grenadine**
	1 tbsp cherry spirits (Kirsch)
	1 tbsp orange juice
into a champagne glass and fill up with	**chilled champagne**

Turkish blood (champagne mix)
(1 serving)

Put	**2 tbsp red wine**
into a champagne glass and fill up with	**chilled champagne**

Black velvet (champagne mix)
(1 serving)

Put	**125 ml/4 fl oz (about $\frac{1}{2}$ glass) dark beer**
into a champagne glass and fill up with	**chilled champagne**
NB. This mixture must be poured very carefully into the glass as it foams a lot	
Connoisseurs mix Black velvet by taking	

Green grass, Blue angel, Soft blossom, Black velvet, Schwyz Turkish blood

one drink in either hand and pouring
them smoothly into the glass at the
same time

Juanito's drink (Illustrated on pages 174-175)

Put	**ice cubes**
into a glass	
Add	**1 lemon slice**
Pour over	**6 - 8 tbsp tequila**
Top up with	**ice-cold clear lemon-ade**

Serve with a straw

Melon cocktail with white rum
(6 servings)

Peel and halve	**1 water melon (about 750 g/1 $\frac{1}{2}$ lb)**

Cut out some melon balls from the middle of the fruit halves with a melon
scoop, remove seeds, and dice the rest
of the flesh

Using a mixer or a liquidizer, purée the melon, and add to taste	
Stir in	**juice of 1 lemon**
	125 ml/4 fl oz white rum

Cover, and leave to stand in a cold
place

Wash	**1 lemon**

in hot water, dry it, and slice thinly
Put the melon cocktail into 6 glasses just
before serving, and garnish with the
melon balls and the lemon slices
Serve well-chilled

Melon cocktail with white rum

Southern comfort tonic

Southern comfort tonic
(2 servings)

Put	**ice cubes**
into 2 tall glasses, and pour over them	**8 tbsp Cointreau**
Fill up with	**tonic**
and stir	
Garnish with	**lemon peel**

Gin fizz

Bring to the boil	**50 g/2 oz sugar**
	3 tbsp water
Allow to boil for a short time, then cool	
Stir in	**125 ml/4 fl oz gin**
	125 ml/4 fl oz lemon juice
Moisten the rims of the glasses with	**lemon juice**
and dip in	**sugar**
Pour the cocktail into the glasses and add	**ice cubes**
Fill up with	**mineral water**
Garnish with	**lemon slices**

Caribbean drink

Caribbean drink
(1 serving)

Put	**3 tbsp coconut milk liqueur**
	2 tbsp white rum
	5 tbsp pineapple juice
	2 tbsp orange juice
	2 - 3 ice cubes
into a cocktail shaker and shake well	
Put	**an ice cube**
into a glass and the drink on top	
Garnish with	**mint**

Party cocktail mix
(1 serving)

Put	**2 tbsp bourbon whisky**
	2 tbsp Campari
	1 tbsp maraschino ice cubes
into a cocktail shaker and shake well	
Pour into a tall glass, and fill up with	**chilled champagne**
Add	**pineapple pieces**
	1 cocktail (maraschino) cherry

Champagne punch

Dip	**6 peaches**
first into boiling water, then into cold water	
Skin, halve and stone	
Peel	**¼ pineapple**
Cut both ingredients into thin slices, and put into a punch bowl	
Add	**juice of 1 lemon**
	juice of 2 oranges
and	**4 tbsp brandy**
Cover, and leave to stand for about 1 hour	
Shortly before serving, fill up with	**2 bottles chilled champagne (or sparkling wine)**

Tempo

Wash	**2 lemons**
	2 oranges
with hot water and slice thinly	
Wash and halve	**500 g/1 lb green grapes**
Remove pips, and put grapes into a punch bowl with	**ice cubes**
Pour on	**10 tbsp gin**
	10 tbsp vermouth
	1 bottle dry white wine
	1 bottle clear lemonade
Cover, and leave to stand in a cool place for about 1 hour	

Tempo

Kuller peach

Wash and dry	**4 medium-sized ripe peaches**
Prick them all over with a wooden cocktail stick, and put them into 4 tall glasses	
Fill up with	**1 bottle chilled champagne**

Lime drink
(1 serving)

Put into a glass	**ice cubes**
and add	**4 tbsp dry vermouth**
	1 tbsp lime juice
Garnish with	**lemon balm**

Lime drink

Exotic punch

Exotic punch

Remove skin and seeds from	**½ honeydew melon (about 500 g/1 lb)**
Wash, dry and stone	**6 - 8 fresh dates**
Cut both ingredients into small cubes, and put them into a punch bowl	
Add	**5 tbsp brandy**
Cover, and leave to stand for about 1 hour	
Peel and slice thinly	**2 kiwifruit**
Wash, dry, and halve	**1 kaki (persimmon)**
and cut into cubes or slices (depending on how ripe it is)	
Put the fruit into the punch bowl	
Pour in	**1 bottle white wine**
Cover, and leave to stand for another hour	
Shortly before serving fill up with	**2 bottles chilled white wine**
	1 bottle chilled champagne

Spanish style red wine punch

Wash	**2 lemons**
	3 medium oranges
in hot water, slice thinly and put into a punch bowl	
Sprinkle on	**125 g/4 oz sugar**
Cover, and leave to stand for about 30 minutes	
Pour on	**1 bottle red wine**
and leave to stand for another 30 minutes	
Shortly before serving, fill up with	**1 bottle chilled mineral water**

Driver's flip - hi partner, good trip

Driver's flip - hi partner

Wash	**1 lemon**
	1 orange
with hot water, then peel lemon thinly, and cut into strips, and slice orange	
Put them in a cocktail shaker with	**8 orange juice ice cubes**
	500 ml/16 fl oz red grape juice
	1 tbsp lemon juice
Shake well, and pour into 4 glasses	
Fill up with	**250 ml/8 fl oz orangeade**
Garnish with lemon strips and orange slices	

Driver's flip - good trip

Beat	**4 ice cubes**
	2 eggs
	3 tbsp icing sugar
	pith of $\frac{1}{2}$ vanilla pod
	250 ml/8 fl oz cold milk
together in an electric mixer	
Put into 4 glasses and fill up with	**375 ml/12 fl oz mineral water**
Sprinkle with	**grated nutmeg**

Three fruit cocktail
(5 servings)

Cut 5 slices from	**1 lime**
Use the rest of the lime to moisten the	

Three fruit cocktail

rims of 5 cocktail glasses, then dip the rims into	**sugar**
Stir together	**250 ml/8 fl oz unsweetened pineapple juice**
	125 ml/4 fl oz Maracuja nectar
	125 ml/4 fl oz grapefruit juice
	125 ml/4 fl oz white rum
Put	**ice cubes**
into each glass and fill with the drink	
Garnish with the lime slices	

Strawberry champagne

Wash and remove stalks of	**250 g/8 oz fresh strawberries**
Pat dry, halve, and put in a bowl	
Sprinkle with	**2 tbsp sieved icing sugar**
Pour on	**4 tbsp strawberry liqueur**
and leave to stand, covered, for about 1 hour	
Divide the fruit evenly between 4 large well-chilled glasses	

Fill up with **½ bottle chilled cham-pagne**

Egg nog
(1 serving)

Whip **2 egg yolks**
1 tbsp sugar

with an electric mixer until frothy, then
add **grated rind of 1**
lemon
1 - 2 tbsp warm

Tomato drink, Cucumber drink

Egg nog

brandy
1 - 2 tbsp boiling
water

and stir
Serve the frothy drink immediately in
champagne glasses

Tomato drink
(1 serving)

Wash and core **250 g/8 oz tomatoes**
Cut them into pieces
Cut into pieces **75 g/3 oz honeydew**
melon flesh

Gradually put both ingredients into a li-
quidizer
Stir in **1 tsp lemon juice**
Season with **cayenne pepper**
Worcester sauce
salt

Cucumber drink
(1 serving)

Wash and halve **250 g/8 oz cucumber**
Remove pips and cut into pieces
Gradually put into a liquidizer
Stir **1 tbsp cream**
into juice
Season with **salt**
pepper
Sprinkle with **chopped dill**
Serve with: **ice cubes**

Put into a glass, and decorate with **whipped cream**
Sprinkle with **sweet paprika**
Serve with: **ice cubes**

**SPICY PICKLES/
PRESERVES**

Harz cheese in oil
(Recipe on p. 186)

Spiced pickled beetroot

Remove from heat and pour over gherkins
Allow to cool, and seal
The gherkins are ready to eat after
about 4 weeks

Spiced pickled beetroot

Carefully scrub under running cold water	**1 kg/2 lb beetroot**
Bring to the boil in and cook until tender	**salted water**
Remove from water, and rinse with cold water	
Skin and slice, if necessary halving beetroot first	
Peel and slice	**5 medium onions**
Layer the beetroot with the onion and	**2 bay leaves crumbled into small pieces**
	12 - 15 whole cloves
	12 - 15 whole allspice
in a bowl	

For the vinegar and sugar solution

Bring to the boil	**75 g/3 oz sugar**
	500 ml/16 fl oz water
	1 tsp salt
Add	**250 ml/8 fl oz wine vinegar**

Sweet and sour fennel

Mustard gherkins

Peel and cut lengthways	**6 kg/13 lb large fully grown firm gherkins or young cucumbers**
Scrape out the centre with a spoon Cut them into finger-long strips, and layer them with in a bowl	**200 g/6 oz salt**
Cover, and leave in a cool place for 12 - 24 hours	
Drain them, and dry them carefully	
Peel	**250 g/8 oz small white onions**
Clean and cut into pieces	**½ horseradish root**
Layer the gherkins, onions, horseradish with	**75 g/3 oz pickling spice**
	3 bay leaves
	15 - 20 white and black peppercorns
	125 g/4 oz yellow mustard seed
in an earthenware pot or in glass jars (Put spices in a muslin bag if preferred)	

For the vinegar and sugar solution

Bring to the boil	**1 ½ l/3 pints wine vinegar**
	1 l/2 pints water
	600 g/1 ¼ lb sugar

Tomato and sweet pepper chutney

Pour solution over beetroot and allow to
soak for some days
Cooking time: about 1 hour

Tomato and sweet pepper chutney

Halve	**2 green peppers**
Remove stalks, seeds, and pith, then wash and cut up	
Dip	**1 kg/2 lb tomatoes**
first into boiling water, then into cold water	
Skin and cut into pieces	
Peel and dice	**500 g/1 lb onions**
Bring these ingredients to the boil with	**200 g/6 oz castor sugar**
	6 whole cloves
	10 mustard seeds
	5 peppercorns
	salt
	paprika
	250 ml/8 fl oz herb vinegar

and cook until vegetables are tender
Put the chutney into jars, and seal when
cold
Cooking time: about 30 minutes

Sweet and sour fennel

Wash and quarter	**1½ kg/3 lb fennel bulbs**

Put into	**500 ml/1 pint salted water**
Bring to the boil, and cook for about 10 minutes	
Drain in a colander	
Bring to the boil	**375 ml/12 fl oz wine vinegar**
	500 ml/16 fl oz water
	125 g/4 oz sugar
Peel and finely dice	**125 g/4 oz shallots**
	3 cloves of garlic
Wash in hot water, dry and slice	**1 lemon**
Put these 3 ingredients, together with	**2 small red chillis**
	2 whole star anise
	1 tbsp green pepper
	rosemary needles

into the hot liquid, and boil for a short
time
Remove from heat
Put fennel pieces into a large jar, and
pour liquid over them
Allow to cool, and seal jar

Sweet and sour pears

Remove leaves and stalks (the stalks may be left on if preferred) of	**2 kg/4½ lb small pears**
and peel	
Put them into	**salted water**
to prevent them turning brown	

For the vinegar and sugar solution

Bring to the boil	**750 ml/1¼ pint wine vinegar**
	250 ml/8 fl oz water
	1 kg/2 lb white sugar
Put	**4 whole cloves**
	1 stick cinnamon

Sweet and sour pears

into a small muslin bag and add to liquid | **1 piece dried root ginger**
Cook the pears in batches in this liquid until they are almost soft, then remove them with a slotted spoon and put them into jars
Boil the liquid a little more, then pour it over the pears
Cover them and allow to cool
After 3 days, pour off the liquid, boil it until thick, remove from heat, and pour over the pears again
Allow to cool, and seal jars

2 - 3 whole star anise

Gherkins pickled in vinegar

Wash | **4 kg/9 lb small gherkins or young cucumbers**
Cover with | **salted water**
and leave in a cool place for 12 - 24 hours
Scrub and rinse the gherkins, and dry each one with a cloth
Remove any discoloured areas

Gherkins pickled in vinegar

Peel | **375 g/12 oz small white onions**
Clean and cut into pieces | **75 g/3 oz horseradish root**
Wash | **dill sprigs**
| **tarragon sprigs**

Layer the gherkins with the other ingredients in an earthenware pot

For the vinegar and sugar solution
Bring to the boil | **1 ½ l/3 pints wine vinegar**
| **300 - 375 g/10 - 12 oz sugar**

Remove from heat and pour enough of the hot liquid over the gherkins to cover them
Allow to cool, then seal

Harz cheese in oil
(Illustrated on pages 182-183)

Combine | **500 ml/1 pint cooking oil**
| **½ tsp white peppercorns**
| **2 peeled cloves of garlic**
| **capers**
| **¼ tsp caraway seeds**
| **1 bay leaf**
| **1 small rosemary sprig**
| **1 small thyme sprig**
| **1 - 2 red chillis**
Cut | **500 g/1 lb Harz cheese**

into pieces (rolls) and put into a tall glass jar
Pour the marinade over the cheese to completely cover it, and leave it to stand for at least 4 - 5 days
Serve with: | **wholemeal, granary, or German rye bread**

N.B. The marinade can be re-used several times

Mixed pickles

Wash | **1 kg/2 lb small firm gherkins or young cucumbers**
Cover with | **salted water**
and leave in a cool place for 12 - 24 hours
Carefully scrub and rinse them
Dry each with a cloth
Remove any discoloured areas
Clean | **1 small cauliflower**

and divide it into florets
(Cover with salted water if necessary to
remove any caterpillars or insects)
Allow to drain
String and wash   **250 g/8 oz green
beans**

Break them into 4 cm/2 in long pieces
Scrape and wash   **500 g/1 lb carrots**
Slice them decoratively with a serrated
knife
Cook cauliflower, beans and carrots one
after the other until they are almost
tender, and drain in a colander
Clean and cut into pieces   **$\frac{1}{2}$ horseradish root**
Peel   **125 g/4 oz small
white onions**

Layer vegetables, horseradish, onions
with   **3 bay leaves
20 peppercorns
10 whole allspice**

in jars

For the vinegar and sugar solution
Bring to the boil   **750 ml/1 $\frac{1}{4}$ pint wine
vinegar
1 $\frac{1}{4}$ l/2 $\frac{1}{2}$ pints water
125 g/4 oz sugar
50 g/2 oz salt**

Remove from heat, and pour over the
mixed pickles
Allow to cool, and seal the jars
Tip: Sealing the jars:
Cut out greaseproof paper circles the
same size as the tops of the jars, and dip
in pure alcohol, rum or vinegar
Lay them over the contents of the jar,
and press down well
Seal the jars with transparent covers

Tomatoes in vinegar

Tomatoes in vinegar

Wash and dry   **2 kg/4 $\frac{1}{2}$ lb small,
firm, ripe tomatoes**

Prick each tomato 15 - 20 times with a
wooden cocktail stick
Put them into jars

For the vinegar solution
Peel   **4 shallots or small
onions**

and cut into rings

Bring them to the boil with   **1 l/2 pints wine vinegar
250 ml/8 fl oz water
25 g/1 oz salt
25 g/1 oz sugar
2 whole cloves
25 g/1 oz peppercorns
25 g/1 oz mustard
seeds**

Remove from heat, pour over tomatoes
and allow to cool
Seal jars

LIGHT DISHES

Muesli to wake you up
(Recipe on p. 196)

Leek soup

Leek soup

Wash and thinly slice	**3 leeks**
Wash again if necessary	
Melt	**1 tbsp butter**
Add	**50 g/2 oz instant porridge oats**

and keep cooking, stirring constantly

Add	**1 1/2 pints instant chicken stock**

and bring to the boil
Boil for about 10 minutes

Stir in	**125 ml/4 fl oz cream**
Season with	**salt**
	sweet paprika
Garnish with	**watercress**
	leek rings

when serving
Cooking time: about 15 minutes

Serve with:	**French bread and butter**
Tip: Stir together	**1 - 2 wedges soft cream cheese**
	a little cream or water

and add to the soup, heating them together

Herb soup

Wash	**1 small leek**
and cut into small pieces	
Wash again if necessary	
Melt	**50 g/2 oz butter**
and sauté the leek in it	

Herb soup

Stir	**25 g/1 oz instant porridge oats**
Add	**1 1/2 pints hot instant chicken stock**
Wash	**125 g/4 oz mixed herbs**

and pat dry
Chop finely, and add to the stock
Purée with an electric mixer, and bring to the boil
Boil for 2 - 3 minutes

Beat together	**1 egg yolk**
	125 ml/4 fl oz cream
and use to thicken the soup	**sugar**
	freshly ground pepper
	grated nutmeg
to taste	
Garnish with	**watercress**

Stuffed red peppers

| Remove stalks from | **4 medium red peppers** |

Cut off tops, and remove cores and pith
Wash and dry

Peel and dice	**1 onion**
Dice	**50 g/2 oz streaky bacon**
Mix onion and bacon with	**250 g/8 oz minced meat (half beef, half pork)**
	1 egg
	3 heaped tbsp fine rolled oats
Season with	**salt**
	pepper

Put mixture into peppers, and put tops

Stuffed red peppers

Birch-Benner muesli

| back on | |
| Dice | **125 g/4 oz streaky bacon** |

and heat it in a pan until the fat runs

| Put the peppers into the pan, add | **125 - 250 ml/ 4 - 8 fl oz water** |

cover, and cook peppers until tender
Cooking time: 50 - 60 minutes

| Serve with: | **rice or mashed potato tomato sauce** |

Birch-Benner muesli

Pour	**250 ml/8 fl oz milk**
	125 ml/4 fl oz cream
over	**200 g/6 oz oatflakes**
and allow to soak	
Wash and dry	**4 apples**

Herb pancakes with quark

Quarter, remove cores, and dice	
Sprinkle	**juice of 1 lemon**
on to the apples	
Peel and slice	**2 bananas**
Peel	**4 oranges**
and cut into small pieces	
Mix fruit and	**50 g/2 oz chopped hazelnuts or blanched chopped almonds**
	2 tbsp honey or
	4 heaped tbsp sugar
with the oats	

Herb pancakes with quark

For the quark

Stir together	**250 g/8 oz low fat quark (curd cheese)**
	4 tbsp cream or milk
Stir in	**1 tbsp grated horse-radish**
	3 tbsp instant porridge oats
	1 - 2 tbsp finely chopped chives
Season with	**salt**

For the herb pancakes

Sieve	**150 g/5 oz plain flour**
into a bowl	
Mix in	**2 tbsp oatflakes**
Make a hollow in the middle	
Beat together	**3 eggs**
	250 ml/8 fl oz mineral water
and put a little into the hollow	

Working from the middle outwards, stir the egg liquid and the oats together, gradually adding the rest of the liquid, taking care that no lumps form
Leave to soak for about 1 hour

Stir into the mixture	**50 g/2 oz grated cheese**
	2 tbsp chopped mixed herbs
Peel and finely dice	**1 onion**
and add to the mixture	
Season with	**salt**
Heat a little of	**4 tbsp cooking oil**

in a frying pan, and pour in a thin layer of the pancake batter
Fry until golden yellow on both sides
Before turning the pancake, add a little more oil
Keep finished pancakes warm, while cooking remaining pancakes
Serve them with the quark cream, and

garnish with	**watercress**

Baked fennel

Clean and halve	**4 small fennel bulbs**
Melt	**50 g/2 oz butter**
and cook fennel in it until tender	
Season with	**salt**
Lay fennel side by side in a greased ovenproof soufflé dish	
Stir together	**2 eggs**
	125 ml/4 fl oz milk
	3 tbsp instant porridge oats
and pour over fennel	
Cut	**400 g/14 oz ham**
into strips and scatter over fennel	
Sprinkle	**125 g/4 oz grated cheese**
on the top	
Put dish into a preheated oven	
Sprinkle the cooked fennel with	**2 - 3 tbsp chopped parsley**

Electricity: 200° C/400° F
Gas : Mark 6
Cooking time: about 30 minutes
Variation:

Use	**celery, leeks, or chicory**
instead of fennel	

Baked fennel

Scrambled egg with oats

Beat together	**4 eggs**
	4 tbsp milk
	salt
	4 tbsp instant porridge oats
Melt in a frying pan	**1 - 2 tbsp butter or margarine**
and add the egg mixture	
As soon as it begins to set, stroke it loose from the bottom of the pan with a spoon	
Continue to heat until no longer runny	
The egg must be soft and in large "flakes" but not dry	
Arrange the scrambled egg on	**4 slices of wholemeal bread**
Sprinkle with	**1 tbsp finely chopped chives**
	125 g/4 oz diced raw smoked ham

Cooking time: about 5 minutes

Marinated button mushrooms
(6 servings)

For the marinade	
Put into a large frying pan	**5 tbsp olive oil**
Peel and crush	**2 cloves of garlic**
Add the garlic to the oil with	**200 ml/6 fl oz water**
	4 tbsp lemon juice
	2 bay leaves
	salt
	pepper
Cover, and bring to the boil	
Boil for about 5 minutes	

Scrambled egg with oats

Clean, wash and drain | **750 g/1 ½ lb small firm button mush-rooms**

Put them in the marinade, cover, and cook gently for 7 - 10 minutes
Add salt and pepper to taste
Allow to cool in the marinade, and let them stand for several hours or over-night
Pour off marinade shortly before serving
Stir mushrooms with | **1 - 2 tbsp chopped parsley**

and arrange on 6 glass plates
Garnish with | **tomato wedges parsley**
Serve with: | **French bread and butter**

Imperial fillet of beef

Stuffed cucumbers

Peel | **1 - 2 cucumbers**
and cut into 5 cm/2 ½ in pieces
Remove centres, and sprinkle them in-side and out with | **salt pepper**

Leave to stand so that the liquid is drawn out

For the filling
Drain and flake | **150 g/5 oz tinned tuna fish**
Shell and dice | **2 hard-boiled eggs**
Mix eggs with tuna fish
Beat | **2 egg yolks**
1 - 2 tsp mustard
1 tbsp vinegar or lemon juice
salt
pepper
sugar

until thick
Gradually beat in | **125 ml/4 fl oz salad oil**

Mix mayonnaise with tuna fish and use to fill the cucumber pieces
Garnish with | **lemon slices tomato wedges parsley**

Imperial fillet of beef
(2 servings)

Wash and dry | **400 g/14 oz beef fillet**
and cut into 2 slices
Rub with | **salt**
pepper
1 tsp Provence herbs
Peel and dice | **1 onion**
If desired, peel | **1 clove of garlic**

and rub frying pan with it
Heat | **2 - 3 tbsp cooking oil**
in frying pan and fry meat slices on both sides
Remove meat from pan, and keep warm
Pour fat out of pan
Melt | **1 - 2 tbsp butter**
in it, and sauté onion until transparent
Add | **125 ml/4 fl oz white wine**
Stir in | **150 ml/5 fl oz double cream**

and bring to the boil for a short time
Season to taste with salt, pepper and | **meat extract**
Stir in | **1 tbsp chopped parsley**
Cut | **2 slices white bread (about 3 cm/1 ½ in thick)**

into strips
Fry them on all sides in | **butter**
Arrange bread strips on a warm serving dish
Slice each piece of meat in half once more, and arrange on the bread in a fan shape with the sauce
Cooking time: about 3 minutes for each fillet
Serve with: | **asparagus button mushrooms**
Variation:
Warm | **3 tbsp brandy**
pour it over the meat, and set alight

Quark dish with raspberries

Put into a small pan | **1 pkt gelatine**
5 tbsp cold water
Stir together, and leave to soak for 10

Quark dish with raspberries

minutes	
Warm, while stirring, until dissolved	
Stir together	**250 g/8 oz full fat quark (curd cheese)**
	75 g/3 oz sugar
	juice from 1 lemon
Beat lukewarm gelatine solution into quark together with	**40 g/1 ½ oz blanched chopped almonds**
	4 tbsp instant porridge oats
Carefully fold in	**300 g/10 oz cleaned raspberries**
Rinse out some little moulds with cold water, and put quark mixture into them	
Put into refrigerator to set	
Turn them out on to glass dishes and decorate with	**raspberries**
and, if desired, with	**whipped cream**

Grapefruit muesli
(2 servings)

Wash and dry	**1 grapefruit**
Cut it in half across, and carefully loosen flesh from membranes with a sharp pointed knife	
Remove white pith and membranes	

Wash, halve and stone	**1 peach**
Cut both ingredients into small pieces and mix with	**150 ml/5 fl oz yoghurt**
	1 - 2 tbsp sugar
Fold in	**4 tbsp oatflakes**
Put mixture into grapefruit halves, and garnish with	**cocktail cherries**

Grapefruit muesli

Omelettes

Beat well	**4 eggs** **½ tsp salt** **4 tbsp milk** **4 tbsp instant porridge oats**
Melt a little of	**2 tbsp butter or margarine**

in a frying pan, and add about ¼ of the egg mixture
Cook until golden brown on both sides
Before turning omelette, add a little more butter
Keep finished omelette warm while cooking the rest in the same way

Serve with:	**sugared strawberries redcurrants raspberries**

Omelettes

Muesli to wake you up
(Illustrated on pages 188-189)

Wash	**75 g/3 oz fresh strawberries**
and drain well Remove stalks, and halve large berries	
Wash	**50 g/2 oz redcurrants**
and drain well Using a fork, strip berries from stems Put fruit into a bowl, and sprinkle with	**2 - 3 heaped tbsp rolled oats** **1 - 2 tbsp preserving sugar**
Pour on	**250 ml/8 fl oz cold milk**

Grape glasses
(2 - 3 servings)

Melt in a pan	**1 tbsp butter**
Stirring constantly, fry	**8 tbsp oatflakes**
until golden yellow, and sprinkle with then fry for a further 1 minute	**1 tbsp sugar**
Wash, halve and remove pips from	**250 g/8 oz white or black grapes**
Stir smoothly together	**250 g/8 oz full fat quark** **1 tbsp lemon juice** **2 tbsp sugar**

Layer the grapes, quark and oats into glasses

Vegetarian's apple
(2 servings)

Wash, dry and quarter	**2 medium apples**
Remove cores, and cut into small pieces	
Mix with	**150 ml/5 fl oz yoghurt** **1 tbsp sugar**
Stir in	**6 heaped tbsp oatflakes**
Variation: Mix in	**grated hazelnuts, washed raisins or a little ground cinnamon**

Tropical muesli

Melt	**1 tbsp butter**
in a pan and fry until golden yellow stirring constantly	**8 tbsp oatflakes**
Sprinkle with	**1 tbsp sugar**
and fry for a further 1 minute, then allow to cool	

Grilled pineapple

Halve strawberries and grapes, and remove pips from grapes	**200 g/6 oz white grapes**
Put all the fruit in a bowl and mix together	
Sprinkle with	**1 tbsp sugar**
Pour on	**4 tbsp cream sherry**
Cover, and leave to stand at room temperature for about ½ hour	
Just before serving, sprinkle with	**1 tbsp finely chopped pistachio nuts**

Grilled pineapple

Put 4 of	**8 slices tinned pineapple**
into a greased soufflé dish	
Spread them with	**2 tbsp marmalade**
and lay the remaining pineapple slices on top	
Melt	**50 g/2 oz butter**
Add to the butter	**125 g/4 oz fine rolled oats**
	50 g/2 oz sugar
	50 g/2 oz blanched chopped almonds
and mix them all together	
Place this over the pineapple slices	
Put the dish in a preheated oven	
Serve hot or cold, garnished with	**strips of orange peel orange segments**
Electricity: 200° C/400° F	
Gas: Mark 6	
Grilling time: about 10 minutes	
Serve with:	**whipped cream**

Strawberry milk shake

Wash and drain	**250 g/8 oz fresh strawberries**
Remove stalks, and purée with an electric mixer or liquidizer	
Gradually stir in	**500 ml/1 pint yoghurt**
	500 ml/1 pint milk
Add	**about 3 tbsp sugar**
to taste	
Stir in	**4 heaped tbsp instant porridge oats oatflakes fried in butter**
Put into glasses, and garnish with	**strawberry halves**
Serve well-chilled	

Peel and stone	**1 mango**
Peel and slice	**2 kiwifruit**
	2 bananas
Wash, halve and stone	**2 nectarines or peaches**
and cut into slices	
Put the fruit slices into a dish and stir in	**1 tbsp lemon juice**
	2 tbsp sugar
Add	**200 g/6 oz yoghurt**
and sprinkle with the crunchy flakes	

Fruit salad with cream sherry

Drain and cut into pieces	**3 slices tinned pineapple**
Cut	**4 peach halves**
into thin wedges	
Peel and slice	**3 kiwifruit**
	1 banana
Wash, drain well and remove stalks from	**200 g/6 oz fresh strawberries**

**DELICATE
SPECIALITIES**

Mixed starters (entrées)
(Recipe on p. 200)

Crayfish tails in shallot zabaglione

Crayfish tails in shallot zabaglione

Thoroughly scrub	600 - 750 g/1¼ - 1½ lb crayfish
under running cold water	
Bring to the boil	3 l/6 pints water
	3 - 4 tbsp salt
	1 pinch caraway seeds
	1 tbsp dried dill tips

and allow to boil for about 5 minutes
Put 2 crayfish into the water head first, and bring back to the boil (they will turn red)
Repeat this process until all the crayfish are in the boiling water, and boil them for a further 5 minutes
Remove their tails from the shells, and allow to cool

For the shallot zabaglione

Sieve the crayfish water, and measure out 250 ml/8 fl oz	
Peel and finely dice	5 shallots
and put them into the liquid with	1 tbsp shallot or tarragon vinegar

Bring to the boil, and allow to boil until all except 5 - 6 tbsp has evaporated

Stir in	2 egg yolks
	salt
	pepper

and heat gently over hot water, while beating with an egg whisk, until mixture has doubled in volume and is light and creamy

Arrange the crayfish tails on a serving dish and garnish with	dill sprigs

Put the shallot zabaglione in the middle of the dish or serve separately

Mixed starters (Entrées)
(Illustrated on pages 198-199)

Thoroughly scrub under running cold water about	1 kg/2 lb crayfish (about 8)
Bring to the boil	2 1/4 pints water
	3 tbsp salt
	¼ tsp caraway seeds
	1 tbsp dried dill tips

Allow to boil for about 5 minutes, then put in 2 crayfish head first, and bring back to the boil (they will turn red)
Repeat this until all the crayfish are in the water, bringing it back to the boil each time a pair of crayfish are added
Boil for about 10 minutes

Line a large bowl with	1 bunch washed dill

Put the still hot crayfish into the bowl, sieve the liquid over them, and allow to cool
Cover with baking foil, and leave in a cold place for 10 - 12 hours
Remove the crayfish from the liquid, break them open, and remove the flesh from the tails
Arrange them on a serving platter

Garnish with 4 crayfish 'noses' (the front sections) and	peeled halved avocado rings mushroom slices watercress dill sprigs
Wash	2 trout (each 250 - 300 g/8 - 10 oz)
under running cold water	
Bring to the boil	125 ml/4 fl oz white wine
	125 ml/4 fl oz water
	10 peppercorns
	1 tbsp wine vinegar
	1 rounded tsp salt

Add trout, cover, bring back to the boil, and cook for about 15 minutes
Remove trout and allow to cool

For the sauce

Bring fish stock to the boil	
Add	150 ml/5 fl oz double cream
and bring quickly to the boil whilst stirring	
Season with	salt
	pepper
	sugar

and pour through a fine sieve
Allow to cool, stirring now and then
Remove head and skin from trout, and

carefully remove bones
Put them on the plate with the crayfish
Pour some of the sauce over the trout,
and serve the rest separately
Serve with: **toast and butter**

Crab salad in its shell

Shell	**4 cooked crabs (each about 400 g/14 oz)**
Slice the crabmeat finely	
Rinse shells out with water	
Remove withered leaves from	**1 head of lettuce**
Loosen remaining leaves from stalk, wash, drain and shred finely	
Wash	**150 g/5 oz celery**
Cut into fine strips	

Line crab shells with lettuce and celery,
and put the crabmeat on top

For the salad dressing
Boil **1 egg**
for about 3 minutes and plunge into
cold water
Allow to cool, then crack, and put into
a bowl
Stir the egg with **1 - 2 tbsp vinegar**

Add	**1 tsp mustard**
	1 tsp salt
	freshly ground pepper
to taste	
Stir in	**3 - 4 tbsp salad oil**
	1 tbsp finely chopped chives

Spread the dressing over the crab and
garnish with **dill sprigs**

Turkey salad with kiwifruit

Cut into strips	**125 g/4 oz smoked turkey breast**
Peel and cut into strips	**1 kiwifruit**
Drain and halve	**125 g/4 oz tinned pineapple slices**

For the salad dressing
Stir together	**1 tbsp mayonnaise**
	4 tbsp yoghurt
	1 - 2 tsp mustard
Season with	**salt**
	pepper
Remove the withered leaves from	**1 - 2 heads of chicory**

Loosen leaves from stalk, wash and

Crab salad in its shell

drain, and line a bowl with them
Put the salad ingredients into the bowl,
and spread the dressing over them

Duck galantine

Wash and dry	**1 oven-ready duck (about 1 kg/2 lb)**
Cut off	**wings**
Remove bones	
Put bones and wings in	**2 1/4 pints salted water**
and bring to the boil	
Cook for about 2 hours	
Clean	**1 leek**
	1 carrot
	1 turnip
	1 parsley spray
Wash and halve	**1 orange**

Put the vegetables and the orange into
the broth, and cook together for about
20 minutes
Pour the broth through a colander, and
put on one side
Lay the boned duck, skin side down, on
a tea towel

Spread on to the duck	**500 g/1 lb pork sausagemeat**
Sprinkle on	**2 tbsp shelled pistachio nuts**
Dice	**125 g/4 oz salted tongue**

and put on top of the sausagemeat
Roll up the boned duck, and wrap
tightly in the tea towel
Sew up the ends, and bind the wrapped
duck round and round with kitchen
thread
Put into the broth, bring to the boil, and
cook for $2\frac{1}{4}$ - $2\frac{1}{2}$ hours
Take care that it is always covered with
the liquid, and add more water if necessary as the broth evaporates
Allow the cooked galantine to cool in
the broth
Remove from the broth, and remove
thread and cloth
Slice fairly thickly, and arrange the

slices on	**washed lettuce leaves**
with	**pickled mushrooms**
	bean salad

For the sauce

Stir	**5 - 6 tbsp redcurrant preserve**
	a little red wine

smoothly together
Serve with the galantine

Belle de nuit salad

Pike-perch and field mushroom salad

Belle de nuit salad

Arrange together	**20 cooked and shelled crayfish (see page 232)**
	1 - 2 slices bottled black truffles
For the salad dressing	
Stir together	**4 tbsp salad oil**
	2 tbsp wine vinegar
	1 tsp hot mustard
Season to taste with	**salt**
	pepper
Spread the dressing over the crayfish	
Garnish with	**1 tomato rose**
	parsley

Pike-perch and field mushroom salad
(2 servings)

Halve and wash under running cold water	**300 g/10 oz pike-perch fillet**
Pat dry, and sprinkle with	**lemon juice**
Leave to stand for about 15 minutes, then cook 5 - 7 minutes in	**125 ml/4 fl oz white wine**
Season with	**salt**
	pepper
Allow to cool and drain well	
Cut stalks off	**250 g/8 oz field mush-rooms**
Wash and drain	
Melt	**2 tbsp butter**
and sauté mushrooms in it for	

3 - 4 minutes	
Sprinkle with	**1 tbsp lemon juice**
and season with salt and pepper	
Arrange mushrooms on	**washed lettuce leaves**
and put fish on top	
Garnish with	**strips of tomato**
	chervil
	chives
For the salad dressing	
Stir together	**1 tbsp olive oil**
	1 tbsp dry sherry
	1/2 tsp mustard
	2 tbsp double cream
Stir in	**2 tbsp finely chopped chives**
and season to taste with salt and pepper	
Pour a little of dressing over the salad	
and serve the rest separately	

Fruit platter with champagne purée and cinnamon knights

Peel, halve, and stone	**1 ripe mango**
	1 ripe papaya
Purée in a mixer with	**2 tbsp honey**
	3 - 4 tbsp Grand Marnier orange liqueur
and leave in a cold place	
Put on to 4 plates	**750 g/1½ lb prepared fruit**
	(e.g. small yellow plums,
	raspberries,
	bilberries,
	cherries,

Fruit platter with champagne purée and cinnamon knights

strawberries,
blackberries,
redcurrants)

and sprinkle with | a little sugar
Cut | 1 loaf raisin bread
into 2 cm/1 in thick slices and cut out
5 cm/2½ in diameter rounds from them
Lay them on a platter
Beat together | 125 ml/4 fl oz milk
1 egg
25 g/1 oz sugar
1 pkt vanilla sugar

and pour over the raisin bread
allow it to soak in a little (but do not
leave to become too soft)
Dip rounds in | about 3 tbsp fine
breadcrumbs
on both sides
Heat | margarine
in a milk pan and fry bread in it on both

sides
Sprinkle with | cinnamon sugar
and arrange on top of the fruit
Stir into the purée enough | dry champagne
to make it a little thinner, and spread it
over the fruit

Beef slices in juniper and red wine sauce

Wash and dry | 750 g/1½ lb topside of beef
Remove the skin if necessary
Season with | salt
pepper
Heat | 2 tbsp butter
in a roasting tin and fry meat on all

Beef slices in juniper and red wine sauce

sides	
Put meat and tin into a preheated oven	
As soon as the meat juices begin to brown, add a little	**hot water**
and replace the evaporated liquid as and when necessary	
Electricity: 225° - 250° C/450° - 500° F	
Gas: Mark 7 - 9	
Roasting time: 45 - 60 minutes	
Put the cooked meat on to a serving dish and cover with baking foil	
Keep warm	

For the juniper and red wine sauce

Peel and finely dice	**4 - 5 shallots**
Add them to the meat juices with	**6 - 8 juniper berries**
and cook for about 1 minute	
Add	**375 ml/12 fl oz red wine**
and bring to the boil	
Boil until all except about 150 ml/5 fl oz	

has evaporated	
Pour sauce through a sieve, and put the juniper berries back in	
Bring to the boil again, and remove from heat	
Stir in	**125 g/4 oz softened butter**
and heat but do not boil	
Add salt and pepper to taste	
Carve meat thinly, and serve with the sauce and	**sautéed mushrooms**

Strawberry cream with strawberry sauce

For the strawberry cream

Wash	**250 g/8 oz fresh**

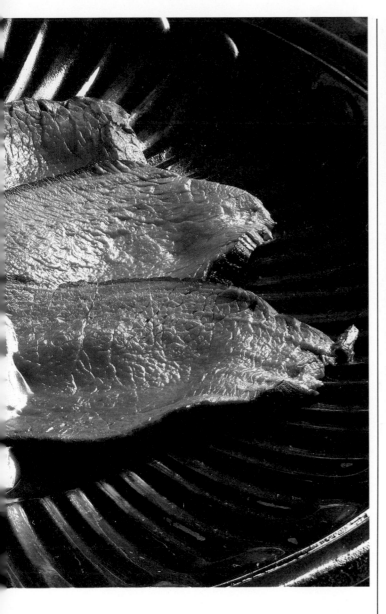

Strawberry cream with strawberry sauce

Stir in lukewarm gelatine solution and
leave in a cold place
As soon as cream begins to thicken,
whip   **4 egg whites**
until stiff and carefully fold them into
cream
Put the strawberry cream into a dish,
and stand in a cold place to set

For the strawberry sauce
Wash   **250 g/8 oz fresh
strawberries**
and drain well
Remove stalks, and rub through a sieve
Stir together with   **2 small glasses
advocaat**

Scoop out balls of set strawberry cream
with an ice-cream scoop, and arrange on
a serving dish
Garnish with   **mint leaves
halved strawberries**

Serve with the strawberry sauce

---

    strawberries
and drain well
Remove stalks and sprinkle with   **50 g/2 oz sugar**
Rub them through a sieve or purée
them in a mixer
Stir together   **2 pkts gelatine
6 tbsp cold water**

and leave to soak for 10 minutes
Warm, whilst stirring, until dissolved,
then leave in a cool place
Beat strawberry pulp with   **4 egg yolks
2 small glasses
advocaat**

over hot water until it forms a thick
cream

**DRESSED DISHES
AND
COLD BUFFETS**
Dressed veal medallions
(Recipes on p. 214-215)

Smoked pork platter

Smoked pork platter
(6 - 8 servings)

Wash and dry	**1½ kg/3 lb boneless smoked pork loin**

Wrap it in a large sheet of baking foil, seal it, and put it in a preheated oven
Electricity: 200° C/400° F
Gas: Mark 6
Cooking time: about 50 minutes
Remove cooked meat from oven, and leave to stand for a short time
Open the foil, and allow meat to cool
Carve it into finger-thick slices, and arrange on a serving dish

Garnish with	**lemon slices**
	bay leaves
Serve with:	**bread roll ring**
	salads

Fillets of beef slices, fruity or spicy

Wash and dry	**2 × 1 kg/2 lb fillets of beef**

Remove the skin if necessary

Heat	**4 - 5 tbsp cooking oil**

in a large frying pan and fry the fillets on both sides for about 5 minutes

Season with	**salt**
	pepper

and put into an ovenproof dish
Pour the frying oil over them, and put in a preheated oven
Turn them now and again while they are roasting, and baste with the liquid
Electricity: 225° - 250° C/450° - 500° F

Gas: Mark 8 - 9
Roasting time: about 30 minutes
Remove the cooked fillets from the oven and allow to cool
Cut each fillet into 14 - 16 slices, and garnish as follows:

Suggestion 1

Drain	**12 tinned apricot halves**
and fill each one with	**a cocktail cherry**

On 3 fillet slices arrange 2 apricot halves

and garnish with	**lemon balm**

Suggestion 2

Purée with an electric mixer	**250 g/8 oz cooked peas**

and rub through a sieve

Stir together in a small pan	**1 tsp gelatine**
	1 tbsp water

and leave to soak for 10 minutes
Warm, whilst stirring until dissolved
Stir the gelatine into the pea purée

Whip	**150 ml/5 fl oz double cream**

and fold it into the purée

Add	**salt**
	pepper
	grated nutmeg
	mushroom soya sauce

to taste
Put it into a piping bag with a rosette nozzle, and pipe a ring around the edges of 6 fillet slices

Halve	**1 - 2 tomatoes**

Remove pips and cores and dice the flesh
Allow to drain on kitchen paper, and use to fill centre of the piped rings

Garnish with	**parsley leaves**

Suggestion 3

Peel and remove the stone from	**½ ripe mango**

Cut it into 12 segments
On 6 fillet slices, put 2 mango slices in the form of a cross, and garnish with

one of	**6 walnut halves**

Suggestion 4

Put in a cold place	**75 g/3 oz tinned goose liver pâté**

cut it into 6 slices, and lay on 6 fillet slices

Drain	**12 tinned mandarin segments**

and lay 2 of them on every slice of pâté

Garnish with	**shelled pistachio nuts**

Suggestion 5

Wash and pat dry	**250 g/8 oz chicken livers**

Remove the skin if necessary

Heat	**1 tbsp butter**

Fillets of beef slices, fruity or spicy

and fry liver on all sides for about 3 minutes	
Season with	**salt**
	pepper
	Italian herbs
Purée in an electric mixer	
Stir into	**75 g/3 oz softened butter**
Add, to taste, more salt, pepper and	**madeira or brandy**
Put mixture into a piping bag with a rosette nozzle, and pipe out rosettes on to about 8 fillet slices	
Shell and slice	**1 hard-boiled egg**
and lay one slice on each rosette	
Slice	**2 - 3 stuffed olives**
and lay one slice on each slice of egg	
Suggestion 6	
Drain	**3 tbsp tinned man-**

	darin segments
and divide them among 3 fillet slices	
Garnish with	**chopped pistachio nuts**
For the aspic	
Stir	**1 pkt gelatine**
	4 tbsp cold water
together in a small pan and leave to soak for 10 minutes	
Warm, while stirring, until dissolved	
Bring	**400 ml/14 fl oz clear tinned turtle soup**
to the boil	
Remove from heat, and sieve	
Stir in	**1 - 2 tbsp madeira**
Add gelatine solution, and stir until dissolved	
Put in a cold place	
As soon as it begins to thicken, spread	

the gelatine solution over the fillet slices
Pour the remaining gelatine solution on to a plate and put it into the refrigerator to set
Cut the set aspic into small cubes, and arrange them on a large platter with the glazed fillet slices

Serve with: **French bread and butter**

Saddle of lamb in pastry

For the quark puff pastry

Sieve **250 g/8 oz plain flour**
on to a pastry board
Make a hollow in the middle
Put **250 g/8 oz low fat quark (curd cheese) salt**

into hollow, and mix with some of the flour to make a thick paste
Cut **250 g/8 oz cold butter**
into pieces and add it to the paste
Cover it with flour, and quickly knead to a smooth dough, working from the middle outwards
Leave it in a cold place for 2 - 3 hours, or overnight

Bone **2 loins of lamb (each about 1¼ kg/2½ lb)**
and trim fat from the 4 pieces
Wash and dry the meat, and place pieces of meat in pairs, tying together with kitchen thread
Season with **salt**
pepper
Provence herbs
Peel and crush **3 - 4 cloves of garlic**
and spread over meat
Heat **3 tbsp cooking oil**
and fry meat on all sides for 5 - 6 minutes
Allow to cool, and remove the thread
Cut stalks of **1 kg/2 lb silverbeet or Swiss chard**

Wash leaves thoroughly, and put them into **boiling salted water**
Cook for 2 - 3 minutes
Transfer to a colander, rinse with cold water, and allow to drain
Wash the stalks, cut into ½ cm/¼ in wide strips, and put into the boiling water
Cook for 2 - 3 minutes, then allow to drain

For the sauce
Peel and crush **1 - 2 cloves of garlic**
Stir them together with **2 tbsp olive oil**

Saddle of lamb in pastry

	2 tbsp white wine vinegar 1 tsp mustard
Add salt and pepper to taste, and mix with the silverbeet strips	
Allow to stand to absorb flavours	
Roll out half of the pastry to a 35 cm/ 14 in square	
Cut off from the sides a 2-3 cm/1-1½ in wide strip and set to one side for garnishing	
In the middle of the dough lay ¼ of	250 g/8 oz streaky bacon (very thin rashers)
and lay about 4 silverbeet leaves on top	
Lay 2 of the 4 pieces of meat on top of that, cover with 4 silverbeet leaves, and then with ¼ of the streaky bacon	
Brush the edges of the pastry with a little of	1 beaten egg white
Fold the pastry over the meat, and lay it, smooth side uppermost, on a baking tray which has been rinsed with water	
Cut 2 small holes in the upper surface of the pastry	
Knead the remaining pastry, roll it out, and cut out decorative shapes	
Brush these with the egg white and stick them on to the upper surface of the pastry	
Prepare the second pastry half with the remaining ingredients in the same way	
Beat together	1 egg yolk 1 tbsp milk
and brush over the pastry parcels	
Put them in a preheated oven	
Electricity: 200° - 225° C/400° - 425° F	
Gas: Mark 6 - 7	
Baking time: about 40 minutes	
Allow the cooked lamb to cool, and arrange whole on a serving dish	
Garnish with	silverbeet
Cut the remaining beet leaves into strips and add to the marinated beet stalks	
Wash, dry and halve	4 medium beef tomatoes (about 800 g/1 ¾ lb)
Remove pulp, and sprinkle the insides with pepper	
Season the silverbeet salad to taste with salt, pepper and	white wine
Put some of it into the tomatoes, and put them on the plate with the meat	
Serve the remaining salad separately in a glass bowl	

Salmon mousse

Wash	500 g/1 lb salmon and salmon head
under running cold water and pat dry	
Bring to the boil	1 1/2 pints salted

Salmon mousse

	water 2 bay leaves coriander seeds dried sage 5 tbsp tarragon vinegar 4 lemon slices
Add the salmon head, and bring back to the boil	
Cook for about 30 minutes, and remove the head	
Add the salmon, and simmer for about 10 minutes (do not boil, or the salmon will become dry)	
Allow to cool in the liquid, then remove the salmon	
Remove skin and bones, and purée fish with an electric mixer	
Stir	2 rounded tsp gelatine 3 tbsp cold water
together in a small pan and leave to soak for 10 minutes	
Warm, while stirring, until dissolved	
Stir in	1 tbsp lemon juice
and stir solution into the puréed salmon	
Whip	125 ml/4 fl oz double cream
until stiff and fold in, together with	2 tbsp chopped dill
Season with	salt pepper
Put the mixture into 4 small moulds which have been rinsed out with cold water, and level the surfaces	
Leave in refrigerator to set, then turn out on to a serving dish	
Garnish with	tomato roses dill sprigs
If desired, arrange	steamed salmon steaks
on the plate with the mousse	

213

Mustard roast

Wash and dry	**1 kg/2 lb boneless pork loin with fillet**
Using a sharp knife, make a deep cut into it lengthways	
Rub with	**salt**
	pepper
For the filling	
Stir together	**2 tbsp hot mustard**
	2 tbsp French spiced mustard
Peel and finely dice	**2 onions**
Peel and crush	**1 small clove of garlic**
Mix these 2 ingredients with the mustard, together with	**3 bunches chopped mixed herbs**

Put the mixture into the pocket cut into the meat, and spread the remaining mixture over the meat
Tie the meat up with kitchen thread, and wrap it in a large sheet of baking foil
Seal the foil, and put it on the wire rack in a preheated oven
Electricity: 200° C/400° F
Gas: Mark 6
Roasting time: about 1 hour
Remove the cooked meat from the oven, and allow to stand for a while
Open the foil, and allow to cool
Remove thread, carve into slices and arrange on a serving dish

Garnish with	**chervil**
	tomato roses
	corn on the cob
	small white onions
Serve with:	**wholemeal, granary or German rye bread**

Meat balls with roquefort filling

Soak	**1 bread roll**
in cold water and squeeze well	
Put it into a bowl with	**500 g/1 lb minced beef**
Peel and finely dice	**1 onion**
	1 clove of garlic
Heat	**1 tbsp cooking oil**
and cook the onion and garlic in it until transparent, then stir into the meat	
Add	**2 eggs**
	2 tbsp chopped parsley
	2 tbsp tomato ketchup

and mix well together, kneading

Season with	**salt**
	pepper
Cut	**75 - 100 g/3 - 4 oz roquefort cheese**

into small pieces
Make 22 - 24 walnut-sized balls from the meat mixture, press a hole in each one, insert a piece of cheese, then make it into a ball again

Roll the balls in	**3 tbsp fine breadcrumbs**

Deep fry them in 2 - 3 batches in hot cooking oil for 5 minutes
Drain on kitchen paper, and serve hot or cold

Roman veal schnitzel

Remove the skin from	**8 veal schnitzels (each about 125 g/ 4 oz)**
if necessary	
Heat	**3 tbsp olive oil**
and fry the schnitzels on both sides for about 2 minutes	
Sprinkle with	**salt**
	pepper
Remove from pan and keep warm	
Fry	**8 slices parma ham (the same size as the schnitzels)**
on both sides in the schnitzel fat	
Add	**15 fresh sage leaves**
and heat together	

Lay 1 sage leaf and then a slice of ham on each schnitzel
Fold the schnitzels over, and fasten 1 sage leaf on top of them with a wooden cocktail stick

Add	**125 ml/4 fl oz white wine**

to the pan juices and bring to the boil
Pour this over the schnitzels, and serve hot or cold

Serve with:	**French bread**
	tomato salad

Dressed veal medallions
(Illustrated on pages 208-209)

Wash and dry	**250 g/8 oz veal fillet**
Remove sinews, and cut meat into 4 equal slices	
Pound them very gently	
Season with	**salt**
	pepper
Heat	**1 tbsp butter or margarine**

and fry meat on both sides for 5 - 6 minutes

Dressed veal medallions, Dressed eggs, Dressed artichoke hearts

Remove meat and lay it on a plate
Sprinkle with | **1 tbsp brandy**
and allow to cool
Stir | **75 g/3 oz tinned calf's liver pâté**
1 tbsp double cream

until creamy
Put into a piping bag with a star nozzle,
and pipe on to the veal medallions
Garnish with | **aspic cubes (page 124)**
quartered cocktail cherries
tinned mandarin segments
thyme leaves
Serve with: | **salads**
toast and butter

Dressed eggs
(Illustrated on pages 208-209)

Shell and halve lengthways | **4 hard-boiled eggs**
Remove yolks and rub through a fine sieve
Stir together with | **125 g/4 oz full fat cream cheese**
1 tbsp double cream
Season with | **salt**
pepper
sweet paprika
curry powder

Put it into a piping bag with a star nozzle, and use to fill the egg whites
Garnish with | **shrimps**
quartered lemon slices
dill sprigs

Dressed artichoke hearts
(Illustrated on pages 208-209)

Drain | **8 - 10 tinned artichoke hearts**
Stir | **150 g/5 oz tinned chicken liver pâté**
2 tbsp double cream
1 tbsp brandy
together until creamy
Put it into a piping bag with a star nozzle, and pipe on to the artichoke hearts
Garnish with | **quartered kiwifruit slices**
chopped tarragon leaves
Serve with: | **French bread and butter**

"The morning after" (hangover) breakfast
(for 6 - 8 people)

Roll up | **8 white herring fillets**
and stand them upright in | **onion rings**
Trim (but do not cut off the green parts completely) and wash | **2 bunches of radishes**
Arrange the herrings, radishes, and | **1 smoked bloater (kipper)**
on a serving platter
Garnish the herrings with | **dill**
Cut | **1 piece Swiss cheese**
1 piece roquefort cheese
into cubes and arrange them on a serving dish with | **tomato wedges**

215

Put	**125 g/4 oz bottled salmon caviar**
into a little dish, sprinkle	**1 tbsp diced onion**
around the edges and garnish with	**chopped dill**
Arrange	**300 g/10 oz smoked salmon slices**
on	**washed lettuce leaves**
and garnish with	**lemon slices**
Put	**mustard and cream sauce (see page 93)**
into a small dish	

Dolores salad

Peel	**375 g/12 oz potatoes cooked in their skins**
and cut into slices or sticks	
Shell and dice	**1 - 2 hard-boiled eggs**
Mix the potatoes and eggs with	**250 g/8 oz fresh peeled prawns**
and arrange in a salad bowl	
For the salad dressing	
Stir together	**150 ml/5 fl oz double cream**
	2 tbsp tomato ketchup
	1 tbsp port
	1 tsp vinegar essence
Season with	**salt**
	pepper
	sugar
Pour the dressing over the salad, and sprinkle with	**finely chopped dill**
Arrange	**about 250 g/8 oz various kinds of salami**
	250 g/8 oz piece of liver sausage
on a serving dish, then put	**mustard and cream sauce (see page 93)**
into a small dish and sprinkle with	**finely chopped chives**

Classic buffet
(for 20 people)

Mixed fish platter	**recipe page 59**
Crispy coated plaice fillets	**recipe page 61**
Vegetables with avocado cream	**recipe page 23**
* Duck with figs	**recipe page 82**
* Roast beef with herbs	**recipe page 75**
* Remoulade sauce	**recipe page 90**
* Fillet of pork Giselle	**recipe page 71**
Button mushroom salad	**recipe page 41**
	(double quantities)

Classic buffet

216

> * the recipes indicated with an asterisk can be prepared the day before, so that they only need to be seasoned again and arranged on serving dishes on the day

Party buffet

Party buffet

Gorgonzola mousse

Stir	**1 pkt gelatine** **3 tbsp cold water**
together in a small pan and leave to soak for 10 minutes	
Rub	**250 g/8 oz gorgonzola cheese**
through a sieve	
Stir it together with	**250 ml/8 fl oz cream** **2 tbsp dry sherry**
Season with	**pepper** **tabasco sauce**
Put into a small bowl over a pan of hot water, and heat	
Stir in the gelatine, and stir until dissolved	
Allow to cool	
Whip	**125 ml/4 fl oz double cream**
until stiff and fold into the mixture	
Put into a mould, and leave in the freezing compartment of refrigerator to set	
Dip base of mould briefly in hot water, and then turn out on to a plate	
Garnish with	**lime slices**

Brown rice salad with crayfish

Put into	**250 g/8 oz brown rice** **750 ml/1½ pint boiling salted water**

Bring back to the boil, and cook for about 20 minutes
Transfer it to a colander, and rinse with cold water
Drain and allow to cool

Heat	**2 tbsp cooking oil**

and fry rice in it, turning the rice constantly
Allow to cool

Shell	**10 crayfish**

Remove the dark intestine

For the salad dressing

Stir together	**4 tbsp salad oil** **2 - 3 tbsp tarragon vinegar**
Season with	**salt** **pepper** **sugar**

Mix the dressing with the rice, and add the crayfish
Allow to stand to absorb flavours and season again with salt and pepper if necessary

Sprinkle with	**finely chopped chives**

Smoked pork with apple in pastry

For the filling

Peel, quarter, core, and slice	**750 g/1½ lb dessert apples (e.g. Cox's Orange)**
Bring to the boil	**125 ml/4 fl oz water** **250 ml/8 fl oz white wine** **50 g/2 oz sugar**

Add apple slices and bring back to the boil
Allow to cook for a few minutes, then drain in a colander, collecting the cooking liquid
Allow apples to cool

Wash and dry	**2 kg/4 lb lean boneless smoked pork**

Put it onto a wire rack in a roasting tin

Heat	**2 tbsp cooking oil**

and brush it over the meat
Put the meat into a preheated oven, and roast for about 25 minutes to brown it

If necessary, add a little of the	**apple liquid**

Remove the meat from oven and allow to cool

For the pastry

Allow	**600 g/1 lb 5 oz frozen puff pastry**

to thaw according to instructions given on packet

Roll out to three times the size of the meat (reserve some pastry for garnishing)

Lay the meat on centre of the pastry, and put layers of apple slices on the meat

Fold the pastry over the meat

Brush the joins of the pastry with a little	**beaten egg white**

and press well together

Lay it, smooth side underneath, on a baking tray which has been rinsed with water

Cut reserved pastry into strips, brush them with the rest of the egg white, and use them to garnish the upper surface of the pastry

Prick the upper surface of the pastry several times with a wooden cocktail stick

Beat together	**1 egg yolk** **a little milk**

and brush over the pastry

Put it into a preheated oven

Electricity: 200° - 225° C/400° - 425° F

Gas: Mark 6 - 7

Baking time: about 40 minutes

Lamb curry

Wash	**about 1½ kg/3 lb shoulder of lamb (bone in)**
and put it into	**boiling salted water**

Remove the scum and cook for about 2 hours

Remove it from the liquid

Remove the meat from the bone, and dice it

Sieve the liquid

Peel and dice	**375 g/12 oz onions**
Melt	**1 - 2 tbsp margarine**

and sauté onions in it

Add the lamb and season with	**salt** **pepper** **garlic salt** **1 - 2 tbsp curry powder**
Fry meat thoroughly, then add a little of	**250 ml/8 fl oz lamb stock**

Stew the meat, replacing the liquid as it evaporates

Sprinkle	**2 tbsp plain flour**

on to lamb, and continue to cook, whilst stirring

Add	**125 ml/4 fl oz lamb stock**
and stir well	
Add	**250 ml/8 fl oz cream**
and continue to cook	
Drain	**400 g/14 oz tinned pineapple pieces**

Add to the curry and continue to heat

Melt	**1 tsp butter**
and fry	**125 g/4 oz nibbed almonds blanched**

until golden yellow

Scatter them over the curry

Cooking time: about 45 minutes (not including pre-cooking of lamb)

Duck en croûte

For the pastry

Sieve	**500 g/1 lb plain flour**
on to a pastry board	
Make a hollow in the middle, put	**3 egg yolks** **125 ml/4 fl oz cold water** **salt**

into it, and mix with some of the flour to a thick paste

Cut	**250 g/8 oz cold butter**

Cover with flour, and working from the middle outwards, quickly knead to a smooth dough

Wrap it in foil, and leave in a cold place

For the filling

Dice	**250 g/8 oz bacon**
Melt	**1 - 2 tbsp butter**

and fry bacon in it until transparent

Scrape and wash	**1 carrot**

and slice it

Peel and dice	**3 onions**

Cook the carrot and onions in the bacon fat

Halve, wash and dry	**1 oven-ready duck (about 2 kg/4 lb)**

Remove fat if necessary, and fry well on all sides in the bacon fat

Season with	**salt** **pepper**
Add	**2 bay leaves** **125 ml/4 fl oz instant chicken stock**
and allow to cook	
Gradually add	**125 ml/4 fl oz white wine**

Cook the duck halves in a covered pan for about 1 hour

Remove lid, and continue to cook until the liquid has evaporated

Remove the duck halves and allow to cool

Mince the bacon and vegetable mixture together with the sediment from the frying pan

Wash, dry and mince **375 g/12 oz veal** and mix with the minced ham and vegetables

Season to taste with salt and **cayenne pepper**
a little dried lemon peel
Pernod

Remove skin and bones from the duck, and cut into medium-sized pieces

Drain **25 g/1 oz tinned truffles**

and coarsely chop them

Roll out the pastry thinly, and use to line a 38 cm/15 in loaf tin (reserve some pastry for the lid)

Layer the meat and vegetable mixture, the duck meat and the truffles in the tin

Roll out the rest of the pastry to form a lid (leave some for garnishing)

Cut some small holes in the pastry lid, lay it on the filling, and press the edges firmly together

Form 2 long thin rolls from the remaining pastry, twist them together, and lay them along the top edges of the pie

Beat together **½ egg yolk**
a little milk

and brush over the pie

Put in a preheated oven
Electricity: 200° C/400° F
Gas: Mark 6
Baking time: 1¼ - 1½ hours
Allow pie to cool in tin

Bean salad with pine kernels

String **1 kg/2 lb young French beans**

If necessary, wash, break them into pieces and put into **boiling salted water**

Bring back to the boil, and cook for about 20 minutes

Drain and allow to cool

Heat **1 tbsp cooking oil**
Roast **125 g/4 oz pine kernels**

until golden brown, and allow to cool

Stir together **6 tbsp salad oil**
3 tbsp aromatic vinegar

Season with **dried oregano**

garlic salt
pepper

Mix the dressing with the beans and allow to marinate

Add more oregano and garlic salt to taste, and mix in the pine kernels

Ham platter

Slice **1 kg/2 lb ham on the bone, or a selection of different sorts of ham**

and arrange them on a wooden platter

Wash **½ small cucumber**

Cut it into decorative slices with a serrated knife

Peel and wash **1 white mouli radish**

and cut it into a spiral with a radish cutter

Clean and wash **radishes**

Cut them into 4 equal quarters, just from the top down to the middle, and then make a cut horizontally across each quarter to cut a half-moon shape in it

Put them into cold water for a short time

Cut **pickled gherkins**

several times from the top almost to the bottom, and open them out like fans

Cut **tomatoes**

into eighths, and remove cores

Wash **parsley**

and remove stalks

Garnish the ham platter with the 6 ingredients

Serve with: **various types of bread and butter**

Cheese platter

Arrange 1 piece each of **emmenthal cheese**
goat's cheese
tilsit cheese
camembert
parmesan cheese
roquefort cheese
gouda cheese

on a platter or cheese board

Garnish with **washed black or white grapes**

KITCHEN TIPS

Only the best tools are
good enough

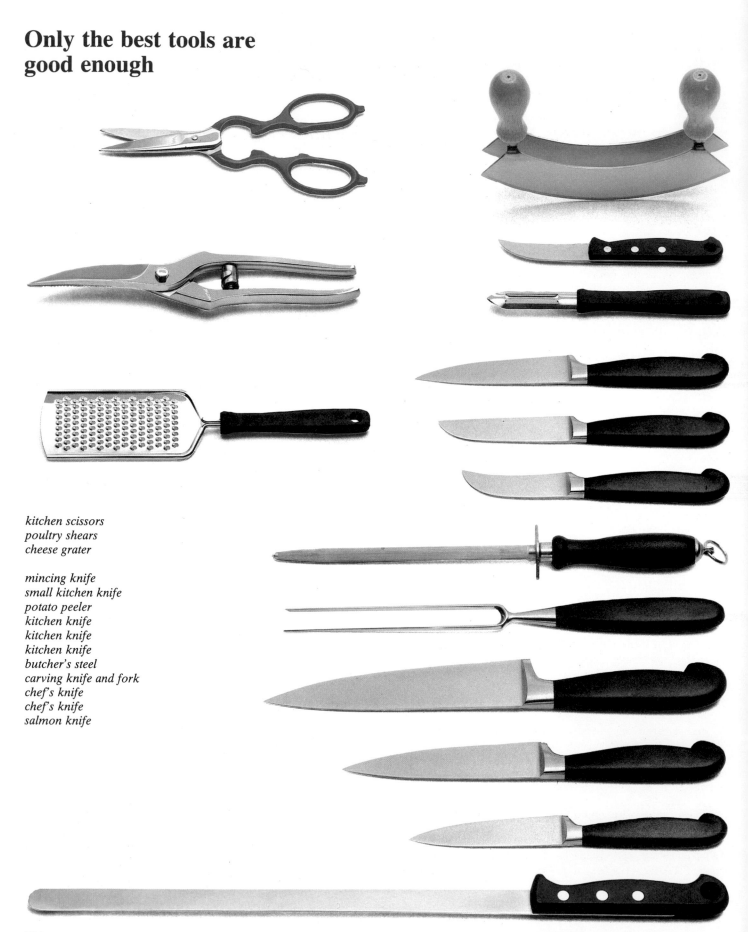

kitchen scissors
poultry shears
cheese grater

mincing knife
small kitchen knife
potato peeler
kitchen knife
kitchen knife
kitchen knife
butcher's steel
carving knife and fork
chef's knife
chef's knife
salmon knife

If you happen to own a hand mixer and an electric processor that does everything from whipping to chopping and mincing, you are very fortunate. And we will assume you have a toaster as well. You can create a wonderful array of cold cuisine dishes with those alone. But there is no point in having them if you do not have the necessary razor-sharp knives. For along with one or two other useful tools, they are the only means of working as precisely as necessary. Even the best tools are only just good enough. So let's have a look at what the well-equipped kitchen should boast:

Kitchen scissors are an all-purpose tool. They can do all sorts of things, from cutting open a packet to chopping herbs. The specially-shaped handles help to open tight lids on jars or bottles, and of course they are perfect for trimming anything from fish fins to radish leaves.

Poultry shears, which have sharp blades and are very strong, are indended for cutting both raw and cooked poultry into portions. They are strong enough to cut bones.

A cheese grater is necessary if you have not got a large grater, or an electric grating attachment. Perfect for small quantities.

A *mincing knife,* double-handled with two parallel curved blades, chops herbs finely and minces vegetables, meat, and fish, whether raw or cooked.

Kitchen knives come in all shapes and sizes for everything from peeling and preparing fruit and vegetables to cutting them up. Among them you will find the chopping knife with its stumpy, pointed blade.

A *butcher's steel* for flat-bladed knives is a must for every professional housewife, even though many housewives already have a mechanical or an electric knife sharpener. It will also sharpen knives with wavy edges, such as bread knives.

A *carving knife and fork* are indispensable for carving large roasts and poultry.

Chef's knives, long or short, are best for slicing both raw and cooked meat evenly.

You'll need a *salmon knife* for slicing a side of smoked salmon into paper-thin, appetising slices.

The *garlic press* is a wonderful invention. You still have to peel the garlic cloves, but the press crushes them.

An *orange peeler* helps to peel citrus fruit in the traditional way, i.e. it removes the pith at the same time.

A *garnishing tool* enables you to form butter rolls and balls, and you can even make grooved butter pats with it.

Egg slicers either slice eggs into eigths, as in the photograph, or into even slices. You can also use them for mushrooms.

An *icing bag* with various nozzles is a must for garnishing and filling with cream cheese, cream, mayonnaise or flavoured butters.

Small, decorative cutters enable you to create attractive shapes from slices of carrot, kohlrabi, cucumber, celery, apple, beetroot, either raw or cooked. There are many shapes available, ranging from 1 cm/$\frac{1}{2}$ in to 5 cm/$2\frac{1}{2}$ in diameter.

garlic press
orange peeler
garnishing tool
egg slicer
icing bag with selection of nozzles
small, decorative cutters

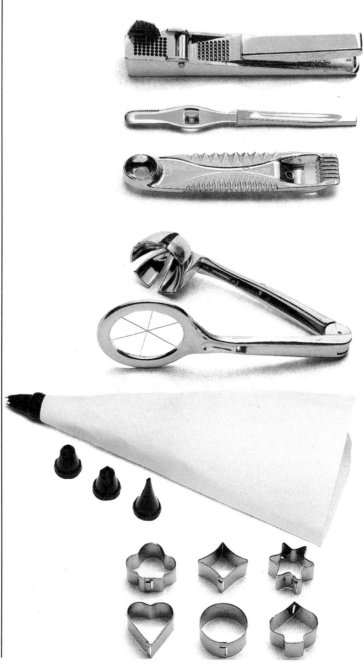

How to clean and fillet fish correctly

Nowadays you can expect to buy cleaned fish portions and fillets from your fishmonger. Or that he will fillet sole or plaice for you, which is not as easy as it looks. But fish does not always arrive on the kitchen table ready for the cooking pot. What about when the keen fishermen of the family bring home their catch, or you happen to buy fresh herrings? Before being prepared for cooking, these fish have to be cleaned, and, depending on the recipe, filleted as well. We show you how to do this in the following photos. You will already know that all fresh fish, whether whole or portions, should be correctly prepared for boiling or baking. A quick résumé: rinse fish briefly under cold running water and pat dry with kitchen paper. Then acidify the fish by sprinkling with either vinegar or lemon juice to make the flesh firmer. Do not add salt until just before cooking, and never leave salted fish to stand. It will draw the water out of the fish and leave it dry and tasteless.

How to clean a herring. Scrape off scales with a sharp knife, working from the tail to the head. Slit the belly open and trim off fins with scissors.

Cut off head, remove entrails and use for fish sauces.

Remove dark lining. Rinse fish under cold water.

Make an incision along the length of the fish as far as the backbone.

Using a sharp knife, cut fillet away from backbone, working from head to tail. Remove any remaining bones.

Skinning the fillets. Before filleting, cut skin around tail end and lift slightly. Then carefully pull skin off fillets, from tail to head.

How to fillet sole. With a sharp knife, cut horizontally into the skin at the tail end and lift slightly. Wrap tail in kitchen paper and hold firmly, and pull the skin back right up to the head.

Remove skin from underside in same way. Insert knife as far as the bone, and cut cleanly down the length of the backbone.

Loosen fish from bones at head end, and cut the fillet off them horizontally.

Carefully remove all 4 fillets, 2 on each side, from backbone.

How to cut up a lobster

There is no doubt that lobster is one of the stars of cold cuisine, whether served cold with delicious sauces and bread, butter, and wine, or as a cocktail, or in canapés. It always has that hint of extravagance so beloved of many, and which, alas, has to be paid for. Lobster is not cheap. On the other hand, there is hardly any other seafood which can delight the palate so much. Delicatessens and fishmongers deal mainly in live lobsters, but also sell them ready-cooked if desired. They are available in sizes up to 50cm/20in long and 1500 g/3½ lb in weight. Connoisseurs consider 500g/1lb lobsters are the best, and have the most tender meat. Lobsters are also sold deep-frozen, and these are a little less expensive.

Live lobsters are grey-brown to greeny-black in colour, and because the shell has two layers, it turns bright red when cooked, as the dark upper layer boils away.

The claws of the lobster are strong enough to easily break your little finger, so do not cut the string or band tying the claws together until it has been cooked. Put the live lobster head first into boiling, salted water, and leave for about ½ hour. Deep-frozen lobster requires only 20 minutes if put frozen into the water.

Lobster can of course also be served hot, but must then be cut up hot, too. Lobster for cold cuisine is cut up when it has cooled, and the best way of doing this is shown in the following photos. You will need a strong, sharp knife or special lobster shears for cracking open the claws. Lobster shears and pins are needed if the lobster is to be eaten out of the shell.

Using a sharp knife, cut lobster open from tail to head, dividing it in half.

Remove intestinal vein, which usually looks like a dark thread, from tail with tweezers.

Remove lobster meat from shell, holding it with one hand, and loosening the meat with the other.

Crack claws in the middle using lobster shears, the back of a strong knife, or a small hammer.

Lay lobster on its back and twist legs one by one out of shell.

Now pull off the sharp upper part and expose the tender claw meat.

Twist large claws off by hand, if necessary cutting the join with the tip of a knife. Leave the smaller claws on.

Before serving, twist off lower claws and remove meat, then slice tail meat and arrange on a dish.

How to dress and carve poultry

Whether you are preparing duck (as in the photos), chicken, pheasant, pigeon, turkey or goose for the cooking pot or oven, the method is basically the same. Frozen produce is of course oven-ready, and all you need to do is thaw, wash, stuff if wished, dress and season it. Fresh poultry is not very different. But should you have an unplucked bird - for instance a pheasant - to deal with, then it has to be carefully plucked, so as not to damage the flesh. Any remaining feathers can be singed off with a gas or spirit flame, and if there are any feather stumps in the skin, pluck them out with tweezers. Then draw the bird, after cutting off the head, part of the neck, and the feet. After that, treat it as oven-ready poultry - wash inside and out, dry, season on the inside and dress. We show how to do this in the photos. Once the bird has been dressed, season it on the outside and lay bacon rashers over lean poultry such as pheasant and partridge.

How to dress a duck.
Lay duck on its back on a work surface. Close opening with skewers or thread.

Tie drumsticks close to body.

Tuck wings behind back skin folds. Lay neck skin flap on breast. Tie wings and skin flap securely.

If wished, lay bacon rashers over dressed duck to help retain moisture and prevent it from browning too much.

How to carve a duck.
Lay duck on its back. Hold steady with carving fork, and using carving knife cut around thigh bone, then cut skin underneath leg to free it from body. Twist a little and lift drumstick up taking thigh bone with it.

Treat wings in a similar fashion, i.e. use knife to cut away from body, using poultry shears if necessary.

Carve slices of breast meat from the top down to the breast bone, then horizontally from the carcass.

Alternative method: Loosen breast meat in one piece from breast bone on both sides, and lay on a chopping board.

Cut these pieces in thick slices. Remove remaining duck meat from bones, and slice.

Meat arranged on a serving platter. Small birds may also be served quartered. Serve pigeons whole.

How to carve a saddle of venison or hare (rabbit)

Whether we are talking of a saddle of venison, hare or lamb, they are all carved in the same way. It must be done carefully and evenly, so that they can be laid back on the bone to look as if it has not been carved at all. Nowadays there is no difference in flavour between fresh and frozen meat, as game matures during the freezing process in the same way that fresh game does when hung. If you have the choice, do not buy ready-larded game, but wrap smoked fatty bacon rashers around it yourself. This method keeps it moist, spicy, and has fewer calories, as it is removed from the meat before serving. Roasting a wild hare or rabbit involves a slight problem, in that the back meat, with the fillets, is so tender that it only takes $\frac{1}{2}$ hour to cook, whereas the legs need 1-1$\frac{1}{2}$ hours. What's the answer? You can either buy just legs or just backs (a half serves one person), or do not put the backs into the oven until the legs are half-cooked. With a tame rabbit both legs and back take the same time to cook, as the meat on both is equally tender.

How to cut up a hare.
Lay hare (rabbit) on its back and hold hind leg. Cut this off diagonally from body, then do the same with the other leg.

Hold one foreleg. Cut away from body at the shoulder, then do the same with the other foreleg, twisting slightly and cutting tendons.

How to carve a saddle of venison. Lay saddle on a work surface, bones downward, and hold firmly. Cut along the middle line down to the backbone. Use the tip of the knife to loosen the meat from the bone horizontally.

Cut hare (rabbit) in half lengthways. Lift back meat from backbone first, in one piece if possible, then cut remaining flesh off backbone.

Slice fillets on the slant, holding meat steady with the carving fork.

Slice back meat, and halve other portions, holding them steady with carving fork.

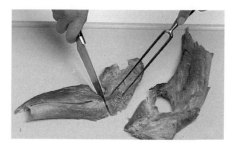

To serve, replace meat slices on the backbone, glaze if wished with aspic, and garnish.

Arrange hare (rabbit) meat on a serving platter, and pour sauce over if desired.

NB If you are preparing just hare legs, which like the backs are available frozen, they should first be marinated. Make a marinade from yoghurt, 2 bay leaves, 3 crushed juniper berries, $\frac{1}{2}$ tsp mustard seed and 1 tsp dried marjoram or thyme. The legs should be covered with the marinade and left for 24 hours. Dry them, and fry quickly on all sides in a little hot fat, then add liquid and braise for about 1$\frac{1}{2}$ hours.

Kitchen herbs and their uses

Herbs, as good for you as they taste, are really the essence of cold cuisine as far as flavour is concerned. Here is a summary of the herbs most commonly used:

Basil: a spicy, peppery herb in season from early summer until autumn. Only the leaves are used. Excellent with pasta, cheese, meat and fish dishes.

Savory: in season from July onwards. Both stalks and leaves are used. Good in all bean dishes and robust meat or pulse salads.

Borage: when fresh, tastes of cucumber, and is a must for all cucumber dishes; in season from May to September. The pretty borage flowers make an attractive garnish.

Parsley: without it, cold cuisine would be extremely dull, as dishwater, both as a seasoning and as a garnish. At its tastiest in the summer, the flat-leaved variety even more so than the curly one.

Pimpernel: this herb, tasting faintly of nuts, is rarely available fresh. But its leaves are perfect in green sauces, salads, herb quark (curd cheese), and herb butters.

Rosemary: the sprigs, with their needle-shaped leaves, give a bitter aromatic flavour to meat, fish, tomato and other vegetable dishes.

Dill: often available in winter and spring when grown under glass, but really at its best when grown outdoors in summer, dill has a fresh, aniseed-like flavour. Essential in green salads, cream sauces and fish dishes.

Tarragon: in season from spring until autumn. An intense, aromatic, slightly sweet flavour. Very good in salad marinades and herb butters.

Cress: or more precisely, mustard and cress, available in boxes all the year round. For salads, cold meats, cold soups and as a garnish.

Sage: in season only in summer, otherwise available dried. A strong, spicy flavour, ideal for Italian salads.

Sorrel: in season from spring until early summer. The delicate, slightly acidic leaves are used in cold sauces, and everywhere that mixed herbs are used, for instance green salads.

Chives: also at their best in summer, but available practically all the year round.

Lovage: also known as Maggi herb, tastes strongly of bouillon, and so should be used sparingly.

Bay: if you have a bay tree, fresh leaves are always available, otherwise they can be bought dried. Essential in fish dishes; also suitable for seasoning roast meat which is to be served cold.

Marjoram: fresh or dried marjoram leaves are used mostly in meat dishes and stuffings.

Celery herb: as highly aromatic and spicy as celeriac. In season in summer and late summer. Good in robust salads, quark (curd cheese), egg sauces and mayonnaises.

Thyme: in season from spring until autumn. Tastes of carnations; sprigs and leaves are used in pork, lamb and game dishes, and in salad marinades.

Lemon balm: a herb which tastes faintly of lemon, equally suited to salads, herb sauces, butters and cheeses; also used in refreshing drinks and cocktails.

Basil

Savory

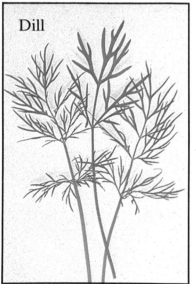
Dill

Tarragon

Lovage

Bay

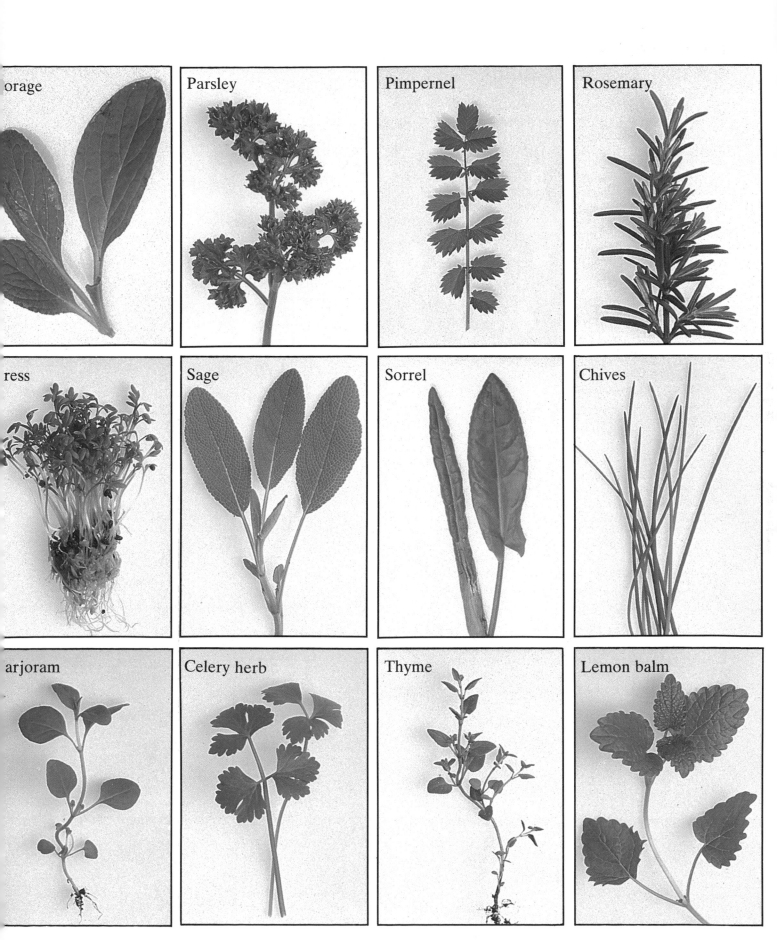

orage

Parsley

Pimpernel

Rosemary

ress

Sage

Sorrel

Chives

arjoram

Celery herb

Thyme

Lemon balm

How to eat shellfish, sea molluscs, and snails

Don't be afraid of strange creatures. If you have never eaten mussels, oysters, snails or lobster, now is your chance to learn the right way to do it. Let's return briefly to lobster, often served cold with sauces. It is usually already cut up, and half of it, complete with claws and legs, lies on your plate. What do you do? As lobster shears and a pin will be provided, approach the creature with confidence. It is easy to remove the meat from both the body and the large claw using the pin and a fork. But there is still tender meat in the joints and the thicker leg sections, so that wherever you cannot reach it with your fork, use the pin to pull the meat out. You may suck the meat from the legs, picking them up in your fingers. With spring lobsters there is a little less work, as they have no claws, otherwise treat them the same.

Crayfish - best when they weigh about 75g/3oz - are a little more fiddly to eat, as you usually have to use just your hands, unless a special crab knife is provided. Twist the claws off at the joints and crack open with the crab knife, then bite out the meat. Break off the legs and suck the meat out of them. Bend the head back and pull out of the shell. Scrape out the shell meat with a small spoon. Finally break off the tail, open at the side, take off upper part of shell and remove intestines. Take out the meat, the best part of the whole crayfish, remove the membrane and enjoy the rest. Allow about 600g/1¼ lb crayfish per person.

Everyone to his own taste - even with lobster and crayfish - for many people dislike all crustaceans. It is the same with oysters - they are not to everyone's liking. Yet there are some oyster fanatics who will consume up to 40 a sitting. The photos show the correct way to open and eat oysters.

Mussels, too, are highly prized nowadays. They can be boiled, stuffed, or baked, and are available tinned or prepared with other ingredients. They can be cooked in a spicy wine marinade and served in deep dishes with the liquid, accompanied by brown or white bread and butter, and beer or white wine.

Which leaves us with snails. Weinburg snails are cooked in special snail dishes, the shells thickly spread with herb butter (containing plenty of garlic), which you are allowed to mop up with your bread. An Alsaçe wine or a Burgundy is the best choice to serve with them. You will need special snail tongs and a snail fork to eat them, as shown in the photos.

Loosen mussels from shells with the aid of an empty mussel shell.

Place oysters domed side down on a cloth, cover, hold steady and force the oyster knife between the shells.

Move oyster knife gently up and down until upper shell is released.

Cut oyster from shell and swallow together with its juices.

Pick up snail shells with snail tongs, holding a spoon beneath to catch any dripping butter.

Remove snail from shell with snail fork and eat.

Stand-by stores for surprise guests

It is not unusual for surprise guests to drop in, and even if they are your best friends who are just popping in to say hello, you still like to offer them something good to eat. Something cold. So you should have in your store cupboard items that will keep indefinitely but can be used on such occasions. Here is a list of provisions which will enable you to swiftly prepare a cold buffet. Of course you will need to fall back on tins and preserves too, and if you need something fresher, use something from the freezer, which is another store cupboard anyway. We are not saying, however, that you have to keep everything that we suggest in the list; just a selection which you choose according to your own requirements. Whatever else you wish to buy is of course up to you. But just a few of these items are enough to prepare a surprise meal for surprise guests.

In the store cupboard: noodles, rice, crispbread, cheese crackers, crisps, packets of biscuits, coffee, tea, nuts; various sauces, including barbecue, horseradish, brown, curry, soy, Worcester, and tomato; tomato purée, mayonnaise, grated horseradish, mustard, evaporated milk, condensed milk, tinned cream.

Preserves: tinned vegetables according to your own taste, a choice of pickles, such as gherkins, mixed pickles, onions; tinned ham, poultry, brawn, corned beef, tinned meat and sausage products, fish such as prawns and sardines; tinned fruit and soups.

In the refrigerator: eggs, butter, milk, sausage which keeps well (e.g. salami), cheese slices, cream, yoghurt, quark (curd cheese), yoghurt-based preparations; vacuum-packed sausage and meat.

In the freezer (your best larder as it can store almost anything): fresh and cooked meat and vegetables; fresh bread (freeze whilst still warm to taste even better); cream, butter, fresh sliced sausage and meat; all kinds of deep-frozen specialities, prawns and other seafood, smoked salmon, poultry, game and even lobster, crayfish and crabs; fruit and ice-creams. Most households have some of these things in the freezer already, and you can add to your stores as best suits your own needs.

Drinks (apart from wine, nearly all of them are easily stored): spirits such as brandy, gin, whisky and liqueurs; beer, sparkling wine or champagne and schnaps - all best kept in the refrigerator although beer can also be stored in the cellar; wine which must be stored in a cool place; lemonade and mineral waters either in the refrigerator or in a cool place. Quantities are up to you!

Finally, a word about rotating your stores: replace and renew with fresh provisions as necessary, using up the older stock so that it does not have a chance to deteriorate.

How to serve your guests, and how guests should serve themselves

It is almost unthinkable nowadays to not offer your guests a drink when you welcome them, or to begin a meal without an apéritif. What drinks to offer? Sparkling wine with or without orange juice, sherry, or cocktails, which can all be accompanied by a few nibbles such as canapés. A secret tip to break the ice between people who do not know each other very well: a small glass of clear schnaps or vodka. One glass is usually sufficient to loosen the tongues and lay the foundations for a successful evening.

If a meal follows which is equally pleasing to the eye and the palate nothing can go wrong. If you have staff who can serve the guests, you have no further worries and everything should go like clockwork. But how many nowadays have staff? So we serve our guests sometimes, and we should make it as easy for ourselves as possible. Cold cuisine guarantees that, for although it sometimes means more preparation, everyone can then help themselves. Cold food should be on the table when guests enter the room: the cold buffet should all be displayed with plates at the ready. The tables are of course already laid.

Then the host and hostess can relax and enjoy the evening with their guests without worrying about anything other than seeing to the drinks, and possibly replenishing the food.

A word on how to lay a table attractively: the cloth must be spotless, the flower arrangements low and unobtrusive so that guests do not have to conduct their conversations through flowers. The colours of the cloth, the flowers and the dinner service should harmonise. If the pattern of the service has an obvious single motif, for instance a flower spray, make sure the plates are placed so that it is the right way up. Lay the serviettes on the plates, and the cutlery in order of use from outside to inside, knives on the right and forks on the left, and the dessert spoon above the plate. Glasses stand at the top right of the plate, right to left in order of use.

You are ready to go. Whether you are serving a selection of cold meat and cheese, a buffet, a champagne breakfast or sandwiches, the traditional order should be observed: first fish, then meat (or sausage or ham), vegetables and/or salads, cheese and fruit or dessert.

Guests help themselves in the order we have described, whether food is served at the table, a cold buffet table, or on a tray of canapés or sandwiches. We hardly need say that no one should start to eat until everyone is served.

By the way, coffee and liqueurs are served by the host and hostess themselves, and are generally the signal that the evening has come to an end, unless guests are genuinely urged to stay on and enjoy the party a little longer.

ALPHABETICAL INDEX IN SECTIONS

INDEX